PORTER

TRINITY and DUKE, *1892-1924*

TRINITY and DUKE

1892-1924: Foundations
of Duke University

by Earl W. Porter

Duke University Press   Durham, N. C.   1964

To

HOLLIS EDENS

Preface

Academic history, if it merits the telling, should be addressed to the total community of higher education and perhaps to the reader of intellectual history as well as the local campus. Although an institutional narrative, like a biography, requires a steady focus on the main character (the institution itself), larger considerations, if sought, will emerge.

Thus, the history of Trinity College is incomplete apart from the context of change in American higher education. For example, by the turn of the last century there had occurred the rise of the modern academic specialties, the acceleration of graduate education, and the evolution of the research scholar. Soon the development of standards in admissions, curricula, and in the professional schools would take place. The national philanthropic agencies had arrived and were becoming a power for change. These and other innovations constituted a challenge to which institutions might respond in different ways but which no institution could ignore.

Here the historian finds himself weighing the claim of institutional singularity against the evidence for similarity. "Every college is different" and with a flavor all its own. Yes, but one may find that the plea of distinctiveness in colleges has rested as much on the possession of resources, the fact of competition, and the inventiveness of catalogue statements as on sharp differences in program, services, or policy. Competition itself, well-nourished by ambition, local pride, and a bit of man's inhumanity to man, may encourage the selection and imitation of models. To its credit, Trinity College kept its sights on the best models, including those beyond its grasp, even as it suffered—and occasionally relished—a reputation for being different.

Nor was Trinity isolated from the difficulties that have prevailed in inter-institutional relationships, the foreign policy of academic life. Two of the college's presidents led campaigns for and against inter-institutional co-operation. The complexities are evident in that Few's drive for a co-operative medical school and Kilgo's crusade against state colleges both failed.

In addition to an interest in these and related problems, I have also considered the special claim of another audience. The generations who have gone to Duke University in recent years have had little opportunity to understand the late history of Trinity College. It has been natural that this should be so. Most of the men who long served to link the present with the past are gone. Much of the story has been told in biography and is necessarily fragmented. More important, those of the later days went to work at Duke, not Trinity. If they knew of Trinity, they surmised that it was small, provincial, Southern. It was a name, and if it was important to them, it was so because it became Duke University.

Somewhat then in a spirit of doubt, I have sought to understand what Trinity College was like, to try with some caution to measure the institution against the colleges of its day. Therefore, I do not offer a full chronicle or a work of reference. There is very little here of buildings, student life, or athletics. The questions that have received emphasis, in addition to the college's growth and resources, have been those dealing with the location of institutional power; the relations with the benefactors and with the Methodist Church; the evolution of academic policies and of the curriculum; and the educational setting of the time. I have also been interested in a few illuminating controversies and in the personalities of men who influenced the story, in particular the presidents, key faculty members, and of course the Duke family, whose support fulfilled the promise of the college and the university.

No one should presume to find a single theme running through an institution's history, but one may report an atmosphere when it overwhelms him. Thus I suggest that the abiding excitement in Trinity College, at lease until the World War, was a zest for intellectual reform, whether applied to a parochial South that would not read books and seemed to demonstrate, even among its leaders, an incapacity to make rational distinctions; to the need for decent college preparation and genuine collegiate education—or merely to a habit of self-criticism. By the end of the war many of the reforms were being won, although no one would claim all the credit for Trinity. The image of embattled intellectual crusaders should not be romanticized, but the thread remains in Trinity's past. It went with the college's capacity for seeming different, something of a stranger in her homeland. To her critics the benefactors were pariahs, the presidents too controversial, and the harping on standards uncharitable. But "the air was fame," and a sense of mission pervaded individuals and got into the bloodstream. It is a heritage worth knowing.

Perhaps to the present generation at Duke other themes will be more suggestive. Obviously, in 1924 Trinity College would bring much of herself into the larger Duke University; sometimes even the obvious may be overlooked. There are familiar overtones in Trinity's persistent need to explain that the Dukes' benefactions did not make the support of others unnecessary. The tie with the Church required a nice balance between cordiality and freedom from control. It was always necessary to adjust ambitions for high academic standards to the educational and economic realities in North Carolina and the South. In modern dress these problems have concerned Duke University too.

I am indebted to many persons for assistance, and some of their names are recorded in the Bibliographical Note and in the text. Here I can thank but a few: A. Hollis Edens, former president of Duke University, for a wealth of warm support and encouragement; Miss Mattie Russell, curator of manuscripts, Duke University Library, for her alertness in directing me to sources and for her interest in the project; and Richard Bassett for carefully preserving his father's papers and for making them available to me. In addition, I gladly join the long line of those who have gone to W. T. Laprade, professor emeritus of history in Duke University, for advice and ideas. I am grateful as well to Richard L. Watson, Jr., professor of history at Duke, for a happy professional and personal association of several years and for an abundance of good counsel. Finally, I thank Agnes W. Wilson for a quantity of excellent typing service and above all my wife, for many hours of hard work and good discussion.

E. W. P.

Urbana, Illinois
July 1, 1963

Contents

Illustrations

TRINITY and DUKE, *1892-1924*

Chapter I

"In the Days of Crowell"

1887-1892

Is this Trinity?' I asked. 'Yes,' they answered in chorus,
'this is Trinity,' rather, I thought, in a tone of apology."[1]
Thus in the spring of 1887 did John Franklin Crowell arrive
in the little North Carolina village of Trinity. He had come, at
the age of twenty-nine, to assume the presidency of Trinity College. For young Crowell it was the beginning of a seven-year
adventure in the South, a period of collision between men and
ideas that was to leave neither the college nor the man ever the
same thereafter.

In the 1880's the farm town of Trinity had some 350 permanent residents. Most of them were farmers, some lived from the
patronage of the college. While not entirely remote, it was
Trinity's ill fortune to lie just at the edge of progress. Services
were limited; one could not buy a newspaper, get a haircut, or
have a tooth pulled. Transportation was a problem; the nearest
railroad station was at High Point, five miles away. A telegram
could be delivered for a dollar service charge. There were, however, compensations. The countryside was pleasant in the midst
of the uplands where the quail hunting was good. The climate
was customarily billed as "salubrious," and there was an arcadian
atmosphere of peace and quiet.[2]

What of the college itself? Although it could trace its descent
from a neighborhood school of the 1830's, the power to grant
degrees dated from 1853 and a formal college curriculum from
about 1856. Ties of democratic tradition and attitude linked
Trinity College with its earliest predecessor. Brown's School-
house, one of the many rural subscription schools, was born of
the determination of Quaker and Methodist farmers and villagers
to see their children grow up literate. In 1839 its principal,

1. John F. Crowell, *Personal Recollections of Trinity College, North Carolina,*
1887-1894 (Durham, 1939), p. 31. Cited hereinafter as Crowell, *Recollections.*
2. Crowell, *Recollections, passim; Carolina Wesleyan,* Jan., 1892 (reprint,
Trinity College Papers, Duke University Library); Augustus W. Long, *Son of*
Carolina (Durham, 1939), p. 176.

Brantley York, converted the school into Union Institute. The union was that of the two church groups sharing a conviction that in a democracy those who wished education could get it, by their own resources if necessary.[3]

In 1842 York left for other work, and Braxton Craven, his young assistant, took over. For the next forty years the institution was the image of Craven's sacrifice and determination. The Institute was an academy with some pretensions to collegiate training, but Craven had higher ambitions. He was in tune with the common school movement of the day and began to experiment with normal training to help provide the teachers that were needed. In 1849 the Institute was incorporated by the state as Normal College, a "people's college," an institution that would emphasize, as had the Institute, the education of "poor boys." Normal never received an appropriation from the state, although the connection provided some prestige, such as state approval of the graduates' teaching certificates. It also made possible a $10,000 loan from the state literary fund to help expand the plant.

But Normal was an unloved child of the state. The lack of financial support, some suspicions about the quality of its work, and frequent charges that it was sectarian made it an unhappy one as well. Its enrollments ranged from 130 to 195, mostly Methodists. Clearly Normal was more Methodist than anything else. The Quaker supporters had participated only in the beginnings of Union Institute. York and Craven were Methodists, and both became ministers. Thus, the religious atmosphere was always present, and Craven turned naturally to the North Carolina Conference of the Methodist Episcopal Church, South, for encouragement and for money. A definite connection began in 1851 with his offer to give aspiring preachers preministerial training. The Church was pleased and in time helped pay for it. The normal training faded, and in 1856 the Methodist Conference adopted the college as its own. In 1859 the name was changed to Trinity College; by this date Craven had deferred his plans to mingle normal training with other college work. The new Trinity sought to grow as a Methodist liberal arts institution and soon began to accumulate a body of alumni and supporters. The graduates tended to become clergymen or teachers.

Prior to the Civil War there was a period of increased patron-

3. The summary to 1887 is taken from Nora C. Chaffin, *Trinity College, 1839-1892: The Beginnings of Duke University* (Durham, 1950), *passim*. Cited hereinafter as Chaffin, *Beginnings*.

age, and the total enrollment reached a high of 238. The numbers in preparatory work and courses of a terminal nature were always comparatively high, but more students sought the full collegiate program leading to a degree. The curriculum was redesigned to make this possible, although a democratic resentment against "aristocratic" leanings kept the alterations in bounds. When the war came, at Trinity as elsewhere in the South, the change was sudden. The college remained open during most of the war years, but with a sharply-curtailed operation. Later it faced the bleak years of the aftermath with few resources. It was 1870 before the enrollment approached that of the ante bellum period.

Craven kept in touch with developments in higher education and in 1869 introduced a few innovations into the curriculum. A de-emphasis of classical studies began, and there was increased attention to the natural sciences, mathematics, and English literature. There was even some interest in engineering and law. With the traditional offerings, Latin, Greek, Biblical literature, and mental and moral philosophy, the new curriculum was little changed until 1887. However, the pattern of alumni occupations shifted with the times. Trinity still produced men who would preach and teach, but others turned to law, politics, and business.

Meanwhile, all the brave gestures to develop a thriving college were conditioned by intermittent crises. Patronage was always subject to the condition of the crops in an agricultural state. The services to "poor boys," reflected in low charges and plenty of credit, made each year a financial struggle. The agricultural depression of the 1870's and the poverty of Reconstruction combined to reduce the enrollment (to a low of 107 in 1875) and to lower the college's prestige. Finally, as Craven struggled with political opposition in the Church, and as the college suffered, his own influence tended to fade.

There were constant efforts to find funds. The answer, all agreed, was a permanent endowment, a floor of dependable income upon which the institution might stand. Other colleges were receiving support from wealthy industrialists, Vanderbilt (also Methodist) in particular. Fortunes had been made in the war and in the industrial boom that followed, and the private colleges were alert to the new opportunities. Lacking a good Samaritan, Trinity turned to its Methodist constituency. But almost everyone was poor. It was a vicious circle: weak resources

6 TRINITY and DUKE

hurt patronage; low enrollments meant low income and inability to develop better resources. And there was always a disheartening difference between pledges of endowment aid and the resulting payment of cash. The spirit was often there, and people offered in good faith, but they rarely had the money when the notes came due. Craven died in 1882, leaving his successor a monument to his own endurance and a body of loyal graduates. A measure of his sacrifice is suggested by the fact that the $10,000 state loan of 1852 had long since been paid by Craven personally. He remained unpaid by the college at his death.

In the next few years others sought to keep Trinity alive. The low point came in 1885 when it was seriously proposed that the property be sold. Three trustees, J. W. Alspaugh, Julian S. Carr, and James A. Gray, all businessmen, offered themselves as a Committee of Management and their money to oversee and help finance the college for two years. This arrangement saved Trinity and provoked a slight flurry of interest and hope. The campus was spruced up, faculty vacancies filled, and new emphasis given to natural science, literature, and business courses. In the meantime a committee, which included the three managers, began the search for a new president. At the same time another drive for endowment began, faltered, and came alive again when Julian Carr made the college its largest individual gift, $10,000. For the first time, Trinity had the beginnings of an endowment.

When the selection committee recommended John F. Crowell and when he was elected president on April 5, 1887, the choice of a Northern man was not mere impulse. The committee of businessmen was looking for progressive management. They knew well the hazards of bringing Church politics into the matter, and they knew that the college required fresh ideas. Indeed, Crowell was not the only Northern man approached.[4]

Crowell was born in York, Pennsylvania on November 1, 1857, the son of a family with Dutch antecedents.[5] His father was a miller, farmer, and brick manufacturer, and Crowell had known a rural small town boyhood. In fact, "the foundations of history"

4. For example, John W. Sanborn, Albion, N. Y., to J. S. Carr, March 26, 1887, Trinity College Papers; Chaffin, *Beginnings*. Crowell's name was given Julian Carr by Horace H. Williams, then a Trinity faculty member, who had known him at Yale. H. H. Williams to W. K. Boyd, Jan. 30, 1922, William K. Boyd Papers (Duke University Library).
5. He was born John Franklin Craul but changed it to Crowell while he was in college. Obituary Record, Alumni Records Office, Yale University (copy in Trinity College Papers); Crowell, *Recollections*.

and "the treasures of philosophy" first reached him through the itinerant book agents who passed his way. He attended school in New Berlin, Pennsylvania, and went to Dartmouth College for a year. In 1880 he entered Yale as a sophomore and received the B.A. in 1883. For two years he served as principal of Schuylkill Seminary at Fredericksburg, Pennsylvania (now Albright College at Reading). In between, he had a year in the Yale Divinity School and another year as Larned Scholar in the embryonic Yale Graduate School.[6] Thus he had qualifications: he was young and had some administrative experience; his religion (the Evangelical Church) was adaptable to Methodist taste; and he was, it was soon evident, completely caught up in the swiftly moving currents of American society.

That society in the latter third of the nineteenth century was aflood with new ideas. There was a pragmatic spirit in the land and a confidence in Progress.[7] In the world of higher education the magic word was Science. Darwin's studies had been digested, as had Herbert Spencer's adaptation of them into social "laws." Every reader could find his own interpretation, sometimes in absolute disagreement with his fellow. But few quarreled about the dependability of the scientific method, which could be made to serve the conservative or the reformer. Moreover, educators had long since found interesting models in Germany, where there was strong emphasis upon science and an accompanying idealism: the doctrine of freedom to teach and freedom to learn, an irresistible combination. For years a trickle of Americans had sought postgraduate study in Germany. Now they streamed to Berlin or Leipzig, where one might apply the laboratory method. There the libraries were open and used, dedicated not to dusty accumulation but to service and growth as students consulted "original sources." Finally, one might see the "seminary" (seminar) in operation, a small group of able students meeting with a master to learn in intellectual intimacy the techniques of research.

6. Crowell's Record, Registrar, Yale Graduate School (copy in Trinity College Papers); Crowell, *Recollections*.
7. This and summary following taken from: Eric F. Goldman, *Rendezvous With Destiny* (New York, 1958); Charles F. Thwing, *A History of Higher Education in America* (New York, 1906); Richard Hofstadter and C. DeWitt Hardy, *The Development and Scope of Higher Education in the United States* (New York, 1952); Merle Curti (ed.), *American Scholarship in the Twentieth Century* (Cambridge, 1953); and Louis Franklin Snow, *The College Curriculum in the United States* (New York, 1907), pp. 171-183.

This new approach to scholarship, altered to suit individual tastes, gradually would become the mark of "a real university." In the 1880's a few institutions were eager to accept and promote the idea. Some had been created in the years immediately after the war: Cornell (1865), Johns Hopkins (1867), and Vanderbilt (1873). In a few years the new philanthropists would bring others into being: Stanford (1885), Clark (1887), and Chicago (1891). In one way or another, the influence was pervasive. At Harvard, the oldest of all, and at Johns Hopkins, one of the youngest, the new ideas had gained vigorous support. Over many years at Harvard, President Charles William Eliot experimented radically with the elective principle, throwing the curriculum open to student choice and liberalizing and equalizing the offerings. At Hopkins President Daniel Coit Gilman had assembled German-trained scholars, using some of the German methods to create an intellectual center of distinguished scholars and carefully chosen graduate students. Soon from the major universities came a generation of American-trained professors who were to take the new learning to other institutions.

Gradually the college curriculum began to give way to the pressures. The modern languages increasingly demanded room from the classical studies. New schools of science appeared, some completely technical. New techniques and data helped science to become increasingly specialized and subdivided, requiring a larger share of the curriculum and greater laboratory facilities. There was talk of a new scientific psychology and new respect for physics and the biological sciences. And there were important changes in the teaching of English, which included a philological approach, emphasis upon analysis and research, and concern for more recent literature.

Perhaps the most dramatic change came with the identification and quick strength of the social sciences and history. Political science and history began to escape from the arms of older fields where they had not enjoyed the identity they would later achieve. In time political economy would become economics and require some attention to statistics. The term "sociology" began to be used to describe a newly aroused concern for the study of man's behavior in groups. The development of the social sciences was based on a belief in their utility as well as discovery of the intellectual satisfaction to be found in new methods of research. The American nation faced a wealth of problems rying for the application of *expertise*. Agrarian unrest, a growing ocialist movement, polyglot cities, recurrent strikes, and swell- ng corporate structures posed the issues of reform and counter- eform; the technique of the specialist might serve both. Fully s important to educators was the need to acquaint the college tudent with the new academic specialties. He was likely to have role in public affairs; at least he should become an informed nember of the democracy.

At Yale Crowell made contact with the intellectual turbulence f his day and became a believer in intellectual progress. In he Divinity School he studied ethics under Noah Porter and the New Testament under the younger Timothy Dwight, refreshing is deep interest in religion and philosophy. But he shopped bout in the graduate school, studying political science (admin- stration and transportation in particular) with Arthur Twining Iadley and psychology with George T. Ladd. Most important f all perhaps, as an undergraduate he sat in the economics lasses of William Graham Sumner. His spiritual inspiration ame from Porter, but he took secular nourishment from Sumner. Chen one of the rare scholarly men-of-affairs, Sumner was active n politics, a productive publicist, and a teacher who "made life is textbook." He was also a leader in the faculty group that ought for and won a new, broader curriculum for Yale, a contest t its height in Crowell's day in New Haven.[8]

With this background, Crowell came to North Carolina. What lid he find? Plainly, the village of Trinity was not prepossessing, or on examination was the college. For a few hours during his irst visit in the spring of 1887, Crowell toyed with the idea of giving it up and going home. The college was still struggling to ecover from Craven's death and to overcome its perennial prob- ems. There was a little money for endowment, but still only one juilding, an uncatalogued library of 10,000 volumes, six profes- ors and two tutors, and a preparatory department with an enroll- nent half as large (fifty-one) as the total taking college courses.

In 1888 a brief study of the state's educational resources, uppropriately by a Hopkins Ph.D. candidate, suggested that Trinity probably ranked fourth among the four largest colleges n the state. Its admissions standards were thought to be "about

8. George W. Pierson, *Yale College: An Educational History, 1871-1921* (New Haven, 1952), pp. 1-163; Crowell, *Recollections*; Harris E. Starr, *William Graham Sumner* (New York, 1925), *passim*.

a year below" those of the University of North Carolina, at Chapel Hill, and Wake Forest College, a Baptist institution.[9] The largest, the university, had ten buildings, an annual appropriation of $27,500, a faculty of 17, and a library of 25,000 volumes. Its enrollment was approximately 200.[10] Wake Forest and Davidson College (Presbyterian) also were better equipped and financed than Trinity. None of the four had more than the most meager resources, but Methodists found the comparison unpleasant, and the constituency revived its efforts to add to the endowment. Meanwhile, the academic program was left to the new president.

The catalogue was ready for the press, but even before he arrived for duty in August, 1887, Crowell was drafting public notices of the changes to come. First was the immediate establishment of required entrance examinations for all who sought admission. Students were tested in six subjects, including United States history. There were no exceptions, and when an objecting applicant sought to barter his patronage elsewhere, he was told he was free to go. Trinity must be truly a college. In the fall of 1887 this policy brought heavy increases in the preparatory department; many students simply did not have the background for Crowell's standards. Later there was less rigidity. Some might qualify if they had a certificate of proficiency from their secondary school teachers. In time, students over twenty-one might be admitted without examination. It was necessary to recapture those who had been discouraged if the college were to have any students. Crowell tinkered with the examination policy throughout his administration, seeking an accommodation between genuine college work and the low level of preparatory training in the state. But he never took the requirement out of the catalogue and always sought to enforce it. At least it was useful in classifying students according to the work they could do.[11] The relative merits of examinations and the certificate system were far from clear nationally, at this time and later. In each case, of course, reliable admissions policies depended upon the nature of the examinations and the administration of the certification.

9. Charles Lee Smith, *History of Education in North Carolina, Contributions to American Educational History,* Herbert B. Adams, ed. (Washington, D. C., 1888), *passim.* Cited hereinafter as C. L. Smith, *North Carolina Education.*
10. *Ibid.*
11. Trinity College catalogues, 1882-1894; *Extra Prospectus,* July, 1887; circulars, Oct., 1887, August, 1889, Trinity College Papers; Chaffin, *Beginnings;* and Crowell, *Recollections.*

The growth of the preparatory department brought other problems. That department might dominate the college. There had been disturbing talk that Trinity was destined to fall back into academy status anyway. Moreover, competition with the academies and high schools would hurt the college. Finally, it was costly. By 1888 Crowell had decided to abolish it. The catalogue of 1888-1889 announced, "The instructors are all fully occupied with College courses."

Crowell brought definite ideas as to what a college faculty should be, especially one that was to teach the advanced work he envisioned. He wanted modern specialists who were zealous to take their learning to the people. He found on arrival a dedicated corps of professors but none who had known direct contact with the new learning. Most were Trinity alumni, some were active and influential in the Church, and there was a former candidate or two for the presidency in their midst. There were marked strengths among them—one or two had been active in public affairs; others were aware of recent advances in their fields, although handicapped by the weak resources of the college. Probably all of them welcomed the opportunity to see how far the college might be able to go.

In the existing organization were nine "Schools" (departments): Latin, Greek, Mathematics, English Literature (which included a little history), Natural Science, Metaphysics, French, German, and Theology. There was a vacant professorship in "Greek and German," and one in English. It was no time for large expansions in personnel; the money was not in hand. In his first two years Crowell was content with two additions, Joseph L. Armstrong in English and Frank E. Welch in Greek and Latin. Both had graduate training, at Hopkins and Michigan respectively, and both had studied abroad. Crowell himself took a new chair as professor of history, political economy, and international law.

The curriculum, however, might be altered free of charge. Crowell decided to draw a sharp line between the work of the sophomore and junior years. He established an Academic Department for underclassmen and placed juniors and seniors in a Scientific Department. In the beginning at least, the same faculty would teach in both divisions. To the required work for freshmen and sophomores were added English and history, now separated, as well as courses in civil government and political and social economy. The new president struggled to make the best of divergent clienteles. Many students were content with a year or so of college work; these were to be given a general foundation, terminal if necessary, with some attention to technological studies. Others would go further and would receive the general preparation to do it.

Between the two was a barrier, the Scholar's Examination, required of all who wished to continue. Here the weeding out process would take place. In the upper division students were free to make many elective choices from among the fifteen schools, which included all the subjects Crowell and the faculty believed themselves competent to teach. At the end of the senior year there would be a final examination and a required graduation thesis based upon original research and defended before the faculty. There was even a mild invitation to graduate study; the unlikely claim was made that several of the schools were "capable of indefinite expansion."

Sizable expansion took place immediately in some areas, especially in Crowell's own field. He offered nine separate history courses in three divisions, constitutional, political, and ecclesiastical. There were courses in political economy (using Sumner's *Problems*), in social science (touching on crime, insanity, and socialism), and in administrative and international law. It seems impossible that the president should have had time for such a load, and Crowell himself thought he should teach less. But there was no one else to do it, and some courses were given twice a week for one semester only. Doubtless, others could be combined.

In other areas, the School of Metaphysics now recognized the existence of modern psychology. English, under Armstrong, was expanded to provide analysis of modern literature and study of Old English. The sciences remained the total burden of W. H. Pegram but were reorganized to give chemistry and physics separate status and a greater portion of the students' time. A smaller collection of interests was combined in the natural sciences, although mineralogy and geology were still differentiated. In a curious departure from the larger pattern, perhaps to make use of the talents of J. M. Bandy, first a course in "road-building," then schools of "mining and civil engineering" were established, at least on paper.

During his first two years Crowell juggled and adjusted this structure, altering the amount of electives occasionally and, indeed, at one point offering four lines of work for bachelor's degrees—in arts, science, philosophy, and letters. In spite of the unwieldy organization, the aim was clear: to bring the intellectual approach into accord with "the best practices." This included an acceptance of the current trademarks of progress, the elective principle, an insistence upon student research, recognition of the new importance of older fields such as English and the sciences, and, above all, pouring into the curriculum the college's, and probably the state's, first comprehensive offerings in the social sciences and history. The pace was fast for Trinity, and one student classified as a junior when Crowell arrived found the curriculum raised under him so quickly that he could not keep up. Four years later he was in the preparatory department.[12]

Meanwhile, Crowell launched a campaign to acquire library and laboratory materials to give the research meaning and to meet the minimum teaching needs. Soon the library received some of the major journals and a few books. The students began reading the New York *Times, Scientific American,* the *Edinburgh Review,* and other publications. Richard Ely's *Political Economy* arrived, along with the Webbs' studies in socialism and John Dewey's new *Psychology.* Crowell traveled widely, begging money and recruiting students—and always soliciting books, manuscripts, documents, bound volumes of periodicals, and items for the scientific museum.[13] He tried to guide the effort. "When in large cities," he advised Methodists, "visit second hand book stores and spend a couple of dollars" for, say, McMaster's *United States History,* Longfellow's *Works* or Strong's *Cyclopedia,* and other items.[14] He wrote for government documents, free state reports, geological surveys, and census materials.

At the same time he demonstrated, and encouraged others to share, what became an obsession: direct participation by the college in "leavening the lump" of public affairs. True, the college should benefit from a variety of lecturers in various fields, and there were a score or more in the first year. More important, however, was the duty of getting into the swim of current issues. On the campus he gave the students practical experience in a mock Congress and in steps toward self-government. In the state

---

12. Robert Lee Durham, *Since I Was Born* (Richmond, 1953), p. 124.
13. Trinity College Papers; Chaffin, *Beginnings*, pp. 424-428.
14. Raleigh *Christian Advocate,* Nov. 14, 1888, p. 1.

he campaigned for tax-supported public schools and, drawing on his work with Hadley at Yale, sought to correct North Carolina's approach to a railroad commission law. He insisted that the faculty take their views beyond the classroom. A college must be "the mother of reform" and "must see with the eyes of prophets."[15] Occasionally this departure from the customary passive role of colleges in North Carolina drew fire, and Crowell found himself in debate with journalists and others who felt that he should run his college and as one editor, Josephus Daniels, advised, let "the people" run the state.[16] After all, he was a Yankee anyway. Unintimidated, he repeated the theme; a college "must not be manned with mummies." The record does not show precisely how his faculty or his constituency reacted, but if there was opposition from these sources, it was quiet. Many were delighted. He was stirring up the state and giving the Methodists a forceful public posture.

Plainly, the campus itself was enlivened by the curriculum, the new reading matter, and the atmosphere. The emphasis was upon hard work. Crowell was proud that at one point only Trinity, of all the state's colleges, required classes on Saturdays, and he warned faculty and students alike about the dangers of inflated grades. The *Archive,* a new student magazine under Armstrong's aegis, was full of the new themes. Library accessions were reported and reviewed as they arrived, and choice articles in the new magazines were pointed out to the student body. From their reading the students began to analyze daily controversy, for instance, the current status of England's Irish problem or the activities of the Farmers' Alliance.[17]

In the research spirit, the seniors combed the little library to get data for their graduation theses. In older days the graduation orations and the debating societies had tended to dwell on personal philosophy and the inner man. The rare political discussion had concentrated on ante bellum days and the evils of Reconstruction. But now the seniors were full of the new excitement. The economic status of the Negro got a hearing, as did the technological revolution. Students asked themselves, and the

---

15. Chaffin, *Beginnings,* pp. 397-458; Crowell, *Recollections, passim.*
16. *Ibid.* Coincidentally, the two editors with whom Crowell had most difficulty were both Methodists, Daniels of the Raleigh *State Chronicle* and T. B. Kingsbury of the Wilmington *Messenger.*
17. *Archive,* Nov., 1887–April, 1892, *passim.*

documents at hand, "Is Agriculture in Need of Government Aid?"; "Can Evolution and Revelation Be Reconciled?"[18] Nor was the faculty untouched. Crowell himself sought new ideas everywhere. He visited Gilman at Johns Hopkins, and he initiated correspondence with Herbert Adams and with Richard Ely. Pegram needed more laboratory equipment and went to other institutions to see "the best models." Others turned to publication, Bandy working up an arithmetic and Armstrong a grammar. Among the older men, Pegram especially welcomed the new regime. He had been as heavily worked as anyone and was relieved when the preparatory department was abolished. Now, he noted, "all have become men of special work and enthusiastic in its execution." Indeed, those who had lived through the recent years felt "delivered as from a siege."[19]

There was encouragement for the young president from other sources. School principals praised the new standards and Crowell's effort to give them guidance in getting their students ready for college. From Baltimore President Gilman wrote that Crowell's plans seemed "sensible and vigorous." Judge Walter Clark of the State Supreme Court, a trustee after 1890 and a man of some scholarly interests, thought Crowell's first day in office had been Trinity's brightest day.[20] Ceaselessly F. L. Reid, who edited the Methodist weekly, the Raleigh *Christian Advocate,* supported the new administration and campaigned for Trinity. Finally, as an educator, Crowell may have been most satisfied in later years to see reactions elsewhere to some of his reforms.

To understand the state of higher education in North Carolina in the 1880's, it is necessary to be aware of the realities that faced each college. The state was wretchedly poor, and the public schools were weakly supported. In 1887 the average duration of the school year was sixty days, the lowest in all the states. A few of the cities had high schools, but a large share of the responsibility of preparing youth for college fell on the host of private academies and preparatory schools. These varied widely in resources and were guided by no uniform standard. There was similar uncertainty in the public high schools, in fact strong feel-

18. Trinity College Papers; Chaffin, *Beginnings.*
19. Raleigh *Christian Advocate,* Sept. 26, 1888, p. 1. The early publications were J. M. Bandy, *An Analytical Arithmetic in Six Parts* (Trinity, 1890) and Joseph L. Armstrong, *A Grammar of English, Parts I and II* (Trinity, 1889).
20. D. C. Gilman to J. F. Crowell, May 25, 1889, J. F. Crowell, Scrapbook, 1891-1910; John F. Crowell Papers (Duke University Library); Walter Clark to J. F. Crowell, Nov. 26, 1889, Trinity College Papers.

ing that they should not undertake college preparatory work. In both types of schools individual principals often had preferences as to which college their students should attend. Some frankly sought to become a "feeder" to a particular college.[21]

The numbers of persons involved in this procedure were minute by present standards. In 1890 the population of North Carolina was 1,600,000. Yet in the school year 1886-1887 the total college enrollment in the state, including all types of institutions, was less than 2,800. In terms of the product, college graduates, the figures dropped sharply. The mortality was high in all institutions. For example, throughout the seven years of Crowell's administration (1887-1894), about one student attained senior ranking for every four admitted as freshmen. The comparable ratio at the state university, which reportedly received a greater share of the better prepared students, was about one in three.[22] And, of course, every college admitted a substantial number with entrance conditions, just as some of those who became seniors did not graduate.

Few went to college, and fewer stayed for four years, and in the South in general the rivalry for students led to aberrations. There were no uniform standards and no accreditation. There was a tendency, not restricted to educators, to look self-consciously and defensively at Northern institutions, and there was a pattern of exaggerated claims and fanciful pretensions. It was common for a college to advertise that its work was "at a level fully as high as Harvard or Yale." The facts were usually uncomfortably discouraging. One measurement of the facilities in North Carolina is suggestive: the largest library, the university's, contained 25,000 volumes in the 1880's. At that time Harvard College had 230,000 volumes and Yale more than 125,000.[23]

Yet, patronage was survival, and in North Carolina the small, struggling institutions watched each other carefully, alert to any change in the balance of trade. The university at Chapel Hill was the strongest college. Its enrollment in the late 1880's was stabilized at 200, including law and premedical students.

21. *Statistical Abstract of the United States, 1888* (Washington, 1889), p. 177; Edgar W. Knight, *Public Education in the South* (Boston, 1922), pp. 415-422; Edwin C. Broome, *A Historical and Critical Discussion of College Admission Requirements* (New York, 1903), pp. 68 ff.; Trinity College Papers.

22. U. S. *Census*, 1890; *Statistical Abstract*, 1888; Trinity College catalogues, 1887-1894; catalogues of the University of North Carolina, 1886-1894.

23. *Report of Commissioner of Education, 1884-1885* (Washington, 1886), pp. 691-782.

There were about five graduate students per year. In some areas, as a college the university was coming abreast of the time, especially in the sciences, and to some extent in literary studies. Entrance examinations were required, and the elective principle was known and implemented. There were two men on the faculty with the Ph.D. degree, and in a few departments "seminary" work was announced. But changes came slowly, and the flurry of activity at Trinity did not go unnoticed. The university was late to welcome the social sciences. President Kemp Battle, trained in law, offered a combination of courses in political economy and constitutional and international law. There was a young historical society and a seminary of literature and philology that sometimes dealt with historical subjects. Not until 1891 did history begin to receive serious attention in the curriculum, when Battle resigned and became professor of history. At the same time the new president, George Tayloe Winston, began to offer a series of courses in the social sciences, including sociology. Increasingly thereafter these areas acquired an important place in the curriculum.[24]

At Wake Forest the new learning also made some inroads. The college had a comparatively large endowment for the time and was occupying a position of relative leadership in the state. Chemistry had been a separate study since 1886, with a Hopkins Ph.D. in charge. There were chairs for English and the modern languages, although history was still linked with moral philosophy. More conservative than some in the late 1880's, Wake Forest was using its strength to support what it had been doing. It was 1897 before there was a professor of history and political science. The elective system was "guarded" against any unwise eliminations in the student program, and in 1891 President Charles E. Taylor noted, perhaps with an eye toward Crowell, that all new departures would be closely scrutinized but none "slavishly followed."[25]

Davidson College was a similar mixture of old and new. Entrance examinations were required, and courses for juniors and seniors were entirely elective. There was a Ph.D. in English, although he also taught psychology and courses in history and political economy. The sciences were slowly developing as great-

24. U.N.C. catalogues, 1886-1894; Kemp P. Battle, *History of the University of North Carolina*, II, 1868-1912 (Raleigh, 1912).
25. George Washington Paschal, *History of Wake Forest College*, II, 1865-1905 (Wake Forest, 1943).

er laboratory facilities were provided. In 1889 a new president, J. B. Shearer, brought other changes: the introduction of book-keeping and commercial law and the announcement that students in history and physics now were encouraged to do independent investigation. There were three Ph.D.'s on the faculty by 1892. Again, the social sciences were slow to receive support. As late as the turn of the century there was one course in history and one in political economy (mingled with logic)—all the responsibility of the professor of English.[26]

In the small circle of educators interested in college work, Crowell's arrival had impact. His emphasis upon the social studies and upon their application to public activities was challenging. Even when it was not influential, it was noticed.

In the midst of the new departures at Trinity and in the pressure of competition, the abiding problem then and later was money. The constituency joined in the endowment campaign, but payments continued to be slow. After 1887 tuition was relatively unchanged. Even then students came and signed notes which were hard to collect. From the beginning Crowell wanted financial reform, a careful husbanding of resources, and he tried to alter the fixation that Trinity was for poor boys who were always to be invited to attend. He urged students to borrow money at home, praised self-help, and sought to reduce credit at the college.[27] But sometimes, as in other colleges, it seemed better to admit a promising student and hope he could pay later. Always there were schemes for fund-raising; the *Advocate* was full of them: "If five wealthy laymen will each pledge $5000 . . ."; "If every Methodist will give 5¢ per week. . . ." Bright ideas were plentiful, including insurance plans and chain-letters, but all hinged on the ability to pay.

Few of the Methodists had money, but the faithful were busy doing what they always did for Trinity—sending her students. Ministers, itinerant by the nature of their profession, sought prospects and sent their names to Crowell, who sent out catalogues or called on students. Trinity students in summer jobs took literature with them. Crowell spent as much time on the road as he could spare. One friend summed it up for many: "He would hardly get any Endowment money [here], but he might get some

26. Davidson College catalogues, 1887-1902.
27. Trinity College Papers; Trinity College catalogues, 1888 ff.

Julian S. Carr

Yours Truly
W. Duke

boys."[28] It was a day when a president with a "full college" in the fall might weep with relief.

Naturally the faculty tempered their interest in the imposing curriculum and the new atmosphere with the reality of pay checks only too reminiscent of the past. Professors' salaries from 1887 to 1890 were supposed to be $1,000 per year, but they were not always paid or paid on time. In June, 1889, the professors petitioned for $1,100 per year and for a schedule of annual increases thereafter. The Board agreed, but the issue was academic. For several months Crowell's salary, $2,000, was unpaid, as he diverted it to the faculty payroll.[29] In brief, the financial situation was little better than in the early years. A burst of enthusiasm under the new administration had helped, as had Julian Carr's gift of $10,000. But even modest improvements cost something, and soon Crowell faced the hopelessness that had haunted Craven to his grave.

Yet, something could be done, and the solution was an obvious one to Crowell: move the college away from the village and into the lifestream of a city. Any student of social science might look about him and observe the urban drift of population. The jobs, the money, and the activity were in the cities. It was common knowledge that many colleges were making such moves; the pages of the *Advocate* regularly recorded them. And Crowell had gained some experience of the trend, in reverse. During one of his years away at Yale, the Schuylkill Seminary over which he was presiding had been moved from the city of Reading to the village of Fredericksburg, Pennsylvania. He had seen the unhappy contrast and felt that the move had been a mistake.[30]

Therefore during his second year he broached the idea, and it reached the trustees as early as December, 1888. The Board was cautious but asked Crowell to sound out the possibilities and report. In the interim, opponents of the idea were alerted and became active in building a backfire of opposition. At the same time several cities were expressing interest, among them Raleigh and Greensboro. In May, 1889, the Board put aside all proposals and debated the issue of the move itself. At length the vote was favorable and a committee was named to bring in proposals in June.[31] The committee decided that $20,500 would duplicate the

28. J. N. Cole to J. A. Cunninggim, March 28, 1889, Trinity College Papers.
29. Chaffin, *Beginnings*, pp. 466-467; Petition, Trinity College Papers.
30. Crowell, *Recollections, passim;* Chaffin, *Beginnings*, pp. 478 ff.
31. *Ibid.*

present building and presented an offer from Raleigh of that amount and a site. Although Crowell spoke vehemently for the move, it was evident at commencement that many alumni were disturbed, and, favoring a cooling off period, the Board postponed action for a month.

In the interval the debate took on full volume as opposing sides sought to influence Methodist opinion. The heart of the opposition rested with the townspeople of little Trinity and with some members of the college faculty. Many people were doomed to lose much if the college departed. Several provided services, in particular rooms for students. Farmers sold their produce in town. Faculty members had long augmented their uncertain salaries by farming, and some of them were influential in the Church. Beneath it all, perhaps, was the old East-West division in North Carolina, the ancient product of topography, climate, and soil. For years it had been reflected in political and economic differences, and it had never been unimportant in Methodist politics. Just at this time, 1889, the Conference was contemplating a split into Eastern and Western Conferences. Western Methodists could not look with favor on the Church's college moving across the new line to the East. Finally, hostility to change itself was fundamental. It was intolerable that the idea should even be discussed.

These perhaps were the real reasons for opposing the move, but as the debate developed, others were forthcoming: the idea was a "whim" and "a fancy,"[32] and destructive at that. The spiritual heart of the old college lay in the village itself where the sainted Craven was buried. The city was the last place for a college; it offered temptations and vice and would corrupt student morals. The move would be expensive in itself, but the costs of operation in a city would be high and would require exorbitant student fees. At length it was natural to attach full blame to Crowell for thinking of it in the first place. A young man from the North could not be expected to appreciate local values.[33] Years later Crowell recalled the force of this feeling, and a student of that day remembered that he became *persona non grata* in the town of Trinity "to a withering degree."[34]

32. Professor W. T. Gannaway, *"Audi Alteram Partem,"* Raleigh *Christian Advocate,* May 29, 1889.
33. A former student believed he grew a full beard to "camouflage" his youth Durham, *Since I Was Born,* p. 129.
34. *Ibid.,* p. 130.

For several weeks the proponents of the move negotiated with the cities. They joined in the debate as the July meeting approached. Crowell was especially articulate on the subject, and his views sum up their argument. It was a useful mixture of the practical and the idealistic.[35]

"All the main creative forces in modern society" were in the cities, and, in turn, the cities needed the intellectual and spiritual transfusion that only a college could provide. Applying Darwin *cum* Spencer, the shift to the city reflected "the inexorable necessity of natural laws which pertain to human society as well as to the world of nature." Yet, "we have left our College standing singularly and severely alone in the country." He reminded the Methodists that the trustees hired him to put Trinity in the front rank; it was his considered opinion that this aim was impossible without a move. Finally, perhaps in response to the personal treatment he was receiving, Crowell burnt his bridges: the village of Trinity, "circumscribed by most uninspiring types of rusticity," gave the college only social poverty. "There are local jealousies that keep a watchful and prayerful check upon any strong, united action for improvement." Sin in the cities? The cities have the machinery to control it, but in the town of Trinity "harlots stalk the streets," and only violence would remove them.[36]

The tide was with Crowell. At the July meeting a proposal to "indefinitely postpone" was rejected eighteen to eleven, and the Raleigh offer was accepted. A small campaign ensued in anticipation of the vote for Conference approval in December.[37] The opposition was not yet beaten. In fact, the chairman of the Board of Trustees, J. W. Alspaugh, who lived in Winston-Salem (in the new Western Conference), regarded the whole effort as "a great wrong in principle and ruinous in its consequences."[38] He would do nothing to help; others were determined to resist to the last. At the Conference the usual arguments were presented, and a move to prevent Crowell from speaking was headed off. He long remembered the moment when he rose. He told them the move meant more, not less, work for him, but he appealed to larger considerations. No personal interest must inter-

35. Raleigh *Christian Advocate*, June 26, July 3, 1889.
36. *Ibid.*
37. Chaffin, *Beginnings*, p. 488.
38. J. W. Alspaugh to J. F. Crowell (note on back of letter dated Aug. 21, 1889), Trinity College Papers.

fere. He offered a vision of what was to be, charting a "Greater Trinity" which bore some of the aspects of a university. He seemed to sweep the audience before him. The vote was 143 to 41, and now the move was certain.[39] When the college left Trinity, the old facilities would be used for a preparatory school.

Almost immediately rumors were heard of a bid from the city of Durham. Recently Raleigh and Durham had made competing overtures to another school, the Baptist Female Seminary (Meredith College). Although Durham's figure had been higher, the final decision had favored Raleigh, and reportedly some of Durham's leaders were stung. Among them, so the story goes, was Washington Duke, a wealthy tobacco manufacturer and a staunch Methodist. Duke had shown only moderate interest in Trinity and had declined to join the Committee of Management of 1885. However, his son, Benjamin N. Duke, had been elected to the Board in 1889, and the Dukes had given the lion's share ($1,000) of a Durham collection for Trinity two years earlier. Two Durham ministers, R. F. Bumpass and E. A. Yates, are credited with urging Washington Duke to make a specific proposal. When the Raleigh offer reached $35,000, he was quoted as saying that Durham would equal that and add $50,000 more for endowment. When Duke agreed to guarantee those figures, Yates wired Crowell to come to Durham to discuss it. At the meeting the group enlisted the aid of Julian S. Carr in securing a site. Carr agreed to give the fair grounds west of the city, known as Blackwell Park. Apparently Washington Duke expected that other local gifts might become a part of the total of $85,000, but in the final offer on March 20, 1890, he underwrote the entire amount. Initial enthusiasm prompted mass meetings in Durham, and enough pledges were reported to make the total $100,000.[40]

But the college was promised to Raleigh, and citizens there sought to equal Durham's offer. The Trinity Board appointed a Committee of Three[41] to discuss the matter with them. It was apparent that Raleigh could not raise enough, and the committee outlined to them the advantages to Trinity if Durham were chosen. Among the arguments were two of special importance. First, since Durham was farther west, the hope for Church unity would be enhanced. There had been talk that the new Western

39. Chaffin, *Beginnings*, pp. 489-490; Crowell, *Recollections*, pp. 152-155.
40. *Ibid.*, pp. 491-498; pp. 162-167.
41. Crowell was one of the three.

Conference (established May, 1890) might erect a rival college. Second, *"The assurance of still greater gifts for the College at Durham are so definite that the Trustees consider the financial prosperity of the College as good as guaranteed for the future."*[42] This last was to prove mischievous.

The Raleigh citizens released the college; they could hardly do otherwise. The trustees approved Durham's offer, and in due course the two Conferences readily followed suit. Now Trinity had obtained a patron and a new local constituency. The college had no way of knowing what it could expect of either, but the tie with the Dukes looked promising.

In 1890 Washington Duke was almost seventy years old and, as the founder of W. Duke, Sons and Company, had built up one of the few large fortunes in the state. It had come quickly in recent years, based on a successful combination of a booming demand for tobacco products, a technological revolution in their manufacture, and enormous family energy amidst fierce competition. In the very weeks in which Duke and his son Ben were discussing the offer to Trinity, a younger son, James Buchanan ("Buck") Duke, the acknowledged leader of the company, was creating the American Tobacco Company, a cigarette combine capitalized at $25,000,000.

It had not always been like that. In 1860 Washington Duke opposed Southern secession and reluctantly saw his state enter the Confederacy. He was conscripted into the Confederate army and returned after the war almost penniless. Before he left in 1863 he had converted his means into raw leaf and stored it away. Once home, he worked this into salable smoking tobacco, in log factories on his farm near Durham and with his sons peddled the product about the state. It was the right mixture of times and men. The great postwar popularity of "fancy yellow" or bright leaf tobacco, then best grown along the Carolina-Virginia border, and the Dukes' salesmanship produced a healthy business. By 1873 the company had moved to Durham for better access to railroad lines, and there confronted the powerful Durham Bull Tobacco Company, among whose owners was another talented salesman and advertising expert, Julian S. Carr. The "Bull" was formidable competition, and by 1881, James B. Duke was directing the family operations into a new venture, the mak-

42. *Proceedings of the Board of Trustees*, 1880-1891, p. 210. Cited hereinafter as *Minutes*, Board of Trustees.

ing of cigarettes—and with quick success. The company expanded to New York in 1884, and in a few years Duke's willingness to gamble on unproved mass-production machinery and a hard, determined, competitive spirit paid off. The American Tobacco Company, formed in 1890, dominated the cigarette market.

Washington Duke, his family, and the Carr family were ardent Methodists, and it is not surprising that Durham should have been a strong Methodist town. Indeed it was company policy for the Dukes to locate a church near every factory to encourage the religious interests of their employees. The town (population 6,000) was almost wholly a product of postwar industrial development. Primarily it was a factory community, and a good place for an ambitious young man to make money in tobacco. Its good works and its leadership naturally fell to the handful of captains of industry who had created it.[43]

The growing concentration of Methodist wealth in Durham had not been overlooked by the Church. The *Advocate*, which tried to reach every Methodist home, reported the healthy situation in Durham and directed its readers to articles praising "consecrated wealth" and to comments on Andrew Carnegie's new Gospel of Wealth, then receiving prestige from the endorsement of the British statesman Gladstone. There is a marked affinity between Carnegie's famous advice to millionaires and the attitude of the Dukes. It may be well here to review the Gospel:

Carnegie shared the philosophy of the day that wealth came to those who had earned it in the struggle for survival, "the fittest." But he insisted that they merely held it in trust and thus faced the duty of disposing of it properly for public benefit. He opposed bequeathing it to one's family and thereby corrupting one's children. He opposed willing it away for any purpose. "He who dies rich, dies disgraced." Rather, he recommended, one should give it away in one's own lifetime when its distribution might be administered. Further, all gifts should preclude indiscriminate charity that would "pauperize" the recipient. Give it to individuals and institutions willing to help themselves, he advised. He offered a list of priorities in the following order:

43. J. S. Bassett, sketch of Washington Duke, *Biographical History of North Carolina*, ed. S. A. Ashe, III, 84 ff.; Chaffin, *Beginnings*; Nannie May Tilley, *The Bright-Tobacco Industry, 1860-1929* (Chapel Hill, 1948), pp. 556 ff.; William K. Boyd, *The Story of Durham: City of the New South* (Durham, 1925), pp. 322-325.

universities, libraries, and medical schools or hospitals. Carnegie's list provided a pattern for giving that the Dukes were to follow all of their lives.[44]

But in 1890 the Durham magnates, the Dukes and Julian Carr, had made relatively small commitments. Washington Duke's offer referred to "the building," not several, and promised an endowment of $50,000, far from enough to guarantee the future as the Committee of Three had predicted. Yet by the spring of 1890 a contagion of excitement led to hopes for a Methodist university. Crowell himself understood what a modern university was, and he had offered a dream to the Methodist Conference in 1889. Before the Durham offer was accepted, Chairman Alspaugh had been converted and in March, 1890, was writing Crowell his belief that Carr would do "much more than he says" for Trinity, adding, ". . . we must not stop at a college, we must have a university. That is what I have always wanted."[45] From Durham E. A. Yates reported his belief that Washington Duke's gesture was "but a beginning. . . ."[46] At commencement Crowell spoke confidently of an endowment of $200,000 by the fall of 1891, the date set for opening in Durham. Earlier he had written Washington Duke of his readiness to outline plans for a greater Trinity, and he had prepared a "Plan of a Methodist University in North Carolina."[47] The constituency was willing. One university in the South, Vanderbilt, was not enough for the growing Church. It was rare to hear a voice of restraint recommend that Trinity concentrate on developing strength as a college.[48]

How did this come about? Washington Duke emphatically denied rumors that he would liberally increase the endowment, and there is no evidence of specific promises from him or Carr beyond those of 1890. Indeed, Duke anticipated that his gift would inspire others. The answer probably lies in the relief and excitement in finding rich benefactors and the need for persuasion in all the negotiations of 1889-1890. The Dukes and Carr

44. Andrew Carnegie, "Wealth," *North American Review*, CXLVIII (June, 1889), 653-664; "The Best Fields for Philanthropy," *North American Review*, CXLIX (Dec., 1889), 682-698.
45. J. W. Alspaugh to J. F. Crowell, March 10, 1890, Trinity College Papers.
46. Raleigh *Christian Advocate*, March 19, 1890, p. 1.
47. Undated. Trinity College Papers, Nov.-Dec., 1890. One of the faculty even ordered "Trinity University" stationery.
48. Raleigh *Christian Advocate*, Oct. 22, 1890, Aug. 26, 1891; and speaking in restraint, Bishop Galloway, June 24, 1891.

wanted Trinity to come to Durham. Crowell and his supporters wanted to come. Both wanted to convince opponents, inside the Church and inside the college, that it was necessary.

In any event, Crowell was always willing to think large and planned accordingly. In the aggregate the dreams took on the dimensions of the multi-purpose state university as it would develop half a century later. The new catalogues began to show an elaborate reorganization, retaining some of the essentials of 1887-1890, but adding a Seminary Department with graduate work in various areas and courses leading to the master's and doctor's degrees. Electives now would be introduced at the sophomore level, and upperclassmen would choose major and minor fields of study. The School of Political and Social Science would gradually attain a separate status and would publish a journal. Science and technology would receive accelerated emphasis, through Schools of Technology and Mines and training in applied fields such as printing and engraving. Later perhaps there would be a textile school "in view of the large manufacturing interests of the South," and there was talk of a High School of Commerce to prepare for business careers. Each day brought fresh ideas: summer courses were envisaged, especially for teachers and perhaps a summer school in the mountains near a good mineral spring. Soon Crowell had plans for a hospital and a three-year medical college—which would be made self-supporting from medical fees! A pharmacy program was outlined, to begin in 1892.[49]

The public service theme of recent years was accentuated. The faculty specialists, who would concentrate on training upperclassmen and graduate students, would help make the college "a bureau of information on all leading interests of the people." Reform and correction would be an institutional service. This required means of communication, and Crowell would be willing "to dispense with a professorship in order to have our own printing press." Moreover, the university extension movement was growing and receiving support, including that of Crowell's old teacher, Timothy Dwight of Yale, and William Rainey Harper, another Yale man. The public was beginning to crave learning, and Crowell thought Trinity should help. He expected that in a few years Trinity's extension enrollments alone would eclipse

49. Trinity College catalogues, 1890-1892; *Supplement to Trinity College Bulletin*, Oct., 1890, no. 6, Trinity College Papers; Raleigh *Christian Advocate*, 1890-1891.

recent enrollments. By 1892 a pilot effort was begun with lectures in Archdale, a village near Old Trinity.

Other college reforms were necessary, and Trinity must lead. The students would be given a real share in the government of the institution. A revolution was called for here. Further, there must be direct connection with the academies to meet them "on the most favorable terms," even if this meant inserting a year between the freshman class and the final year of preparatory training. Somewhat on a note of anti-climax and lacking a resolution of the problem of poor secondary education, the college re-established its preparatory department.[50]

Crowell took these plans to the largest audience he could reach. He began an educational column in the *Advocate* and by the spring of 1891 was traveling the state organizing mass meetings among the Methodists. His aim was to develop among the constituency a "parliament of experience" through discussion of educational planning—and incidentally to quicken interest in Trinity College.

The grandiose plans seemed to require more faculty, of course, and the need was accentuated by the unwillingness of some of the old faculty to make the move to Durham. Accordingly, Crowell continued to recruit new men from the graduate training centers. Two came from Yale, William Price (French) and M. Austin Aikins (Philosophy). Others, J. M. Stedman from Cornell and C. B. Hinde from Hopkins, became the first full time professors of biology and physics. An ambitious, research-minded Hopkins Ph.D., Stephen B. Weeks, attracted by the "Renaissance" he perceived at Trinity, arrived to become professor of history. From among the recent Trinity graduates a corps of young instructors was assembled, including John Spencer Bassett, William Ivey Cranford, and B. B. Nicholson. Their contact with the new scholars was to persuade each later to go off to Yale, Hopkins, and other institutions for graduate study. Another instructor, Robert L. Flowers, just out of the Naval Academy, came to teach mathematics and electrical engineering—and remained for half a century.[51]

The enthusiasm and cosmopolitan air of most of the new personnel provided more of a university atmosphere and contrib-

50. *Extra Official Bulletin, Trinity College,* Aug. 1, 1891, no. 10, Trinity College Papers.
51. Trinity College catalogues, 1890-1892; Chaffin, *Beginnings,* pp. 460 ff.

uted to a certain secularizing of the college. In the new faculty the students discovered an intellectual toughness they had not known before. Weeks found that his beginning students tended "to gape," although the upperclassmen were eager and thoughtful. There was a tendency to accept provincialisms like the Mecklenburg Declaration, which Weeks sought to correct.[52] There was "a vast amount of bibliolatry," although Weeks said that Aikins in philosophy had more problems there. The rather exacting Methodist Discipline, which abjured dancing, drinking, and wordly amusements, was a little confining. One professor spoke ironically of smoking a cigar and hoped it was not a mortal sin. He found it hard to deal with his nervous attacks, which he had treated elsewhere with doses of wine, a pint at a time.[53]

A degree of secularization was evident also in the new charter obtained in 1891 that authorized the move to Durham. The Board of Trustees was no longer permanent or self-perpetuating. Now the thirty-six members were chosen for six-year terms, twelve by each of the two Conferences and twelve by the graduates. The Conferences were free to make their choices, but the board would determine how the alumni might proceed. A clause in the old charter granting "ownership" of the college to the Methodist Church in North Carolina was deleted. Of course it was a compromise of the varying centers of power, and a rather adroit one: the Board had to open its membership to outside influence. The competing Conferences might name trustees, but alumni, and surely Crowell was thinking of the new alumni, would have a voice. Through the lay alumni who could be elected and through the Durham location and the influence of its lay patrons, the religious and the secular might be balanced.[54] Crowell was proud of his work. He thought the new management would be more representative, that there would be fewer of the "inbred type of custodian."[55] It was a charter calculated to align the college with the progressive thought of the state, he believed —in short, the attitudes that had brought Crowell to Trinity in 1887.

52. Stephen B. Weeks to Herbert B. Adams, Oct. 10, and Oct. 31, 1891, Herbert Baxter Adams Letters (photostats, Duke University Library).
53. William Price to J. F. Crowell, June 17, 1889 and Sept. 2, 1889, Trinity College Papers.
54. Chaffin, *Beginnings*, pp. 500-503; Crowell, *Recollections*, pp. 190-193.
55. J. F. Crowell, East Orange, N. J., to W. K. Boyd, Feb. 4, 1922, Boyd Papers.

Expansive thinking had led to an expanded building program by 1891. In addition to the Main Building, a College Inn was planned with the aid of an additional gift of $15,000 from Washington Duke. Crowell wished to give a building in memory of his wife, who had died in 1888 (and from whom he had inherited some money), and thought at first of a library. Later, he decided on a Technology Building, and this too was planned. Finally, six faculty residences were under construction. These projects were beyond the original plan, and their actual cost exceeded estimates. Gradually construction needs ate into the fund set aside for endowment. But the hazards were not yet apparent. The new curriculum and the corps of lively professors were ready, the government was tailored for the future. It only remained to finish the new campus and move into it in September, 1891.[56]

In August disaster caught up with the dream. The tower of the Main Building, defective from faulty masonry and possibly faulty architecture, fell and with it tons of new brick. The loss was $6,000 in cash and a great deal more in prestige. The opening was delayed, and for another year the college remained in limbo at Old Trinity. Enemies of the move called the calamity a judgment of God. It did seem to shake confidence.

One uncertainty had given Crowell some uneasiness many months before, the college's relationship with its patron. A controversy developed at the commencement of 1890. J. R. Webster, editor and publisher of *Webster's Weekly* in Reidsville, was given the honor of presenting some medals. Webster was active in Democratic politics and served a major tobacco-growing county. Therefore he disliked the Dukes on at least two grounds: they were Republicans, and they were operating the new tobacco trust. He had been tireless in his attacks. Thus, when Webster was honored at commencement, Ben Duke was indignant and felt that the family had been humiliated. He said that he and his father might "wash our hands of the entire affair."[57] Crowell apologized, explaining that the students had chosen Webster, who was an alumnus, and that it had been a minor ceremony that Crowell had not thought important enough to attend.[58] That seemed to settle it, but it must have set Crowell thinking. A few weeks later he was inquiring of Judge Walter Clark if Washing-

56. Chaffin, *Beginnings*, pp. 505 ff.; Crowell, *Recollections, passim.*
57. B. N. Duke to J. F. Crowell, June 14, 1890, Trinity College Papers.
58. J. F. Crowell to B. N. Duke, June 19, 1890, *ibid.*

ton Duke's offer was legally binding. Clark doubted that Duke would change his mind, but he advised that there was no legal contract. In case of his death, the old man's executors might choose not to pay what had been promised. Clark's advice was that "it would be well to put it in a different shape."[59] In these early days of their new relationship, both the college and the philanthropists were feeling their way.

Of more immediate concern was the continuing problem of money. In 1890-1891 Eastern North Carolina was in sore financial condition, and endowment pledges suffered. In that year at Trinity less than one-half of the tuition had been collected, and in June, 1891, one-third of the professors' salaries remained unpaid.[60] When the tower fell in August, the crisis merely deepened. The Executive Committee of the Board concluded there was no hope of meeting the salary budget and asked for faculty agreement on a salary ceiling, which apparently might be revised downward. The faculty was sympathetic but thought the proposal vague and potentially a heavy burden on them. They preferred a bird in the hand and offered a counter suggestion, let each professor be paid $100 per month at the end of each month. The trustees agreed and sought to fund the budget by short-term notes, signed by the president and treasurer and drawn on the Board itself.[61] This procedure had been followed the previous spring and was to become a frequent resort in succeeding years.

Another source of tension in the last years at the old location was caused by uncertainty as to whose duty it was to direct the building program in Durham. These operations seemed to move very slowly. Most of the staff work fell to Crowell, who was expected to do all things left undone. Yet during this period he was keeping his hand in a variety of academic interests. He was alert to the new scholarly societies being organized across the nation and prepared several papers that he delivered at national meetings.[62] He took time, admittedly "in the midst of growing official duties," to work on a series of popular articles for the *Progressive Farmer*. In 1891 he offered a *Program of Progress* to the General Assembly of North Carolina, urging greater public

59. Walter Clark to J. F. Crowell, Sept. 8, 1890, *ibid.*
60. Treasurer's Report, 1890-1891, *ibid.*
61. *Minutes*, Board of Trustees, 1891-1900.
62. Trinity College catalogues; Trinity College Papers, 1891-1892.
In 1889 Crowell belonged to the American Academy of Political and Social Science, American Institute of Civics, American Economic Association, and American Statistical Association.

support for the schools and advocating more attention to highways, flood control and conservation, railroad lines, a geological survey, farm credit banks, and other reform measures. He also continued to promote a plan to establish a chain of Methodist "feeder" schools to supply Trinity College. The new charter provided for this plan and authorized the trustees to acquire the properties and administer them. The idea was an item in the Methodist university dream.[63]

However, as economic conditions worsened, a few trustees wanted to concentrate all forces upon the college itself "until we get her well established and in safe working order."[64] A statement of this view in June, 1892, warned that Washington Duke already "feels that the church in this State has not manifested any appreciation of his donation" by making its own contribution to the endowment. The statement specifically asked that no more money be spent for acquiring feeder schools, but the Board voted it down.

At this time increasing faculty disaffection became apparent as well. Crowell's inclination was to work out most of the academic details of the college himself. This attitude began to pinch the professors by the spring of 1892. A list of questions about the separate responsibilities of the faculty and the president was presented to the Board and resolved almost wholly in the president's favor. His authority to approve or veto any action of the faculty was emphasized. However, the Board stated that no professor might be dismissed without a hearing.[65]

Although the principal faculty complaints apparently stemmed from inadequate funds and from Crowell's authoritarian tendency, a glimpse at the teaching load is at least informative. In 1892 Stephen Weeks reported, without complaint, that during the year he had given a two-hour course each week to twenty-eight "sub-freshmen" (preparatory students) in American History; two hours of General History to thirty-eight freshmen in two sections; three hours of the History of the Middle Ages and Modern Europe to nineteen sophomores; two hours of General Church History to three theological students; three hours of French History to three juniors; and three hours of American and North Carolina History to three seniors. After Christmas two of

63. Trinity College Papers.
64. *Minutes*, Board of Trustees, 1891-1900, p. 49.
65. *Ibid.*, pp. 50-53.

these classes had been combined.[66] Weeks's load was probably typical.

This would have been sweatshop teaching even if the college could have paid for it. But it could not. In that year Crowell himself was due $1,900 of his $2,000 salary. In June, 1892, estimates for the coming year showed an income of less than $12,000 and a faculty payroll of $16,000. Not included in resources was a $3,000 pledge from B. N. Duke to be paid "if necessary."[67] Nor were any other college expenses included in the figures given. Retrenchment was the only answer, and the Board decided that five of the fourteen members of the faculty must go. After discussion, the five were re-elected but given a year's leave of absence without pay! Some went off to further graduate study.

To cap the succession of miseries, in late May, 1892, Ben Duke, who was planning a summer's trip abroad, resigned as a member of the Board and as treasurer of its Executive Committee. He hoped the resignations would be promptly accepted.[68] The apparent disaffection of the patron was an omen. A time of troubles awaited the college in Durham.

66. Stephen B. Weeks, "Report," 1891-1892, June 6, 1892, Trinity College Papers.
67. *Minutes,* Board of Trustees, 1891-1900, pp. 44-54.
68. B. N. Duke to J. W. Alspaugh, May 17, 1892, B. N. Duke Letterbook, B. N. Duke Papers (Duke University Library).

Chapter II

A Time of Troubles

1892-1894

The last commencement at Old Trinity was held in June, 1892, and during the summer the faculty and the college moved their belongings into the raw new buildings at Durham. The move marked the end of the more leisurely days in Randolph County and the beginning of two years of unrelieved tension and struggle.

Throughout the summer Crowell sought to build up enrollments sufficient to fill the new dormitory rooms. He launched an advertising campaign in surrounding states to round up boys, and friends helped refute continuing complaints that the new Trinity was going to be too expensive in its fancy new home. A movement by the *Advocate* produced dormitory furnishings that the college had no money to purchase. By fall Crowell thought "the tide of murmur" was moving in his favor.[1] Enrollments in all departments totaled 180, and there were 104 students in the new Trinity High School back in Randolph County. Combined, this total was an increase of fifty-five over the previous year.[2]

On the other hand, in the summer of 1892 the lot of the farmer in North Carolina was unimproved.[3] The farm problem was chronic, and as always, economic distress was reflected in the ability of Trinity's patrons to pay fees and of the Methodists to give to the college. By August the financial problem of the previous spring was unresolved, and a committee of the Board confessed that it could devise no plan that would promise a solution. Again, the Board borrowed on short-term notes to pay overdue salaries and to get cash for moving expenses.[4] In opening the college, Crowell found himself smothered by details, including a host of housekeeping and maintenance activities.

1. Trinity College Papers, *passim*, including J. F. Crowell to J. F. Heitman, Trinity, N. C., Sept. 14, 1892.
2. Trinity College catalogue, 1892-1893.
3. *Progressive Farmer*, June 28, 1892—Sept. 6, 1892.
4. *Minutes*, Board of Trustees, Aug. 3, 1892.

When classes began, there were still unfinished buildings, no electric lights, unfurnished rooms, "much incompetent help and an inadequate amount of funds to do anything." Hopefully, he wrote Ben Duke, who had returned to New York from Europe, "It will be a glad day when you return."[5]

As cold weather drew near, the new heating system in the Inn proved balky, students complained, and physical discomfort heightened the sense of desperation. A few days before the dedication ceremony, E. A. Yates, who was a trustee, sent Ben Duke an appeal for help. Yates concluded that the building program had been too expansive, frittering away as it did any reserves for endowment. He and Crowell personally were in debt $600, and this was "only a drop in the bucket." He thought the Methodists appreciated the Duke gifts and wished to contribute, but they were poor and could not. He warned, "We are really in *danger of a collapse*. It will be a disgrace to us for this to take place." If only all the debts could be paid, the college might get along by itself.[6]

In New York Duke was not inclined to be stirred. Probably he had just seen a letter to his brother from an elderly minister, asking for money and lecturing "Buck" on the transitory nature of wealth. The old clergyman hoped Duke's prosperity "does not drown your soul in perdition."[7] In a few days Yates received his reply. Ben's pent-up irritation produced, for him, an unusually comprehensive comment:

> I predicted, when the question of moving to Durham was first agitated, that just such a state of affairs as now exists, would be the case and the more I looked into the past history of the institution, the more convinced I became. . . . The prediction of some of my Durham friends, that if my father's gift was made unconditional, the Methodists of the state would rally to the support of the College with their means so that an ample endowment fund would be provided and thus success would be assured were entirely wide of the mark and have in no wise been verified. . . . Under the circumstances failure is inevitable sooner or later, and I think the sooner the better. . . . The people of Durham have done their full duty in connection with this enterprise. . . . I do not for one moment regret that the gift of my father has been used as it has, for if the life of the College depends upon the in-

5. J. F. Crowell to B. N. Duke, Sept. 23, 1892, B. N. Duke Papers.
6. E. A. Yates to B. N. Duke, Oct. 7, 1892, Trinity College Papers.
7. R. S. Webb to J. B. Duke, Oct. 11, 1892, *ibid.*

come from that portion of his contribution mentioned for endowment, it would still be the failure that it now is. From what I
know of the past history of the College it has always been more
or less a failure, and from the standpoint from which I view the
situation, the future of it bids fair to be the same.

I know just what you and Dr. Crowell have and are under-
going, and you certainly have my sympathy, and I can say frankly, that no enterprise with which I have ever been connected has
caused me half the trouble and worry and loss of sleep, as my
short connection with the work since it began operations at Durham. . . .[8]

Meanwhile the college put the best face on its condition, and
on October 12 an elaborate dedication ceremony was held on the
porch of the Inn. A procession marched from town, and the
merchants joined to make it an occasion. Business firms closed
for the period of the exercises in tribute to "Durham's Glory."[9]
Colonel E. J. Parrish, speaking for the mayor, praised Crowell
and noted that he was overworked. "Give him the reins and
plenty of grease, and all will be well." The buildings and grounds
were presented and accepted. Crowell had been ill but delivered
a strong address on the mutual benefits bound to accrue to Trinity
and the city. The college would provide "truth" and would expect from the people financial support. He hoped both would
understand each other.

He also took occasion to sound a call for freedom. Trinity had
the duty to warn and to counsel and must be free from restraints.
He turned prophetic:

There will, therefore, come times when the teachings—the utterances of teachers in this institution—may for a time be unpopular
and distasteful. But the truth is the thing that must be taught.
Therefore, this College cannot expect always to be crowded with
students. It may have to first train a remnant to proclaim new
prophecies and lead the people away from the idols of the times.[10]

Meanwhile, the financial problems were becoming unbear-
able. In mid-November the trustees reviewed the situation.
Literally, the college owed everybody: more than $5,000 in facul-

8. B. N. Duke to E. A. Yates, Oct. 14, 1892, *ibid.*
9. Durham *Daily Globe*, Oct. 8, Oct. 12, 1892.
10. Raleigh *Christian Advocate*, Oct. 12, Oct. 19, Oct. 26, 1892. Fresh in
Crowell's mind was a recent public exchange with the editor of the Wilmington
Messenger about a Trinity faculty member's right to run for office on the Populist
ticket. Chaffin, *Beginnings*, pp. 404-409; Crowell, *Recollections*, pp. 121-125.

ty salaries for the previous year still unpaid, and already behind $300 in the new year. The series of notes drawn on the Board were unmet, three of them to Crowell for $2,570. There were overdue bills for coal, water, newspaper advertising, books, stationery, furniture, even for insurance premiums on the buildings. A committee had found comfort in estimating total assets, almost wholly in buildings, at $182,000. But these paid no bills, and expenses for the current year would be $17,900. The income from tuition was listed as $4,500 and included $2,300 still due for the present term.[11]

With or without the patron, Yates pushed for a tighter operation and offered a plan which was accepted. A treasurer and a finance committee would be elected, all of whom "shall reside in Durham." The committee would have complete authority over expenditures and must meet to endorse every item of payment. Those chosen were all Durham businessmen, Virginius Ballard, as treasurer, and H. J. Bass, W. H. Branson, and E. J. Parrish. None was a trustee, and Yates offered an amendment to the college charter that would make them Board members *ex officio.*

The amendment contained other proposals. It gave the trustees power to declare any place on the Board vacant and to fill it, subject to the confirmation of the Methodist Conferences; and it contained this proviso, "All trustees provided for in the Charter of Trinity College shall be nominated by the Board subject to confirmation by the conference in which they respectively reside." The charter of 1891 had made no mention of nomination, merely stating that the Conferences and the alumni were to "elect" trustees in groups of twelve. The amendment was endorsed by the Board.[12]

At the November meeting the trustees reached for the one resource, the assets in property, and authorized the Executive Committee to fund the floating debt by mortgaging the property and to put an agent in the field to collect unpaid pledges and new gifts. This last appealed to Ben Duke, who agreed to help pay the agent's salary.[13]

Before they left, the trustees had to deal with faculty dissatisfaction, some of which had turned directly against Crowell. The details are not well recorded, but the unrest rose out of a compound of unpaid salaries and Crowell's disposition to

11. *Minutes,* Board of Trustees, Nov. 16-17, 1892, pp. 73-77.
12. *Ibid.,* pp. 77-82.
13. J. F. Crowell to B. N. Duke, Nov. 22, 1892, Trinity College Papers.

ignore the fact that some of his faculty were as fully trained as he in the new learning. Some members of the faculty began holding "irregular" meetings or complaining to Board members and to students. After a series of hearings, the Board issued a statement. It expressed sympathy with the professors' difficulties but expressed full confidence in Crowell and asked him "to be as courteous and sympathetic towards the Faculty as his great heart will suggest."[14]

Ben Duke held to his earlier determination to resign from the Executive Committee but was persuaded to remain on the Board. By early December Trinity's misery had persuaded him to lift his hand, and he offered a matching plan to the Board and to the Conferences. He would help create an endowment by insuring the lives of fifty men for $10,000 each until the plan became self-sustaining. As a condition, the two Conferences would bind themselves to find the money to meet Trinity's annual expenses. When the plan was found to be questionable legally,[15] Ben offered another scheme, on behalf of himself, James B. Duke, and their sister, Mary (Mrs. Robert E. Lyon). They would jointly give $7,500 per year for three years if the college would raise $15,000 each year for the same period. Part of the gift would be used to fund sixty scholarships, and the remainder would be spent as determined by the donors.[16]

The Conferences quickly accepted the offer, and each agreed to an assessment. They also accepted, without record of discussion, the charter amendments proposed by the trustees.[17] However, when the bill passed the legislature there were changes from the original proposal.[18] There was no refer-

14. *Minutes,* Board of Trustees, Nov. 16-17, 1892, pp. 78-83; Crowell, *Recollections,* pp. 203 ff.; Charles Lee Raper, *The Church and Private Schools of North Carolina* (Greensboro, 1898), pp. 190-193. Cited hereinafter as Raper, *Church and Private Schools.* Raper was on the faculty at the time and one of those who later resigned.

15. *Minutes,* Board of Trustees, Dec. 1, 1892. The plan is in the Trinity College Papers. Its legality is discussed in F. L. Fuller to B. N. Duke, Dec. 13, 1892, B. N. Duke Papers. Insurance laws required "an insurable interest." There was the possibility that the families of the men insured might rightly claim the insurance.

16. *Journal of the North Carolina Annual Conference of the Methodist Episcopal Church, South* (Raleigh, 1893), pp. 51-52. Cited hereinafter as *Journal, N. C. Conference.*

17. *Journal,* N. C. Conference, 1892, pp. 20, 52-53; *Journal of the Western North Carolina Annual Conference of the Methodist Episcopal Church, South* (Greensboro, 1892), pp. 14, 42. Cited hereinafter as *Journal,* Western Conference.

18. *Private Laws of the State of North Carolina, 1893* (Raleigh, 1893), pp. 416-417.

ence to the *ex officio* membership of the treasurer or finance committee. The Board might declare a place vacant temporarily, but when the Conferences next met they were to fill all vacancies. There was no mention of the Board's power to nominate all trustees.[19] When Trinity's trustees met in May of 1893 they resolved that the four business managers were *ex officio* members anyway, and in 1893 the four Durham men were confirmed by the North Carolina (Eastern) Conference.[20]

One item of special concern to the Western Conference that year was intercollegiate football. To the great satisfaction of the students, Crowell had introduced the modern game to Trinity on his arrival. Other Trinity supporters were greatly pleased after the team defeated the university in its first game in 1888. Crowell was a strong believer in all sports, competitive or otherwise, and saw many positive benefits. The physical conditioning was fundamental to good scholarly work; the pleasure itself was important; and the games united the students and faculty.[21]

Yet, as Eastern colleges developed competitive leagues, and as accounts of brawls, injuries, and occasional sprees reached North Carolina, many Church leaders campaigned against "match play." Parents occasionally complained to Crowell, and even his steady supporter, F. L. Reid, editor of the *Advocate,* was unrelenting in his attack upon the immorality of intercollegiate football. He feared the consequences of Trinity's policy. At the Western Conference of 1892 an official warning was issued by the Board of Education. "While not presuming to dictate" to the Trinity trustees, the Conference thought the practice was "a source of evil, and of no little evil, and ought to be stopped."[22]

19. *Journals of the Senate and House of the General Assembly of the State of North Carolina, 1893* (Raleigh, 1893). Senate *Journal,* pp. 527, 546, 635, 811. House *Journal,* pp. 363, 641, 1049.
20. *Minutes,* Board of Trustees, May 3, 1893, p. 91; *Journal,* N. C. Conference, 1893, pp. 21, 53. The record is blank as to discussions or compromises that may have led to the new wording. It seems unlikely that this was a strong bid for greater secular power at Trinity. All seemed to agree that the Methodist Church owned the college. Later in practice the Board did receive nominations from *its own* committees from each Conference and from the alumni, and the Conferences regularly accepted names submitted as nominations from the Board. Yet, the original wording was set aside in the bill of 1893. Perhaps it was altered in deference to Conference sensitivity as to where final authority lay. The importance of the episode lies in its being remembered later in the charter "codification" of 1903.
21. Chaffin, *Beginnings,* pp. 442-447; Crowell, *Recollections, passim;* J. F. Crowell, *Annual Report of the President of Trinity College to the North Carolina Conferences of the Methodist Episcopal Church, South* (Autumn, 1893), pp. 21-26. Cited hereinafter as Crowell, Conference Report, 1893.
22. *Journal,* Western Conference, 1892, p. 44.

The Eastern Conference took no action.

With the new year there were more urgent problems at Trinity. Business conditions worsened nationally with some major industrial bankruptcies and a collapse of the stock market. The Panic of 1893 was on. Bank failures were recurrent, and agricultural prices dropped again, ushering in a prolonged depression that was to be severe in the West and South for the next three years.[23] January in North Carolina brought fourteen inches of snow and temperatures ten degrees below normal.[24] At Durham Crowell's mail was full of letters from the college creditors. Once merely insistent, now they were demanding.

By the terms of the Dukes' offer, one dollar of the $7,500 gift would be paid when two dollars from other sources were collected. The conditions simply could not be met. The finance committee appealed to ministers and others urging heavy collections to make the Dukes' gift possible.[25] Crowell pressed Ben Duke and his father for immediate aid, citing "the high aims of which only a few in each generation are capable. . . ."[26]

The Dukes were receiving hundreds of other appeals and responding to many of them. A few of their own enterprises were suffering. Small gifts were going out to other colleges, to the Durham poor fund, the Oxford Orphan Asylum, to retired preachers, and to a variety of individuals and churches over the state. Ben Duke, who directed the family charities in North Carolina, was reluctant to authorize the expenditure of the pledge until there was some indication that others were going to contribute.[27]

Spring brought no relief, and word came from Old Trinity that the teachers there were having a difficult time getting enough to eat.[28] At the same time, Crowell and his Board Chairman, J. W. Alspaugh, were struggling to hold off creditors, including the banks from which the college had borrowed. Alspaugh feared that unless something were done, he and Crowell, as endorsers, would be sued.[29]

It was, therefore, no shock when the smoldering resentments

23. Chester W. Wright, *Economic History of the United States* (New York, 1941), pp. 873-876.
24. *Progressive Farmer*, April 11, 1893, p. 6.
25. Raleigh *Christian Advocate*, March 1, 1893, p. 3.
26. J. F. Crowell to B. N. Duke, March 6, 1893, Trinity College Papers.
27. B. N. Duke Letters and Letterbooks, 1893.
28. J. F. Heitman to J. F. Crowell, April 13, 1893, Trinity College Papers.
29. J. W. Alspaugh to J. F. Crowell, April 26, 1893, *ibid.*

on the campus again erupted. One faculty member later gave his opinion of the causes of the demoralization:

> The truth is that neither the president, faculty nor trustees were alone to blame; all three together had made the mistakes that brought on the crisis. The president had driven his faculty from him by his insincerity, by his attempt to absorb all the power into his own hands and by not paying any attention to the experience and requests of his colleagues. The faculty were perhaps too ready to find fault and to talk the failings of the college to the student body and to the world. The trustees are to be blamed for allowing such enormous extravagance in building and in not keeping themselves acquainted with their institution's affairs and real condition.[30]

By late April Alspaugh was receiving resignations. He reacted coolly. He suspected it was "more of a money or pay question than anything else," but he was wary of faculty insistence upon greater control of college affairs. He was not prepared to yield.[31] When the trustees met in May, Crowell reported much suffering from the depression, "much discontent, a good deal of disagreement, and a general want of cordial and effective cooperation." He described the differences within the college as "conscientious" but assured the trustees that there was no neglect of duty or student unrest. He hoped the Board would act, and he offered some recommendations.

He pressed for the collection of the Conference assessments and urged a general pruning of expenses. He asked that the Executive Committee be reorganized to include men living in Durham "within ready call of the president." He urged that the immediate problem, the college debts, be attended to, and he recommended that the faculty resignations be accepted. New replacements should be advised of a Code of Laws and Regulations that had been drawn up and was being offered for approval. He asked that faculty appointments now be bound by written contract and that the Board agree to three-year "tenure" for all professors and assistant professors. The tenure proposal did not offer much protection. Faculty members might be released for cause *or* if their services became unnecessary, and then with three months' notice.[32]

30. Raper, *Church and Private Schools*, p. 192.
31. Alspaugh to Crowell, April 29, 1893, Trinity College Papers.
32. *Minutes*, Board of Trustees, May 3-4, 1893, pp. 93-95.

At the evening session of the first day, the Board accepted the six resignations in hand. Two more were submitted the following day and accepted, although one, that of Robert L. Flowers, was later withdrawn. These resignations left the college with five of the twelve faculty members who had begun the year in Durham. Crowell was ready with one replacement, Jerome Dowd in economics, who was duly elected. The remaining replacements were to be elected at the commencement meeting in June.[33]

The new code, which was approved, formalized procedures that had developed from the experience with the finance committee, and it specifically stated duties and responsibilities. In effect it made the Executive Committee a board of management, which, with the finance committee and the president, would run the college between the infrequent and poorly attended Board meetings. The Board did not approve of Crowell's tenure proposal. Rather, the committee would receive presidential recommendations about dismissals and was directed to hold hearings in each case.

The president received a grant of power in line with the Board's earlier response. In addition to making recommendations as to personnel, he was empowered "to lay out curricula, prescribe requirements for admission, to approve textbooks and the mode of teaching. . . ." He was directed to confer frequently with the faculty, to appoint all committees, and to serve as the means of communication between the Board and the college. The faculty were left to their teaching and to reporting on its results. They were empowered, with the president, to determine degree requirements and make proposals to him, but all faculty actions were subject to the president's approval.[34]

At the May meeting the Board estimated the total floating debt at about $36,000. The mortgage plan had been delayed (because the deed to the campus had been lost). Now a committee was directed to fund the debt by selling $40,000 worth of bonds. The security was the college real estate and all the equipment.

It had not all gone smoothly for Crowell. Some of the disaffected faculty members had talked to trustees, and a minority in the Board had favored asking Crowell to resign. But the in-

33. *Ibid.*, pp. 107, 117-118.
34. *Minutes*, Board of Trustees, pp. 97 ff.

fluence of Ben Duke and Julian Carr had prevailed, and he was re-elected.[35] Stephen Weeks, one of the first group to resign, was bitter over the results. His salary was $900 in arrears. He thought "the defects, the inconsistencies, the doubtings, the lies of Crowell have permeated the State." He had talked with one trustee, John R. Brooks, and found him "very sick" over the result of the meeting. Weeks had invited Brooks into his study

> to help him feel my loss a little more keenly. I showed him all my N. C. collection of books & Mss. I got him very much interested in my work, he became enthusiastic & *then* wanted to know what I wd. do next year. Told him I was going to leave the State & take my N. C. library, the finest with possibly one exception in existence, away with me. The good doctor's voice grew husky & this morning in talking with another member he simply broke down.[36]

But Weeks was encouraged to wait. Crowell might be forced out at the June meeting. One of the students reported a general belief that Crowell was to have been dismissed in May. "Everybody knew that Crowell or the faculty would have to go."[37]

Certainly, the minority remained unpersuaded that the right alternative had been chosen, Brooks in particular. He was then a presiding elder in the Western Conference and a powerful Methodist leader. He had headed or been a member of delegations to the Church's General Conferences, and his name had come up for bishop. He was elected to the Trinity Board in 1892. After the trustee meeting, Brooks talked to Ben Duke about asking Crowell to resign and suggested the name of James Atkins of the Western Conference as a successor. Atkins was a minister and president of Emory and Henry College. He had received an honorary degree from Trinity in 1890. At this time, and later, groups of disaffected Methodists of the Western Conference

35. Stephen B. Weeks to H. B. Adams, May 5, 1893, Adams Letters; J. S. Carr to B. N. Duke, May 27, 1893, Trinity College Papers. Crowell said that he was told that both his name and that of James Atkins of Asheville were presented to the Board for election. He refused to compete for the position, leaving it to the Board to decide if it wished to keep him or not. Crowell, *Recollections,* pp. 210-11.

36. Weeks to Adams, May 5, 1893, Adams Letters.
The collection was sold to the University of North Carolina Library some years later.

37. J. F. Shinn to his father, May 7, 1893, Thomas J. Shinn Papers (Duke University Library). Weeks had said the students were entirely with the faculty, but Shinn, whom Weeks thought his best student, was "very well pleased with the present arrangement." For Weeks's high opinion of Shinn, see Weeks to Adams, May 25, 1893, Adams Letters.

would turn to him when positions of leadership were to be filled. A few days later Brooks sought Duke's aid in a movement to ask Crowell to get out at the June meeting. Crowell, he warned, "can not rally W.N.C. to Durham, but Atkins can draw our people to a rival institution within our bounds at Asheville and elsewhere." He said a member of the faculty had told him that Crowell "has lost his hold on the faculty, students &, he believed, the public; that he is largely a failure as a teacher, preacher & financial manager; that his theology is a mixture of orthodoxy and heterodoxy, & that his administration is wholly unsatisfactory to those who know most about it." Finally, he argued, "Let us not yield our convictions as some of us did last Thursday,"[38]

Three weeks later Ben Duke received an overture from Julian Carr on the same subject. Carr had come to feel "that we have got to make a change at Trinity College." He had heard from Brooks and Atkins. He believed that if Duke and he suggested that Crowell resign, he would do so. But he did not wish to influence, and would not try if Duke thought Crowell the right man.[39] Among others in the movement was N. M. Jurney, a minister and a trustee from the Eastern Conference. Jurney was a friend and sometime associate of Duke in various enterprises. He urged, "We must not let sympathy—or sentiment—or friendship cause us to make a mistake. There must be a change."[40] The record discloses no answer from Duke to these overtures.

When the Board met on June 7, financial worries received first priority, in particular the need to raise some money immediately for emergencies. Negotiations to sell the bonds to an insurance company were moving slowly. Again, the other members turned to Ben Duke. He and Jurney agreed to lend $5,000 jointly, to be repaid from the first Conference collections and the first money received from the bonds.[41] Next, Crowell was ready with faculty replacements and a salary schedule.

When the Board turned to its political problem, Crowell read letters he had received urging him to resign. A "pivotal" allegation in one from Brooks was that the Dukes would advance no more funds so long as Crowell held the presidency.[42] Infuriated,

38. John R. Brooks to B. N. Duke, May 8, 1893, Trinity College Papers.
39. J. S. Carr to B. N. Duke, May 27, 1893, *ibid.*
40. N. M. Jurney to B. N. Duke, June 3, 1893, B. N. Duke Papers.
41. *Minutes*, Board of Trustees, June 7, 1893, pp. 127-128.
42. Crowell, *Recollections*, pp. 41-42.

Crowell resigned. The decision came, he noted, after careful deliberation and represented the "settled conviction" that "for the past year more or less, you have as a body, with noteworthy individual exceptions, ceased to accord to my administration either the just consideration or the moral support necessary to effect the purposes for which you called me to this office." He expressed his love of the college and referred to the trials of the past six years. He was forced to confess that his confidence had been shaken in Christian institutions like Trinity.[43]

Brooks could not persuade the Board to accept the resignation. A pledge of support for Crowell was approved, and he agreed to withdraw his resignation upon three conditions: that a public statement of confidence be issued and signed by every trustee; that the athletic policy be left to the president, faculty, and students; and that $2,000 more be raised for faculty salaries.[44]

Crowell had not been present at all of the debates. He was told that Ben Duke had denied the assertion that he and his father were unwilling to support Crowell.[45] Perhaps the new loan was denial enough. Crowell thought the student body generally neutral, but a communication "signed by a large number" reportedly expressed confidence in Crowell.[46]

For Stephen Weeks, now it was all over; he and the others were out, and he was "profoundly thankful such is the case." At the meeting "Ephraim was joined to his idols." He was done with Crowell, but he was going to take pains to expose him. In the meantime he was waiting for his pay, promised in a few days, ". . . and they had better hustle about mine if they don't want a law suit on their hands." Trinity was a "den of robbers" anyway.[47]

Publicly the college minimized the struggle. In the *Advocate*, F. L. Reid asked Methodists to rally around Crowell and the college and cautioned against Church criticism of any Methodist institution.[48] The public statement authorized by the Board referred to the "difficulties and embarrassments" as incident to the problem of moving. Now the crisis of the first year was over, and Trinity had a bright future. The trustees were convinced that Crowell was too valuable to be lost. The major difficulty in find-

43. *Minutes*, Board of Trustees, June 8, 1893, pp. 131-133.
44. *Ibid.*, pp. 134-137.
45. Crowell, *Recollections*, p. 213.
46. *Minutes*, Board of Trustees, June 8, 1893, pp. 137-138.
47. Stephen B. Weeks to Adams, June 10, 1893, Adams Letters.
48. Raleigh *Christian Advocate*, June 14, 1893, p. 2.

ing a new faculty, the statement noted, had been the abundance of applications, one hundred in all, from "all parts of the Union and leading educational centres of Europe." The students had done well under some inconveniences, and the college was recommended to all as deserving of support. "The future of the college lies with the church which owns it." The statement was signed by the members of the Executive Committee, now composed of Chairman Alspaugh, the four Durham businessmen, and Ben Duke.[49]

During the bleak year just passed the work of the college had not borne much resemblance to the university plan envisioned in 1890. Indeed, after the fall of the tower and attendant difficulties, even the existing organization had been streamlined. A departmental structure replaced the complex divisional arrangement. Yet, Crowell clung to some of the original apparatus. Four separate bachelor's degrees with separate curricula continued to be offered, and the professional schools were still listed.[50]

In his review of the year, Crowell made it clear that a relatively simple program actually had been provided. And by 1894, with a smaller faculty and with the removal of "nonessentials" from the curriculum, it would be simpler still. Some students had quit under the burden of eighteen hours of classes per week; this had been reduced to sixteen. The work of the law school was being transferred to political science after a summer's trial as a separate department. The technological studies had not been given at all because of the lack of funds, and the theological department and its B.D. degree were entirely abolished.[51] This last had been an undercurrent in some of the trustee discussions. There was a feeling that Trinity was wrongly competing with Vanderbilt in this area, as well as a traditional sentiment that literary training was sufficient for ministers. "Let theology take care of itself."[52] In the future, courses in Bible would become electives for the Bachelor of Philosophy degree.

49. *Special Report of the Executive Committee of the Board of Trustees on the Conditions and Prospects of Trinity College* (Durham, June 20, 1893), Trinity College Papers. B. N. Duke had been re-elected to the Executive Committee at its meeting of June 14, 1893. *Minutes of the Executive Committee of Trinity College.* Cited hereinafter as *Minutes,* Executive Committee.
50. Trinity College catalogues, 1890 ff.
51. *Ibid.*; Crowell, Conference Report, 1893.
52. Bishop E. R. Hendrix of the Western Conference in the Raleigh *Christian Advocate,* Dec. 7, 1892.

There was also a liberalizing of the number of electives. Now A.B. candidates might freely choose over sixty per cent of their total program.[53]

Crowell continued to fret about college preparation. Performance on the entrance examinations was discouraging, and the students from rural schools did most poorly. Trinity was not strong enough financially to reject all who could not pass, nor, apparently, were other colleges. The "demoralization" of secondary education, poor textbooks, and the frequent change of teachers merely emphasized a general and often correct belief "that a boy can get into college whether he is fully prepared or not." Crowell insisted, however, that Trinity still would admit only those who appeared worth betting on academically.[54]

As president during the years in Durham, Crowell was tormented with a drudgery of detail. His days were filled with a host of maintenance chores: locks did not work; lights burned out in the Inn; a mattress was lost. Or there were disciplinary problems: too much swearing, drunkenness, noise, improper dress, or card playing.[55] Somehow he maintained and encouraged a determined academic posture. Cold or underpaid, students and faculty worked together on a lively campus.

In the political and social sciences Crowell believed that Trinity was "several years" in advance of most colleges. "I must warn you," he advised a new member of the faculty, "that this institution both in its policy and its construction is regarded as ahead of the age. . . . Can you join us?"[56] During his years at Trinity, Stephen Weeks had contributed to this attitude, especially in his zeal for collecting historical materials. In the spring of 1892 he had organized, with Crowell's support and that of other members of the faculty, the Trinity College Historical Society. He campaigned for gifts to the library, books, documents, newspapers, and other items, aggressively seeking to rescue rare materials. For a time he served as librarian in addition to his other duties.[57]

The ferment was rather general, even during the grim year 1892-1893. Crowell had not given up on university extension.

53. Crowell, Conference Report, 1893.
54. *Ibid.*
55. J. F. Crowell, Notebook, Dec. 9, 1892 ff., Crowell Papers.
56. J. F. Crowell to Olin Boggess, June 10, 1893, Trinity College Papers.
57. Nannie M. Tilley, *The Trinity College Historical Society, 1892-1941* (Durham, 1941), pp. 8-22.

He had duly joined the national association and established a lecture series for the townspeople as well as students. Armstrong found time to publish an article on the gerund in nineteenth-century English literature. Weeks was constantly writing, as was Crowell, and the students filled the *Archive* with their own papers and those of the faculty. Crowell tried to launch a series of publications on taxation, beginning with an effort of his own. By the fall of 1893 he was hoping to establish a quarterly, to be edited by the college faculty.[58]

The students continued to deal with current controversy. E. C. Brooks wrote on North Carolina education, and Luther Hartsell attacked the trusts. Hartsell spoke for the farmer and concluded that combination inevitably forced down the prices of the things the farmer sold and increased the prices of what he bought. He did not spare the cigarette trust, that "large monster."[59] The students also heard regularly through the *Archive* from J. S. Bassett, '88, now working on his doctorate in Baltimore. Bassett urged the literary minded to shake off the doctrinaire style of the old South and look to the present and the future. He advised those who could to get away after graduation, to the North if possible, and get some perspective.[60]

The students were impatient for the new self-government Crowell had promised. In 1891 he had pushed a bill through the legislature that incorporated the campus as Trinity College Park, a municipality with its own governing officers. All advanced students and all over twenty-one were "citizens" and made up a legislative council. The college would remain *in loco parentis* only to the underclassmen who were minors. For safety purposes, the president and trustees continued to hold final authority. It was an exciting dream to the boys, its beginning for some reason, perhaps faculty resistance, postponed during the first year. The troubles of the second year in Durham prevented it from becoming truly effective.[61]

Another unrealized vision was the school of technology. Crowell thought that he saw great opportunities for a mingling of technical training and research in the service of business and industry in the South. Shortly after he arrived at Old Trinity he

58. Raleigh *Christian Advocate*, March 22, 1893; Trinity College Papers, *passim*.
59. *Archive*, 1892-1894.
60. *Ibid.*, Feb., 1893.
61. *Laws of North Carolina, Private and Public, 1891*, pp. 1238-1239.

had talked to Thomas A. Edison in Charlotte and was impressed with possibilities for developing the state's mineral wealth. He believed there were opportunities in engineering and agriculture. But in Durham the money was never available, and machinery and equipment that had been ordered were undelivered.[62]

Nevertheless, Crowell was unabashed by poverty; he kept things churning. He hoped that a normal school course at Trinity would prepare "head-teachers" for the preparatory schools, and he offered a program of ten courses for a full year, yielding a certificate upon completion.[63] Two of the new faculty replacements had some newspaper experience; accordingly, training in journalism was announced for the fall of 1893.[64] He dared to open a course of Biblical exegesis for Sunday School teachers, emphasizing Biblical criticism. Always he sought to take advantage of the Durham location. The students made arrangements to take the local census. A night school in telegraphy was announced for the benefit of young men in Durham. Not least, arrangements were made to get the daily weather forecast from Raleigh by wire and announce it to Durham by flying flags from the tower of the Inn.[65]

Doubtless, the depression contributed to the college's success in filling the faculty vacancies—although there was no rush from the European centers. Three former instructors, Bassett, Nicholson, and Cranford, came back from Hopkins, Virginia, and Yale (Bassett, effective 1894), and three other replacements from other graduate schools joined them. Crowell was alert to sound out new men on their disposition toward harmony in the college community, and he questioned applicants rather closely. He obviously believed that the teachers were appointed to teach, and little time was left for politicking. Almost everyone taught from fifteen to twenty hours per week in addition to committee assignments and disciplinary duties.[66]

Across the nation and in North Carolina the hard times continued through 1893 and 1894, but Trinity's fortunes seemed improved in the fall of 1893. The sale of the bonds had been arranged. Ben Duke and his business partner, George Watts,

62. Crowell, *Recollections,* pp. 175-182.
63. *Announcement,* Normal School For Teachers, Trinity College Papers; Raleigh *Christian Advocate,* Aug. 8, 1893.
64. Raleigh *Christian Advocate,* Aug. 9, 1893.
65. *Ibid.,* Jan. 25, June 7, July 5, and Aug. 30, 1893; Durham *Daily Globe,* Jan. 9, 1893.
66. Raleigh *Christian Advocate,* Aug. 16, Oct. 18, 1893; Trinity College Papers.

arranged for the Travelers' Insurance Company of Hartford, Connecticut, to buy the entire $40,000.[67] At one stroke the floating debt was paid off.[68] At the same time Ben Duke pressed for more action by the two Conferences to try to meet their share of his matching proposal.[69]

At the college there was optimism. Enrollment was up 15 per cent. The heating system was improved, and the newly initiated student government plan at least was being tried. Crowell felt secure enough to permit himself an indiscretion in his annual report to the Conferences in December. The Board of Trustees had left the football issue in the college's hands, and match play had continued, although at least one of the faculty disapproved.[70] Crowell decided to reply strongly to the warning of the Western Conference of the previous year. In his report he reviewed his arguments, favoring the game as essential to the college. By contrast, "compulsory physical exercise is a bore." He reminded the constituency that Trinity had beaten the university again in October, and that the victory had done much to arouse the pride of her friends. The warning of last year had not been discussed by the Conference at large. He wondered if the statement had really represented the will of the Church or whether, "like many other statements that get into our Conference records, this one was passed unchallenged, as though it would do no harm if it did no good." He stated that the college could best deal with the matter and promised that it would be watchful to eliminate or forestall abuses. He asked that no action be taken this year.[71]

The Western Conference opened in Charlotte on November 29. Crowell presented his report on the third day and it was referred as usual to the Board of Education.[72] Soon Crowell had signs that he had struck a nerve. On December 1 he and W. H. Branson (of the college finance committee) wired Ben Duke. They urged that Parrish, whose Methodist ties went back many years, come to Charlotte. Parrish could not, but Ben replied that J. S. Carr would go.[73] The trouble was clear when the Board of

67. B. N. Duke to Travelers' Insurance Co., Sept. 21, 1893, B. N. Duke Letterbook.
68. *Minutes*, Executive Committee, Oct. 17, 1893, p. 10.
69. *Minutes*, Board of Trustees, Dec. 8, 1893.
70. W. H. Pegram to B. N. Duke, Nov. 23, 1893, Trinity College Papers.
71. Crowell, Conference Report, pp. 21-26.
72. *Journal*, Western Conference, 1893, p. 13.
73. Telegrams, "Crowell and Branson" to B. N. Duke, Dec. 1, 1893, and B. N. Duke to J. F. Crowell, Dec. 1, 1893, B. N. Duke Papers.

Education presented its report at the last session. The Board had found Crowell's comments "neither courteous nor correct." He had devoted three and a half pages to the religious life of the students and more than five pages to athletics. The Board insisted that the statement of 1892 did represent "the intelligent will of the Conference" and requested the president of Trinity College to carry the Conference's views to the faculty and to report later "what is to be the future position of the College. . . ."[74]

As Crowell reconstructed the events, he rose to speak, but the Conference, expectant as always about the announcement of new pastoral assignments, wanted an immediate vote on the report. Angered, he said that he would regard acceptance of the report as a condemnation of his administration. The vote was prompt, perhaps unanimous, and in support of the Board of Education. Stunned by the "ruthless, blind severity of collective action," Crowell decided he was through. For him it was always the instant he could not forget. The "agony of standing alone" remained fresh for forty years.[75] He accepted the vote as final. He stopped the intercollegiate contests, including those in other sports, citing the will of the Church. After all, "the College was theirs and not mine."

In the weeks that followed, Crowell was quiet about his decision to leave. It may have been tentative. He applied to the School of Political Science at Columbia for a fellowship and was one of the eight selected.[76] Meanwhile, he continued with his presidential duties. A librarian was badly needed, and he made an arrangement for a recent graduate to combine the work with clerical duties in his office. He had to find two faculty replacements. One, for the chair of English, was Edwin Mims, who came highly recommended and with a master's degree from Vanderbilt. Crowell was elected president of the new North Carolina Association of Colleges, which met at Trinity. He accepted an invitation from Nicholas Murray Butler to speak on "The Future of the Small College" at a meeting in New Jersey. He sought important speakers for the Trinity lecture series, failing with William Jennings Bryan, but getting Woodrow Wilson. Apparently he sought to leave the college with as few convulsions as possible. When Bassett wrote of the "ominous" fact that he

74. *Journal*, Western Conference, 1893, p. 61.
75. Crowell, *Recollections*, pp. 239, 247.
76. R. Gordon Hoxie, *et al.*, *A History of the Faculty of Political Science, Columbia University* (New York, 1955), p. 56.

The College Inn—later known as "Epworth"—part
of the original campus in 1892
etching by Louis Orr

Crowell Technological Building housed the schools of physics, chemistry, biology, and engineering.

had seen Crowell's name in Columbia's list of fellows, he was reassured that there was no wholesale shakeup and urged to come on down next fall as planned.[77]

When the trustees met in May of 1894, it was apparent that the mortgage had saved the college. All debts were paid, and there was a small surplus. Estimated income for the new year would cover expenses if the Conferences raised $2,000 each, a sum they usually could manage. Economies were still necessary, but the availability of rent-free houses was a useful supplement to salaries. The arrangements with the various academies (there were now ten of them) were agreeable so long as they cost Trinity nothing, and the Board agreed that a uniform curriculum should be prepared to guide them.[78]

At the afternoon session on May 2, Crowell presented his resignation and then withdrew from the meeting. It was a temperate letter. He wrote that the college had passed the critical stage, that the foundations for growth had been laid. He expressed appreciation for all who had helped to accomplish so much in spite of "triflingly inadequate means." The Board voted, unanimously, not to accept his resignation, and the students petitioned him to reconsider.[79] But he remained firm. Alspaugh sought to convince him that he had made a mistake. Crowell replied that the resignation was necessary "to avoid a collapse. . . ." He and his wife were not willing "to live in an atmosphere in which our influence is to be poisoned with those with whom we have to deal."[80] The Board had little choice but to accept his decision, at least for the moment, and appointed a committee to consider applications for a new president and to report at the June meeting.

A confused, angry session took place on June 12-13. Apparently those unreconciled to Crowell's leaving made it difficult for any other candidate to be discussed. Several names were presented, including those of Bassett, Judge Walter Clark, and James Atkins. Bassett and Clark declined to run. Alspaugh, reporting for the committee, said it had nothing to report. It was

77. J. F. Crowell to J. S. Bassett, April 28, 1894, Crowell Letterbook, Crowell Papers.
78. *Minutes*, Board of Trustees, May 1, 1894, and *Minutes*, Executive Committee, May 1, May 18, 1894.
79. *Minutes*, Board of Trustees, pp. 169-171.
80. J. W. Alspaugh to J. F. Crowell, May 24, 1894, Trinity College Papers; Crowell to Alspaugh, *ca.* May 26, 1894, Crowell Letterbook. Crowell had married again in April, 1891.

suggested that the matter be postponed until September and that Crowell stay on until then. This proposal was received with opposing reactions. Finally, a new committee, three from each Conference, was named, and Alspaugh was instructed to call another meeting in thirty days to elect a president.[81]

In the meantime the conflict continued. N. M. Jurney bombarded Ben Duke with messages. Ben had tried to get Crowell to stay but apparently had joined others in accepting his decision. Jurney was still strong for Atkins but was finding opposition, especially from the Durham group. In late June he reported that there was a plan afoot to elect Bassett as chairman of the faculty and let Crowell go to Columbia, presumably to return later as president. Jurney was strongly opposed to this idea and appealed to Duke to lend his influence "to let us blow it up."[82] Duke replied that he favored Atkins but would not write the letter requested. He was in New York and not feeling well. ". . . I do not care to enter into the contest. . . . I do not propose to let such matters bother me and harass me longer."[83]

When the Board met on July 3 Crowell's resignation was accepted. By this time, Jurney had withdrawn Atkins' name, and the joint committee had agreed on Collins Denny, professor of philosophy at Vanderbilt and a rising young Methodist minister. An invitation was extended to Denny, but he declined to accept.[84] Jurney had not been happy about withdrawing Atkins' name, and he was irritated. Now, he complained, "Ballard, Bass & Co." were running the college and would want "some other whang doodle fellow."[85] In fact, another name was being seriously considered, and in mid-July the Executive Committee (Alspaugh, Branson, Ballard, and Bass) met with the selection committee and decided to send a delegation to Spartanburg, South Carolina, to see if "Prof. Kilgore [*sic*]" would be suitable. He was. When the Board met again on July 31, John C. Kilgo was unanimously elected.[86]

At the same meeting the Board paid tribute to Crowell. He had come to Trinity "in perhaps the most critical moment" of her life, had assembled a modern faculty, and moved the college to

81. *Minutes*, Board of Trustees, June 12-13, pp. 186-189.
82. N. M. Jurney to B. N. Duke, June 25, 1894, B. N. Duke Papers.
83. B. N. Duke to N. M. Jurney, June 28, 1894, B. N. Duke Letterbook.
84. *Minutes*, Board of Trustees, pp. 191-192.
85. N. M. Jurney to B. N. Duke, July 14, 1894, B. N. Duke Papers.
86. *Minutes*, Board of Trustees, p. 194.

Durham. His pressure for higher standards had stimulated Trinity and the whole state. He had given his money as well as his effort, and his work would abide.

Crowell left Durham and Trinity in mid-summer and began a new career. He was not yet thirty-seven, and the adventure in the South was over. He went to Columbia for a year and taught economics and sociology at Smith College while finishing his Ph.D. Then he spent a year at the University of Berlin. In the years that followed he became a specialist in finance and expert on commerce, serving in government agencies, with the *Wall Street Journal*, and in his later years as a financial consultant. Occasionally he lectured at various universities but did not take another permanent academic position. He continued to write, largely on economic subjects.[87] In 1929, at the age of seventy-two, he completed his *Recollections* of Trinity, and the memories were bittersweet. He had kept in touch with Trinity and was familiar with the new Duke University. He had lived to see many of his seeds come to flower; he seemed to fear that his work was not appreciated. It was. In 1917 Trinity gave him an honorary degree; many have testified to his lasting influence.[88]

87. Obituary Record, John Franklin Crowell, Alumni Records Office, Yale University (copy in Trinity College Papers); Crowell Papers, *passim.* Crowell died Aug. 6, 1931.

88. H. H. Williams to W. K. Boyd, Jan. 30, 1922, Boyd Papers. "Dr. Dred Peacock on the Early Days of Trinity," *Duke University Alumni Register,* XVI (Jan., 1930), 31.

Chapter III
Kilgo: The Holy Wars
1894-1903

In mid-August of 1894 Trinity's new president arrived and took charge. He was a commanding, fighting, preacher-president, and his personality, containing a curious mixture of the idealistic and the practical, was to dominate and to drive the college forward. For the next sixteen years, little Trinity was to be tormented and inspired; they were years of excitement, controversy, and success.

John Carlisle Kilgo was born on July 22, 1861, the day after the Battle of Bull Run, in Laurens, South Carolina. He grew up in a parsonage life wherein spartan necessity and religious zeal combined to place a constant emphasis upon spiritual aims. Life was not easy, duty was clear, and "one got in such a school a clear idea as to what should claim his faith and love."[1]

In the irregular fashion of the itinerant minister's son, Kilgo attended various public schools and for a time Gaffney Seminary. In 1880 he entered Wofford College (South Carolina) as a sophomore but left at the end of that year. Apparently he suffered from eye trouble, although there was a hint that "uninterrupted application to books" and the sedentary scholarly life were unappealing. He taught school for a year and then moved into his natural home, the church. He joined the South Carolina Conference and for the next six years preached in the various circuits assigned him.

He was a quick success as a preacher. He had great confidence, no uncertainty about his call, and a kind of absolute pitch in the pulpit. And he was always a challenge to his audience. His brother likened him to St. Paul in his capacity to inspire

1. This and the summary following from Paul Neff Garber, *John Carlisle Kilgo* (Durham, 1937), especially pp. 1-16. Cited hereinafter as Garber, *Kilgo*. Additional insights may be found in J. S. Bassett, "John Carlisle Kilgo," *Biographical History of North Carolina*, ed. S. A. Ashe, I, 352. For Kilgo's contacts in the South Carolina church organization, see *Report of the Proceedings of the Investigation of the Charges Brought by Justice Walter Clark against Dr. John C. Kilgo* (Durham, 1898), *passim*. Cited hereinafter as *Proceedings, Kilgo-Clark*.

controversy. "I doubt," he said once, "if my brother during his entire ministry ever preached a sermon or delivered an educational address that did not result in dividing the crowd. . . . The pulpit was his throne, the privilege to occupy it his delight."

Soon he became a young man to watch in the Methodist organization. In 1888 he was made financial agent to Wofford College, entering a post that had led to higher things for his predecessors; two became bishops. The financial agent at Wofford faced the same problem as his several counterparts at Trinity—to inspire the Methodists to send their children to the college and to give it their money. South Carolina was no richer than its neighbor, but Kilgo had some success. In six years he got cash and pledges amounting to almost $50,000, an amount double that which Trinity was accustomed to receiving. Kilgo also gained a familiarity with the realities of operating a denominational college. During the period at Wofford he organized in some detail the argument for "Christian Education" that he was to advance ceaselessly at Trinity, and in the process of collecting money he became somewhat disillusioned about the dependability of a Methodist constituency as a source of permanent income. "Our benevolence is far behind our wealth," he wrote. "The future historian will write us down as a rich people with small institutions."

During his years at Wofford he sought to complete his education, and after three years of private study with Henry N. Snyder, a member of the faculty and later president, he earned a master's degree. To him, Snyder always was his "university," and from Snyder he gained an appreciation of the profit in reading. At the same time Kilgo served on the Wofford faculty, teaching "metaphysics and political science" and learning something of the attitudes and problems of the professor.

Kilgo's traveling and his platform success placed him constantly before the Church and its leaders. He came to know men in power well and to develop an interest in the ecclesiastical organization and the practice of church politics. In time he became secretary of the Conference Board of Education, and in 1894 he was elected a member of the delegation to the General Conference, always a coveted honor. By this time he was being mentioned occasionally as college-president material, and a few weeks before coming to Trinity he had refused the presidency of Hendrix College (Arkansas).

On September 19, 1894, when Kilgo, then thirty-three, stood before the Trinity College community to deliver his inaugural, the audience saw a sharp contrast with his predecessor. Where Crowell was rather squarely built, Kilgo was drawn on finer lines. He was of medium height, wiry of build, and gave the suggestion of frailty. His face was thin, his nose acquiline, and a tendency to baldness was beginning to emphasize his high forehead. His eyes were sharp and challenging. Where Crowell was an indifferent speaker, Kilgo's rich voice was like a musical instrument, and he played it with assurance. Where Crowell's instincts were always intellectual, scholarly, Kilgo was forever a preacher.

In the words he spoke there was call to duty.[2] Unlike Crowell, he offered no dreams but foresaw a hard path ahead; colleges were built slowly. Yet, with Crowell, he warned that there was much shoddy educational practice in the South. Too many claimed too much in their advertising and did not deserve the patronage they sought. Students entered too soon and ill-prepared. A strong system of preparatory schools was essential, and the college that fought this idea in reality fought itself. There was also a regrettable and expensive tendency to squeeze charity from the college, rather than make it an object of giving. "The Southern father must learn some self-denial at home, and not impose it all upon the college."

However, most of his remarks were on a different series of themes. He had profound respect for the power of ideas. "Every thought has left its mark somewhere." History was littered with the wreckage of false ideas and honored by the monument of great ones. This emphasis on ideas naturally took one to the role of the church college, based on the noblest idea of all, Christianity. It was not the church's option but its *duty* to educate, and the aim was to produce "the highest and noblest type of man." This was the essence of Christian education, whose apostle Kilgo soon became. He pitted "Caesar" against Christ, clearly implying that Caesar represented all that was corrupt or weak in politics, and he wondered if democracy was not reaching a precarious point in abandoning all to mob rule without leadership. Who then was to guide public opinion? The church college, "independent of every ballot and trickster, standing true to the high standards of right and justice. . . ." It was "the one hope of our

2. Manuscript, inaugural address, "Christian Education," Trinity College Papers. Among various printed versions, see *Archive*, VIII (Oct., 1894), 4-18.

salvation from the fury of the rabble and the helplessness of the multitude." The inaugural was a glowing speech, and it excited the Methodist loyalties while it preached hard-headed management.

Kilgo was fully aware of the existing situation at Trinity and understood the problems he faced. The situation was apparent in the unrest left in the wake of Crowell's departure. The needs were two: money and unity. In the months that followed he moved toward their solution.

The money problem was most immediate. The mortgage had funded the debt. However, there was no reserve resource, no foundation for the future. The slender reeds, tuition fees, income from the tiny endowment, and uncertain collections from the Conferences, made an annual operation possible only with the aid of gifts. Kilgo's experience had taught him that the Church would not endow the college. It was believed that Washington Duke had become disillusioned about helping Trinity, although Ben Duke had been its means of survival during the two years in Durham. But Ben's gifts were not large; he was not yet forty and still building his fortune. As Kilgo weighed the uncertainties, he settled on one course, an effort to convince the Dukes, especially Washington Duke, that within Trinity lay the seed of success.[3]

Before Crowell had left, the trustees had launched a summer campaign for money and students, enlisting the aid of the faculty and paying their travel expenses. By early summer L. W. Crawford, who continued to serve as financial secretary, was encouraged.[4] He thought the effects of the depression were passing; moreover, he detected a growing interest in Christian education. However, by fall Crawford was disconsolate. He had barely collected his salary and expenses, and, "if the people have the money, it is impossible for me to get much of it." In the meantime Ben Duke continued to make the annual supplement of $7,500 for the family.[5]

Kilgo lost no time in making an impact on Durham. He preached in both Methodist churches his first Sunday in town,

3. In the summer of 1894 Washington Duke wrote a Trinity student who wanted a loan: "I feel that I have done enough for the present." Washington Duke to Charles G. Self, Aug. 29, 1894, B. N. Duke Letterbook.
4. *Minutes,* Executive Committee, June 26–Nov. 7, 1894.
5. B. N. Duke to V. Ballard, Sept. 18, 1894 and Oct. 30, 1895, B. N. Duke Letterbook.

and his pulpit power was never stronger. Pegram sent word to
Old Trinity, "he has captured Durham completely. . . ."[6] By
early fall Ben Duke was among his admirers: "He is a very
strong man in every way."[7] For his part, Kilgo was slowly developing his plans. While he learned the ways of the college and
lacked money, he described his objectives in general terms.
Trinity must become "the centre of the noblest and highest influence," he wrote Ben Duke. "I have no ambition beyond this,
and am not crazy to vie with the fraudulent fads in Southern
colleges."[8] The relationship with Washington Duke was personal
and directly related to the Church. Whereas Crowell had represented the modern college man to perfection, it is doubtful that
he was able to command the skill in personal relations that
came naturally to Kilgo. To Washington Duke the new president
seemed familiar, reminiscent of the Methodist circuit riders he
had known and comforting as a counselor and companion. When
Kilgo preached Christian education, as he soon began to do, he
linked the college with the Church in Duke's mind. Kilgo's biographer suggests that the close relationship came early and lasted
to the elder Duke's death.

During his first year in office Kilgo stumped the state, speaking for Trinity and for Christian education and getting acquainted with the constituency. By May, 1895, he was ready to
spell out his financial aims.[9] In brief, they were to cut all other
expenses in order to pay the faculty what they deserved. He
offered a brisk businesslike approach, eliminating maintenance
help in the summer months, even dropping the clerk-librarian to
concentrate on the "internal force of the College." The new
policy would include a hard-boiled view toward credit for room
and board. Students who could not pay their living expenses
should be discouraged from coming. At the same time, he argued,
low salaries were Trinity's weakest point. He urged the trustees
to concentrate all funds in this direction. "Your faculty costs you
less than the faculty of any other institution of like grade, yet
your professors are specialists. . . ." He got agreement that all
professors' salaries would be set at $1,200 per year and a house or
lodging for each. He suggested a goal of $1,500.

Most important, he pushed strongly for endowment. He re-

6. W. H. Pegram to J. F. Heitman, Aug. 23, 1894, Trinity College Papers.
7. B. N. Duke to Solomon Pool, Oct. 10, 1894, B. N. Duke Letterbook.
8. J. C. Kilgo to B. N. Duke, Jan. 26, 1895, B. N. Duke Papers.
9. Kilgo's report to the Board, Minutes, Board of Trustees, May 1, 1895.

fused, as he put it, "to play at this question." He set out to get ten chairs, underwritten at $25,000 endowment each, and had won a significant victory when he announced that Washington Duke had made another matching proposal: he would give Trinity $50,000 if others would find an additional $75,000. It was the first large effort from the old man since 1890 and proof of a revival of his interest in Trinity.

Ben Duke was pleased with the report to the trustees and with the situation. He wrote A. H. Meritt, who was coming back to the faculty after a leave of absence in Europe, "I have never felt so confident about the success of Trinity College as I do at present." There was "entire harmony" on the campus, and the only problem was finances; he believed that Kilgo would solve that. He mentioned his father's proposal and added, "I am sure the hand of God must have been in Kilgo's selection. . . . I think he is one of the greatest and best men in every way I have ever known. . . ."[10] A month later at the June meeting of the trustees, Kilgo announced a gift of $5,000 from Ben Duke for improving the campus grounds. Also announced was a plan for a building which would combine a chapel and a hall to accommodate large gatherings. It would be a memorial to Braxton Craven and would be erected from alumni contributions. The trustees themselves pledged $3,100, of which $2,500 was promised by Ben Duke on behalf of himself and the family.

In the midst of this encouragement, the college and Kilgo had to deal with a series of flank attacks that were to become chronic in the years to come.[11] On the college's part, resistance to them became a reflex. One of the issues was the opposition of moralists and some churchmen to tobacco in general and increasingly to the cigarette in particular. At the same time, a violent campaign was developing against the tobacco trust, said to be the cause of low prices in the markets. The two campaigns tended to become interwoven, and both of course were directed against the Dukes. As the family and the college became more closely identified, it became customary to attack them together. A complication was the impassioned political

10. B. N. Duke to A. H. Meritt, May 2, 1895, B. N. Duke Letterbook. Meritt was a friend of Ben Duke and had tutored his children.

11. The most concentrated period of attack covers the years 1895-1900, although it did not end in 1900. The best sources are *Webster's Weekly* and the *North Carolina Christian Advocate* for the period. Kilgo's reaction is best treated in Garber, *Kilgo*.

spirit of the late 1890's. The growing power of the agrarian movement, as seen in the Populist party, and the hazard that in North Carolina the Populists might "fuse" with the Republicans was an ominous prospect to those who were determined that North Carolina should remain Democratic. It had been so since Reconstruction. As unabashed Republicans, then, the Dukes made good targets for those who disliked cigarettes, trusts, Republicans, men of wealth, or the individuals and institutions identified with them. Kilgo's appearances in the state, and his campaign for Christian education (soon a campaign against state colleges) alienated other groups and offered a personal target that was irresistible—and frequently vulnerable.

The complaints and charges came from several directions and points of view. One general theme was clear: the Dukes robbed the farmer to give Trinity "blood money"; by accepting it the institution was endorsing tobacco, especially the cigarette, which was a danger to health and morals; Trinity's policies were affected, if not dominated, by the "heartless trust" that espoused selfish economic views and an "alien" political party. In time the dissident Methodists in the Western Conference could be appealed to on other grounds as well: Trinity had strayed far from the ideals of Craven; it was indifferent to the "poor boy" (and later the poorly prepared boy); and the new managers of the college at Durham were hostile to the high school that had been left at Old Trinity.

From time to time one or a mixture of these complaints was expressed in many organs of opinion, but the leading sources were two. One was John R. Webster, editor and publisher of *Webster's Weekly,* who had irritated Ben Duke as early as 1890. The second was a faction in the Western Conference. Webster's readers were tobacco farmers whom he taught to believe that the trust was destroying them. He was proud to have been the first to spot its malignancy and to his death denounced the Dukes and their tie with Trinity College. A spokesman for discontent in the West, although far more moderate than Webster, was L. W. Crawford, the financial agent of 1894, sometime candidate for the Trinity presidency, and after 1896, one of the editors of the *North Carolina Christian Advocate.*[12]

12. Recurrent schisms and mergers of the Methodist newspapers reflected the tensions between the Conferences. After 1894, one paper, the *North Carolina Christian Advocate,* served both with co-editors. From 1896 to 1899 Editors

In the summer of 1895, at the end of Kilgo's first year, the pattern described had not fully developed, although Webster's views were well known. By October, however, the *Advocate* and secular papers had begun to reflect sentiment in the West, which questioned the Church's acceptance of Trinity's help from the Dukes. Had Trinity been bought by the cigarette trust? Kilgo consulted his friend and mentor, Bishop W. W. Duncan, who advised him to go his way, but to be cautious about publicizing his views. Kilgo would always find it hard to take such advice in a crisis, and he replied to the attacks in the *Advocate* and elsewhere. He asked questions that he thought answered themselves. Why were only the Methodists and a Methodist college attacked as beneficiaries of the trust? The Dukes had many charities. Were there political implications behind this? To the Church critics: why was it wrong for Trinity to take tobacco money and right for a minister to be paid with it? When one writer asked how Trinity could give Christian education when it was supported from such a source, Kilgo said it was just as easy for Trinity to give a Christian education as it was for other Duke beneficiaries, such as the Oxford Orphanage, Guilford College, and others, to do their work. Characteristically, ably, and perhaps with some truth, in these and later replies he sought high ground. Trinity was being attacked from low motives; the ultimate aim was to hurt the college.

As has been said, the battle lines were not clearly drawn in 1895, but Kilgo was determined that insinuations would be answered. He arranged for a special meeting of the trustees in November, a few days before the annual meeting of the Western Conference. He told the trustees that it was "an imperative necessity to take a decided, positive stand" against the recent criticism. The Board did so, expressing its view that the Church should either defend its benefactors or return their gifts. The statement noted that the college was never more worthy of Church support and asked the Conferences to express their positions "in very positive terms."[13] Both passed resolutions. To-

---

T. N. Ivey and Crawford were in open warfare, displaying opposing editorials on pages one and eight. This was the "double-barreled" *Advocate*, an unrivaled source for signs of Conference enmities. After 1899 each Conference had its own paper until a final consolidation, to the *North Carolina Christian Advocate*, in 1919.

13. *Minutes*, Executive Committee and Board of Trustees, Nov. 13, Nov. 20, 1895.

bacco was not mentioned, but expressions of appreciation to the Dukes were approved, as were pledges to try to match Washington Duke's offer.[14]

By early 1896 the college had another financial secretary, A. P. Tyer, a trustee from the Western Conference and the man who had brought Kilgo to the attention of the college when the search was being made for a president. Tyer was devoted to Trinity and eager in his work; he met with much vocal support but little money. By spring Ben Duke was again discouraged about the Methodists' matchless inclinations. Tyer had collected no more than $600 in cash since January. At the spring meeting the Board renamed the buildings[15] but could do little about the financial situation. By mid-summer with the need to finish paying salaries and to anticipate fall expenses, the annual emergency arose. Ben Duke sent a check for $2,500, which paid all debts and left a small surplus. When Tyer reported to the Executive Committee in early November, he gave a disheartening report. "Our people have never been trained to give to the College, and as a people they have never given to it."[16] A few days later he wrote Ben Duke that the Dukes were the only hope. He asked for $500,000 and permission to allow the trustees to name Trinity "Duke College."[17]

Duke left no record of an answer, but from this period it appears that the Dukes had decided that their support of Trinity probably was going to have to be permanent. In December great news was given to the Eastern Conference at Kinston. In a letter dated December 5, 1896, Washington Duke said that he would give $100,000 for endowment if the college would admit women.[18] He expressed his disappointment that there had been so little response to his matching proposal but was pleased with the "wise and progressive" management of the college and with the quality of its faculty and student body. He believed Trinity would succeed. And he added, "I say to you frankly, the confidence I have in the present administration of the affairs of the College, and the hope that it will be continued along the same

14. *Journal*, Western Conference, 1895; *Journal*, N. C. Conference, 1895.
15. The Main Building became the "Washington Duke Building"; the Inn, "Epworth Hall"; and the Technological Building, the "Crowell Building."
16. *Minutes*, Executive Committee, Nov. 6, 1896.
17. Andrew P. Tyer to B. N. Duke, Nov. 16, 1896, Trinity College Papers.
18. Washington Duke to J. C. Kilgo, Dec. 5, 1896, Trinity College Papers.

ines, has been the main influence in encouraging me to make his offer."[19]

The condition required that existing regulations be altered to permit the admission of women "on an equal footing with men." The presence of women at Trinity was not new. As early as 1878 the Giles sisters had taken degrees at Old Trinity, and women had attended the college in an irregular fashion over many years. Crowell's modernization plans had included women, and in 1892 the Board had agreed that they would be admitted to classes, "but not to residence on the campus." The condition of 1896, accepted by the Board the following spring, meant that Trinity now had made a complete commitment to coeducation. Soon a dormitory, the Mary Duke Building, was provided by the Dukes, and beginning in September, 1897, women began to arrive in modest numbers.

Kilgo gave Washington Duke credit for the "prophetic vision" of women's education, but for some years Kilgo himself had belonged to the new reform movement that was beginning to insist upon equal higher education for women.[20] The cause had received impetus from the spread of coeducation in the public schools and in the state universities of the Midwest. The South and East had been slower to respond. Indeed, as recently as 1888 the historian of education in North Carolina had doubted that anyone would dare propose coeducation at the university or the denominational colleges. The need was the greater because the few women's colleges were poorly supported and were just beginning to make their curricula equal to the institutions for men. In some instances there remained an emphasis upon the cultural arts, elocution, and commercial training.[21]

The reaction to the gift must have gratified the elder Duke. Wires and letters poured in from all over the state. All agreed that it heralded a new era in North Carolina and to some extent in the South. The president of the state college for women, Charles D. McIver, thought it marked the death of discrimination against women. As the news reached a wider audience, there was a run of letters from delighted women over the country. In-

19. *Ibid.*
20. Garber, *Kilgo*, p. 141. There seems to be no recorded reason for the condition; it may have come in memory of Washington Duke's daughter who had died not long before.
See Thomas Woody, *A History of Women's Education in the United States,* II (New York, 1929).
21. C. L. Smith, *North Carolina Education*, pp. 117-130.

deed, Washington Duke was offered, and declined, the vice-presidency of the National Suffrage Association.[22]

By 1897 it was clear that Kilgo had begun to conquer his major problem, finances. He had convinced Washington Duke that Trinity merited further support, and Duke was stirring himself to provide it. Due credit may be given Kilgo for winning Washington Duke's confidence without concluding that Duke's alleged decision to cast Trinity off was permanent. He is reported to have told Kilgo on arrival that he never expected to give Trinity another dollar.[23] Yet Ben Duke, though frequently complaining, continued to keep the college alive in 1892-1894. It may be argued that from the moment the college arrived in Durham, the Dukes were unlikely to let it fall. Aside from their interest in it, which grew from its proximity, its failure, evident to all in their home town, would have seemed to be their failure. And they were used to success.

Of course the new financial security contributed to the second objective, unity. The emphasis upon faculty salaries and the ability now to pay them, a more handsome campus, and a general feeling of confidence encouraged the constituency. The problem of football that had tormented Crowell was solved quickly. Kilgo tolerated a few games in the fall of 1894, but by December of that year intercollegiate football was abandoned. It would remain so for twenty-five years, although match games in other sports were encouraged.[24] However, it was in the Christian education crusade that Kilgo built up a strong core of support—and opposition—that he was never to lose.

Christian Education

Kilgo did not invent the Christian education theme. He brought it with him from South Carolina and he found it in North Carolina when he arrived. To some extent, of course, it was a natural claim for any church-related college. One might properly advertise this unique contribution just as public institu-

22. Letters to Washington Duke, Dec., 1896, Trinity College Papers and B. N. Duke Papers.
23. Garber, *Kilgo*, p. 90.
24. *Archive*, VIII (Nov., 1894), 33; (Dec., 1894), 33; Trinity College catalogue, 1895-1896, p. 75. The Board of Education of the Western Conference was happy to leave in Kilgo's hands "certain matters criticized at our last Conference." *Journal*, Western Conference, 1894, p. 24.

tions later would emphasize their democratic character or their absence of sectarianism. But in North Carolina for at least seventy-five years the philosophy had been mingled with hot competitive struggles between the denominational colleges and the state university.[25] When the state agricultural and normal colleges were opened in 1889 and 1891, the competition merely became hotter. Who threw the first stone? Who can say? The denominational colleges of North Carolina were established in the 1830's to teach the faithful and frequently in protest against the presumed infidelity of the university. Sometimes the state resisted granting them charters, or limited the property which they might own. Over the years leaders in each of the major Protestant denominations had separately or jointly led a series of protests concerning immorality at Chapel Hill, the balance of denominational representation among the university trustees, or the right of the state to levy taxes for the university's support.

In the 1880's there had been battles in the legislature over the amount of appropriations the university should receive. Compromises produced a period known as the "lull" from about 1888 to 1892. But the depression that had closed in by 1893 emphasized again the desperate competition for students. The university's privilege of granting scholarships or making possible easy credit became the target, and "unfair competition" the complaint. It was also disturbing that so many "denominational students" were attending state institutions. The presidents of Wake Forest and Davidson Colleges, C. E. Taylor and J. B. Shearer, assumed leadership in a new crusade, Shearer with the "Apex Bill" which sought to remove gradually the university's right to teach undergraduates. The bill repeated an old theme: make the university a "real" university, not merely another college, and let it concentrate on training graduate and professional students. Thus, the university would be the "apex" of education in the state, and funds would be freed for the common schools.[26]

By 1893 the churches, especially the Baptists, were turning to the people for support. The Methodists began to pass resolutions, but in Crowell they did not have a leader with a taste for

25. The best treatment of the long battle is Luther L. Gobbel, *Church-State Relationships in Education in North Carolina since 1776* (Durham, 1938). Cited hereinafter as Gobbel, *Church-State.*
26. *Ibid.*, pp. 137-138.

a fight against state institutions.[27] Crowell was deeply religious and not uncertain about the moral discipline to be gained in a denominational college. He also knew enough about universities to know that North Carolina did not yet have one, and he too resented the undue pretension he thought he saw at Chapel Hill. But he did not find secular and Christian education incompatible. He believed that there was room for all: "It is not war but welfare that we are after."[28]

However, to Kilgo high principle was involved, and characteristically, he made principle serve a useful end. Soon after his arrival at Trinity he had received friendly suggestions from those who hoped he would not enter the conflict. Perhaps he had made up his mind before he came. To an early inquirer about his attitude toward state aid to higher education, he was cautious. The college had not considered it "authoritatively." However, as president, he would "take care of Trinity at all odds."[29] And he added, "Personally, I do not believe in free higher education by church or state." Accordingly, he soon converted Trinity's Duke Scholarships to a loan program and then spent his first two years speaking for Christian education. He did not participate much in a legislative battle of 1895, largely led by the Baptists, but his positiveness for Christian education could be interpreted as negativeness toward state colleges.

By 1896 he was committed. Looking toward the next legislature, a union was made with young Josiah W. Bailey, editor of the Baptist newspaper, the *Biblical Recorder*, and for the next two years the two were to fight as a team.[30] Each organized his church. Kilgo made his Christian education speech the classic statement, wrote pamphlets, toured the state, and inspired Methodists with his arguments and his pulpit appeal. Preachers were organized to spread the word and establish Trinity recruitment headquarters in every town. Bailey hammered away in the *Recorder*, and Kilgo established in Durham the *Christian Educator*, a monthly newspaper that carried the argument.

27. Resolutions are in the *Journal*, Western Conference, 1892, p. 41; and 1893, p. 38. Crowell's sentiments are in "The Future of the Small College," *Proceedings*, National Education Association, 1894, (St. Paul, 1895), pp 797-803; and Crowell to W. K. Boyd, Feb. 4, 1922, Boyd Papers. Crowell wrote Boyd, "I believed in every feature of the State's work with a whole heart."
28. Crowell in *Proceedings*, cited above.
29. J. C. Kilgo to F. P. Hall, Oct. 10, 1894, Trinity College Papers.
30. Gobbel, *Church-State*, pp. 148 ff., and Bailey-Kilgo correspondence, Trinity College Papers.

An obvious tactic was to secure formal resolutions from the Church,[31] perhaps the Trinity trustees, as well as district and annual Conferences. Usually such expressions took the form of a strong plea for greater support of the public schools, a pledge of support of Christian education, and a protest against the taxing power which took money from Methodists to support competing secular colleges. The legislature was asked to discontinue funds for free scholarships at state colleges and to limit appropriations so that tuition fees would meet much of the operating costs. Sometimes a protest was registered against the expansion of the state's "technical" schools into the liberal arts.[32]

As the battle developed there was extravagance on all sides. Journalism was noisy in those days, and personalities were easily attacked. Motives were candidly examined and held suspect. Bailey and Kilgo, both still in their thirties, seemed to infect each other with the exhilaration of the campaign. At one point Bailey, dramatically recording new vigor in the fight, wrote Kilgo that it was not "Luther, Melancthon and Calvin after all. Let it be Hasdrubal, Hannibal and Alexander." He signed off "from the camp of Hannibal," but noticed that "God is on the ramparts."[33]

Through his public appearances and his speeches Kilgo drew to himself much of the personal comment. To some he was a hero. The people in Mann's Chapel wanted to name a post office after him. He was endorsed wholeheartedly by the State Superintendent of Public Instruction, who welcomed aid in the biennial competition with Chapel Hill for state funds. However, he was a villain to his opponents, and there was some opposition even in his own camp. Not all of the resolutions were easily passed. Sincere friends of Trinity thought the campaign a mistake and probably futile. Again, the Western dissidents found another reason to groan about how Trinity had changed.[34]

In the perspective of a later day, the crusade was selfish and

31. *Christian Educator*, 1896-1898. Washington Duke's gift of $100,000 was put to service. His letter was dated Dec. 5, 1896, but the announcement was delayed and made at the Eastern Conference at Kinston on Dec. 10. The "Kinston Resolution" was adopted at that time.

32. See especially the "Kinston Resolution," *Journal*, N. C. Conference, 1896, p. 14-17.

33. J. W. Bailey to J. C. Kilgo, Aug. 6, 1897, Trinity College Papers.

34. Trinity College Papers; *North Carolina Christian Advocate*. One loyal dissident was Charles L. Raper, an alumnus and former member of the faculty. In his *Church and Private Schools of North Carolina* Raper described Kilgo's fight as "intense and able, though it seems that he has accomplished very little thereby."

intolerant. Sometimes Christian education seemed a bit un-
Christian. The Christian educators attacked the university for
not providing a true religious environment but insisted that it
could not do so as a state institution. It was not yet a university,
but they proposed to convert it to one upon a base of perhaps a
half-dozen graduate students. Early in 1897 its annual appropriation was something over half that of the University of North
Dakota and less than one-tenth that of the State University of
Ohio.[35] Moreover, the possessive attitude of the Christian educators toward "denominational students" had serious implications:
most students of the day belonged to some church; if all attended
a church college, who would be left for the public institutions?
They did not say.

On the other hand the idea of adequate state support for
higher education had not won a place in the minds of the people
—in part perhaps because of the long denominational opposition.
It is true that at this time from the Midwest came rumors of a
menace to all denominational colleges, the "Michigan Idea" that
the state should take over all of higher education.[36] Perhaps this
helped persuade religious leaders that their colleges were in
mortal danger.

When the legislature met in 1897, the turning point had been
reached, and the Christian educators were soundly defeated. The
university supporters had fought behind the scenes with skill and
gained great support. Today it seems implausible that the people
at large would have been willing to abandon an institution that
had been in existence for over a hundred years—one indifferently
supported at best. The legislators did not reduce but increased
the university's appropriation (if only by $5,000) and doubled
that of the agricultural college. They also earmarked $50,000 for
the public schools, half of the amount the church and school
leaders wanted, but enough to encourage them. At the time both
camps carefully supported the request for public schools;[37] their
agreement probably made it easier to pass that part of the legislation. More important to all the colleges, the development of
the public schools would in time produce more candidates for
college, thus relieving the competitive strain. Kilgo and Bailey

35. E. A. Alderman, inaugural address, in the *University Record*, Jan. 27,
1897, *Extra Number*.
36. For example, Charles E. Taylor to J. C. Kilgo, July 6, 1896, Trinity College
Papers.
37. Gobbel, *Church-State*, p. 156.

continued to campaign for Christian education, but it was clear that the war was over. The *Christian Educator* was discontinued at the end of 1898, although Kilgo never relaxed his hold on the idea that Christian education was the prerogative and the glory of the church college.

What was Christian education as Kilgo saw it?[38] What did it actually mean on the campus? The question is not easily answered. Christian education was more a matter of institutional attitude, less a matter of educational practice. Almost always it was expressed in general terms, although what it was not sometimes could be stated specifically. Clearly, it was education which emphasized character, Christian character. The importance of this lay in Kilgo's belief in the "absolute power" of education in making character. Colleges, he said, had differing capacities to exert this influence. Christian education, with its emphasis on character, bred students more patriotic and more democratic—than did secular education. A Christian college was inherently free because it was beyond political power. In time he settled on a comprehensive definition: Christian education "is that education that assumes Christ's estimate of all things and seeks to develop manhood in the light of His ideals and by His methods and inculcates His truths as the fundamental truths of personal and social character."

Christian education was not a number of things; it was not a religious campus atmosphere, however pious the faculty, or active the Y.M.C.A. (thus brushing away religious activity at state institutions). It was not simply "cheap" morality. Christianity was a dogmatic religion, and sinners found salvation in faith, not merely in ethical principles. Nor was Christian education sectarian; it was bigger than any denomination and free of intolerance or narrowness. In preparing his arguments for the public battle, Kilgo sought definitions from others. From religious leaders he received similarly general statements. Christian education was "a process of culture" that produced Christian character; it was broad in its recognition of the "supreme fact"

38. Kilgo's views are recorded in his *Christian Education: Its Aims and Superiority* (Durham, 1896); *Our Dilemma; Into or Out of Christian Education* (Nashville, 1897); D. W. Newsom (ed.), *Chapel Talks by John Carlisle Kilgo* (Nashville, 1922), cited hereinafter as *Chapel Talks*; and Sermons and Speeches, Kilgo Papers. Definitions are in correspondence, Trinity College Papers, and the *Christian Educator*.

of Christianity above the narrowness of secular institutions that did not—and of course could not—provide this type of education.

From Christian educators Kilgo received somewhat more specific comments. For example, according to the president of one church college, it was precisely the same education as that given by the best institutions, but with the addition of the Bible, Christian Evidences, and Christian Ethics in the curriculum. It meant that the faculty were Christian and that the college was controlled by a church. Under such influences history, philosophy, and science naturally assumed a different aspect.

But, again, what did Christian education mean on the Trinity campus? It meant four years of a required one-hour course in Bible. Students were expected to attend church and Sunday school. There they often heard Kilgo preach that all truth was dependent upon ultimate religious truth, and that literature, science, history were incomplete without religion. The faculty were almost wholly men who were active in religious work. Bassett, Mims, and Cranford wrote frequently for the *Advocates*; Flowers and Cranford edited the *Christian Educator*; Pegram was an ordained minister, and Meritt preached often. Others were active in student religious groups or as Methodist lay leaders. All of this interest and effort combined to insure faculty acceptance and endorsement of the Christian education campaign, and most of the professors helped fight that battle. As to what Christian education meant in the individual classroom, one cannot say. Presumably, Trinity's specialists remained specialists. Significantly, Mims once wrote, "Christian Education has locked up within it the destinies of many men and women."[39] Perhaps each individual arrived at his own understanding of the doctrine. An examination of the academic interests of the college under Kilgo will reveal that Christian education, whatever it meant to its adherents, did not preclude an awareness or desire for the "best" education.

The College, 1894-1898

With a determination to choose the best models and a capacity to use resources wisely, Trinity's progress would be determined by the funds in hand and in sight. Kilgo was never un-

39. Edwin Mims to the Board of Trustees, May 13, 1896, *Minutes*, of that date.

certain about this and stated it bluntly, in one form or another, throughout his career. "There is a lot of cheap talk in the world," he said once, "about education costing nothing, but it is not true. Education is a matter of money. . . ."[40] Increasingly this argument, as well as those dealing with Christian education, and the public battles Trinity fought, influenced Washington Duke. In June, 1898, he announced a second gift of $100,000. He believed Trinity had a "definite policy" and that it had the "key to many of our problems." It needed more resources and, as in the past, he was aiding it from "a desire to build up our people and advance the Kingdom of Christ." He was aging rapidly now (he was seventy-eight), and he confidently left to younger men the task of working out problems of the day.[41] Two years later he was to make another gift of $100,000, and these sums, supplemented by a series of smaller gifts from Ben Duke, were to give Trinity a security and a chance undreamed of in the days of Crowell.

Although the new wealth would make possible important academic changes, they began slowly in 1895. Kilgo inherited the faculty of Crowell: W. H. Pegram, chemistry; Robert L. Flowers, mathematics; William I. Cranford, philosophy; Olin Boggess, Greek and French; John S. Bassett, history and political science; Jerome Dowd, political economy and social science; Edwin Mims, English; M. H. Arnold, Latin and German; and M. H. Lockwood, physics. For the most part, this was the group recruited in 1893 and included Crowell's university-minded students who had gone off for graduate training.

With the faculty's advice, and in consideration of the tight financial situation, Kilgo in his first year introduced some modifications.[42] Trinity had been offering three baccalaureate degrees, the Bachelor of Arts, Bachelor of Philosophy, and Bachelor of Science. The practice of offering three degrees was an earlier fashion, rapidly going out among the modern colleges. It was said, and Kilgo agreed, that the multiple degree notion weakened the standard of the traditional Bachelor of Arts. Therefore, the new plan offered three lines of work (one took the "A," "B," or "C" course), all leading to one degree, the A.B. Actually the difference from the pre-1895 program was a technical one. Each

40. *North Carolina Christian Advocate,* July 24, 1901, p. 8.
41. Washington Duke to J. C. Kilgo, June 6, 1898, Trinity College Papers.
42. Trinity College catalogue, 1894-1895, published 1895.

of the three divisions was matched to each of the old degree programs, and the earlier distinction, the requirement of Greek for admission to the old A.B. program (now "A") was preserved.

Courses "A" and "B" differed in that one might take German or French for Greek in "B"; otherwise they were almost identical. Course "C," the counterpart of the science degree, also permitted a substitute for Greek and differed from the others in an early exposure to biology and in requiring fewer courses in English and the social sciences. Common to all three were two years of Latin, of English, and of mathematics; chemistry, logic, and philosophy in the junior year; and, one most important change and the hard core of Christian education, four years of a one-hour course in Bible, required of all students and taught by Kilgo. Aside from some juggling (influenced by the loss of Crowell in the social sciences), the major change was the introduction of Bible and a rather sharp reduction in electives. The latter was an abrupt departure, the amount of junior and senior electives being cut in half.

More important and far-reaching changes were being discussed at this time in the areas of college admission requirements and preparatory training. A few colleges, most notably Vanderbilt, had reached the point where they could afford to push for new standards. Accordingly, in November, 1895, Chancellor James H. Kirkland of Vanderbilt and W. M. Baskervill of his faculty led in the organization at Atlanta, Georgia, of the Association of Colleges and Preparatory Schools of the Southern States. The aims were to establish lines of communication between the colleges and the schools, to elevate and agree upon standard admission requirements, and to mark a clear line between college and preparatory work.[43] Trinity was represented at the charter meeting by Edwin Mims (he had been Baskervill's student at Vanderbilt), and Trinity with five other institutions accepted the new, higher admission requirements. Members also had to agree to separate or eliminate preparatory work from their college organization and to enforce the admission requirements by written examination. Certificates of admission still might be given students from selected schools where the work was sufficiently advanced. The

43. *Proceedings of the First Meeting,* Association of Colleges and Preparatory Schools of the Southern States, Nov. 6, 1895. Cited hereinafter as *Proceedings* Southern Association. The original members were Trinity, Vanderbilt, Washington and Lee, the Universities of North Carolina and Mississippi, and the University of the South.

equirements were modest enough, and became effective over a
period of years, but the weakness of Southern colleges is evident
n the fact that for four years only the six original members could
meet, or chose to meet, the requirements of the association. Kirk-
and believed that the requirements in Greek kept most colleges
out.[44]

Trinity's young faculty, encouraged by Kilgo's ebullience and
he new financial resources, thrived on the Southern Association's
appeal to quality. Promptly the new requirements were accepted,
and soon a bulletin was issued stating them and containing suggestions for the secondary schools.[45] The requirements were
more demanding than those Trinity had enforced earlier. The
specification as to Greek was the same. In English different
exts were now recommended. However, general history and
geography were additions, and in Latin Cicero replaced Vergil.
n mathematics now one must have pursued algebra "through"
not "to" quadratic equations. As in the past, the student following the "B" or "C" program did not need to offer Greek.

The college began to keep its own list of "accredited" schools
and to revise it in the light of experience. Admission by certificate was possible from these schools; otherwise examinations
were required. In a few years the faculty would be pressing the
Southern Association hard to enforce the standards more rigor-
ously.[46]

The departmental offerings reflected the attitudes and interests of the faculty.[47] Kilgo's course in Bible frankly set out "to
acquaint the student with the truths of Divine revelation." Both
Testaments were covered, and special attention was given to the
evidences of Christianity, a traditional approach in the denominational college. In English Mims was no technician but a lover
of literature. He announced that "all details—grammatical, philological, and irrelevant matters" would be secondary to the task
of understanding a heavy load of reading. He believed philology
was best studied by the graduate student. A little more balance

44. *Proceedings,* Southern Association, 1896-1898.
45. *Requirements for Admission and Suggestions to Teachers of Secondary
Schools* (Durham, 1898); Trinity College catalogues, 1895 ff.; *Proceedings,*
Southern Association, 1896 ff.
46. Trinity College Faculty Communication to the Southern Association, Nov.
8, 1902, Trinity College Papers.
47. Trinity College catalogues, 1895-1898. The summary following is from
an analysis of the course descriptions.

came to this field when, perhaps for questionable reasons,[48] Kilgo determined to have a second man in English. When Mims went off to Cornell to take his doctorate in 1896, William P. Few, a South Carolinian and a Harvard Ph.D., replaced him. When Mims returned, Ben Duke agreed to carry Few's salary. Together Mims and Few were able to provide the drill work in composition and grammar as well as literary studies. Later they made up the strongest department in graduate work.

History under Bassett prospered among the required courses but Bassett was heavily overworked. The versatile place Crowell had held in the faculty was not filled, and for years Bassett carried courses in political science and taught all the French. He was always busy as well with his own writing, with the college library, and as the permanent mentor of the Trinity College Historical Society, and he was constantly growing in his field. Soon he dropped the emphasis upon the ancient world in his introductory courses and began to push North Carolina and Southern history. He offered a course in "contemporary history" and began to preach the "history is life" message. Indeed, he hoped that his treatment of the Renaissance might not be inappropriate to the "Renaissance spirit in the South at the present time."

Dowd's work in "political and social science," offered only to upperclassmen, was, by modern labels, economics and sociology with the emphasis upon sociology. He alone of the faculty chose to state that "the principles of Christianity" were applied in class —to economic and other problems. He and Bassett clung to the practice of assigning original library papers, and Dowd concentrated on field trips to hospitals, prisons, and the legislative sessions in Raleigh. His lectures were organized by topics and problems, and he did not ignore trusts and monopoly, socialism, or child labor.

In the sciences and mathematics the college was relatively weaker in these years, if not in the quality of the faculty then in their need for versatility and in the poverty of laboratory equipment. Pegram was able to concentrate on his field chemistry, but occasionally offered astronomy, mineralogy, and

48. In the summer of 1896 Kilgo heard that Thomas Hume, English professor at the University of North Carolina, had said Trinity was two years behind the university in English. Kilgo wrote Hume, who politely denied that he had made the statement. It may have set Kilgo thinking; when Mims came back, Few was kept on. With Cranford and Bassett doing double duty in the languages, a second man in English seems luxurious. Kilgo-Hume correspondence, June 24 July 9, July 11, 1896, Trinity College Papers.

geology. Lockwood, a physicist, shouldered all of the courses in the biological sciences. Both physics and chemistry were offered only at the junior level and beyond. Flowers in mathematics managed to offer two graduate courses but at some sacrifice; it appears that he had to elevate the undergraduate work to meet the new Southern Association requirements, and from 1896 to 1898 he was helping to edit the *Christian Educator*.

For several years there was difficulty in providing sufficient staff in the languages. In 1895 Boggess taught Greek and French, and Arnold, Latin and German. The college offered four years each of the ancient languages, two years of German, and one of French. When both men left in 1896, Bassett and Cranford shared Boggess' load, and Meritt absorbed that of Arnold. This arrangement was to continue, with some aid from a handful of graduate students, until 1899. It was not until that year that the modern languages were put together and several years later before a distinction was made between the Romance languages and German.

In philosophy Cranford, though burdened with Greek, was able to offer logic-psychology as a required course for juniors and as a prerequisite to the senior requirement in philosophy. He offered also two graduate courses. By 1897 he had reduced logic to a subdivision of psychology. After 1898 he was free of Greek and able to offer work toward a "major" in his field. Gradually he sought to develop a somewhat more difficult series of courses for the potential graduate student.[49]

The references to graduate work should not be misleading. There was no concentration of courses or students before 1900, and in that year but sixteen students were so classified. Only gestures could be made in this direction. In 1895 the master's degree requirement was altered to permit only resident students taking three graduate courses to qualify. Later this was increased to five. In effect, in the years before 1900, most of the faculty offered a course or two, and the effort produced some assistants to help with the teaching. But for many years Trinity's "specialists" were to deal almost wholly with undergraduates.

Away from the classroom the young professors (the average age in 1898 was thirty-three) somehow made time for the extras. Most of them wrote or lectured constantly. Kilgo was proud that the faculty had given one hundred addresses and prepared

49. Trinity College catalogues, 1895-1898.

forty papers for publication in 1896. The papers often were articles for the newspapers, frequently the Church paper or the *Archive,* but usually were on professional subjects. Mims, Bassett,
and Dowd, whose fields were more susceptible to popular discussion, were able to satisfy editors at the national level. Some of the
papers were published in *The Dial, Gunter's Magazine,* the *American Magazine of Civics,* and the *Outlook.*[50] Students and faculty
alike contributed to a series of *Historical Papers* begun in 1897
under Bassett's supervision and published by the historical society.

In one form or another everyone collected. The historical-
minded, as in Crowell's time, sought pamphlets and old records,
and there was a zeal for relics, Confederate battle souvenirs, rare
coins, arrowheads, and the like. For their part, the scientists
sought to stimulate the students in developing homemade laboratory equipment. It was good teaching and a useful supplement
to limited resources. During the summer minerals and biological
specimens were collected. The whole college constantly campaigned for library materials. Kilgo started early with a Christmas appeal. Potential donors were asked to give a specific volume that was badly needed, or in the case of the Dukes perhaps
a set of volumes.[51] By 1898 the library holdings were listed at
10,000 volumes (about 2000 had been left with the high school
at Old Trinity). Gifts and purchases that year totaled 571 volumes. There was progress in cataloguing and classification, with
student help, and an increase in the library fee (to four
dollars per year). By 1898 Trinity could afford its first full-time
librarian, J. P. Breedlove.

Kilgo was well aware of Crowell's troubles with the faculty
and began early to forestall a recurrence. He was careful to
channel such matters as curriculum changes and honorary degree
decisions through faculty hands. After 1898 a faculty committee
on courses of instruction was established. Perhaps the president's
limited personal contact with advanced scholarship was an advantage; the young Ph.D.'s might be turned loose to the college's
benefit. But Kilgo himself was always alert to the absolute indispensability of library materials and equipment, the need
for higher standards, and the growing pressure for tenure policies.

50. *Christian Educator,* 1896, *passim.* The *Educator* contained regular news
items of college activities as well as the Christian education message.
51. Trinity College Papers, correspondence and memoranda.

And what he did not know he could find out quickly. In 1898 two-thirds of his professors had made personal contact with graduate learning in America or abroad, and half held the doctorate or were in the process of earning it. As the economic resources accumulated, it was also possible to make life a bit more comfortable. By 1898 salaries averaged $1,400 per year, and for many years free housing was provided in addition[52]—a standard at about the national average but far below that of the wealthy universities.[53]

Kilgo in Battle

Clearly, by 1898 the college was a much stronger institution, more stable than the shaky structure Crowell had tried to hold together a few years before. The tie with the patrons was strong and looked promising. The tangibles might be easily counted off, but the spirit and atmosphere came from the personality of Kilgo. His role was to lead, to inspire, and in so doing to dominate. Although he traveled a great deal, his campus audience was frequently before him—in his weekly chapel talks, in Sunday sermons in the Durham churches, and in his regular classes in Bible. What he said and how he said it were rarely dull. He had a gift for the arresting phrase and for dramatic exaggeration. Indeed, in a moment of attack, there was an occasional suggestion of abandon. A glimpse at his favorite themes is suggestive:[54]

Central to all the exhortations was a call to personal courage. Life was a battle to Kilgo, and he reached instinctively for martial figures. "God never gives a great man to a small age. It would be a waste of heroism." The gentle virtues of Christ were admirable; He was indeed the Prince of Peace, but hardly "a soft, inoffensive person." Of course people want peace, but they want and need truth far more. "No, sir, we want truth, we want truth if it brings war. We want truth if it brings destruction." Naturally, honor and truth applied to all things, including cheating in class or general misbehavior. "A man may mend a lack of

52. *Minutes,* Executive Committee, June 23, 1898.
53. John J. Tigert, "Professional Salaries," *School and Society,* XV (Feb. 25, 1922), 208.
54. Much of the following is taken from notes and copies of speeches and sermons in the John C. Kilgo Papers (Duke University Library) and from Newsom's *Chapel Talks.* Kilgo's views on many subjects also are carefully noted in Garber, *Kilgo.*

knowledge; he cannot mend a shattered conscience." What about public opinion? It was overrated. A "real man" led public opinion, he did not follow it. Micah, for example, was woefully in the minority "but gloriously in the right." Could prudence be recommended? "A prudent youth is a coward." Could one be too blunt? "Bluntness, bluntness . . . Be a man! My God, if truth does not make a man of a fellow it makes nothing." There was a similar appeal to independence in material things. Trinity's student body was heavily rural and frequently poor. Kilgo believed in strength-through-adversity. "Four cent cotton ought to purchase a ten million dollar conscience." Indeed, poverty was peculiarly related to the college student. "Many of you come to college because you are too poor not to get an education."

On other targets Kilgo also found the range: the influence of heredity? It was overworked and was a means of "indicting the graveyard." Leadership came from inner resources. Solitude? Yes. Men are never at their best in a crowd; the mob cannot think. Newspapers? A bad record, we need good ones, "not papers that dump into our homes the gossip of the land." Politics? Frequently immoral and dominated by partisan objectives. Sectionalism in the South? We must outgrow it. "There are men who will never leave Appomattox."

True to his calling, Kilgo did not let the campus forget that religion was always greater than learning, or that learning was always serious business. There was, he felt, too much faddism in intellectual "broadmindedness." To some, "the breadth of a man's mind is measured by the number of points from which he may view the world."

One looks in vain for an ordered "philosophy" here. Kilgo was a preacher, not a thinker. One who knew him well and admired him recalled, "I never did know what the man was talking about, but whatever it was, I was for it."[55]

One theme was constant, a stern call to duty. Yet, the admonitions were thrilling to the students and made Kilgo seem less unapproachable. There was a kind of optimism in it all, a call to greatness, and an assurance that if one were strong enough and brave enough—and willing to stand alone if necessary—he might conquer anything. One may also assume that some of Kilgo's message was scarcely new in a time and in a community familiar with religious oratory. The difference was that Kilgo

55. Interview, Gilbert T. Rowe, Sept. 14, 1959.

said it better than most, and he could put it in picturesque terms. Above all, he was a personality, and his courage, which seemed unlimited, could stiffen the spines of others. What he said on the campus he would say anywhere. His battles with the press, with politicians, or with some elements of the Church became Trinity's battles.[56]

An acutely personal battle with one of his trustees began in June, 1897, and was to capture the attention of the state during the summer of the next year. The so-called Clark-Kilgo controversy had mixed elements of comic opera and war to the knife.

Judge Walter Clark was a leading Methodist layman and a graduate of the University of North Carolina. He had become a justice of the State Supreme Court in 1889 and a trustee of Trinity College in 1890. He owned a good Civil War record and was active in politics. His judicial reputation was enhanced by substantial scholarly interests and a prolific pen. He was friendly with Crowell and had helped with the charter amendments of 1891. He had been one of Crowell's favorite candidates for the Trinity presidency in 1894. At the time Clark had withdrawn his name but had served on the selection committee that chose Kilgo. He had been seriously mentioned as a Democratic candidate for governor and had refused the almost certain nomination in 1896. In that year the Democracy suffered its worse defeat since Reconstruction. The dreaded fusion of the Republican and Populist parties took place and controlled the legislature, and a Republican governor sat in the Capitol. Some of Clark's social and economic views were advanced for the time. He waged war against the trusts and monopoly and what he believed to be railroad control of politics in North Carolina. He advocated an income tax; the popular election of senators, judges, and postmasters; and many legal and economic reforms.[57]

As antagonists Clark and Kilgo were well matched. Both had a personal following and both were able, strong leaders. Each had a measure of fanaticism and a gift for invective in his advo-

56. Holland Holton, a student under Kilgo and later a member of the faculty, offered this candid description: "He personally awarded scholarships, interfered frequently in matters of discipline even after the office of dean was well-established, and felt free at any time to influence student elections. . . . Kilgo was the biggest personality with whom most of us ever came in contact." *Trinity Alumni Register*, VIII (Oct., 1922), 213-215.

57. Clark's record and views are covered in Aubrey Lee Brooks, *Walter Clark: Fighting Judge* (Chapel Hill, 1944); and in Brooks and H. T. Lefler (eds.), *The Papers of Walter Clark*, I and II (Chapel Hill, 1949). Cited hereinafter as Brooks, *Clark* and *Clark Papers*.

cacy of a cause, and each was a hard-hitting fighter, especially in the public arena.

If there were personal differences between the two men prior to the meeting of the Trinity trustees in June, 1897, they are unrecorded. At that time the struggle began when Kilgo asked the Board to approve four-year tenure for the faculty.[58] Clark reported for a committee that considered the recommendation and that did not approve it. He said he feared "legal entanglements." A few days later Kilgo heard that Clark had said that Kilgo's proposal was calculated to insure the protection of his own tenure as president. Kilgo was, of course, a member of the faculty.

Here began a series of letters between the two, beginning with Kilgo's brief inquiry of Clark, asking if the reported comment were true. Clark denied the statement, asked for its source, and soon the letters grew longer and more heated. The correspondence ended with Kilgo's promise to take the matter before the Board the following year and Clark's admission that he had indeed said substantially what Kilgo had heard. In his last letter Clark was more specific: he had sensed Kilgo's "growing unpopularity" in the state. Clark, who was an advocate of free silver then currently in debate, had also heard that Kilgo had attacked such views. He reviewed Kilgo's church-state fight and his attacks on the state university, and then he exploded a bit: there was public sensitivity to moves by "Northern multi-millionaires" to capture educational institutions by gifts, and there was a feeling that the Dukes' gifts to Trinity were likely to infect the students with a "political heresy foreign to the faith of their fathers," i.e., Republicanism. He warned that public opinion might not approve of this influence, if it existed, and that adverse public opinion had hurt the University of North Carolina in the past. If Kilgo did not adjust to popular sentiments, "wealthy syndicates may give you money, but the public will not send you boys."

At the board meeting the following year, June, 1898, Kilgo presented the correspondence, and a committee reviewed it. The committee gave Kilgo its endorsement, condemned Clark's suspicion of motives on the tenure issue and stated as "the sense of the

58. Garber's *Kilgo* and the works on Clark cover the incident from partisan points of view. Each advocate seems determined that his hero should emerge a "liberal." The best sources are the *Proceedings, Kilgo-Clark* and R. B. Boone [compiler], *Suppressions and Omissions of the So-Called "Minutes" of the So-Called "Investigation" of Dr. J. C. Kilgo* (1898). Here one may weave his way through a maze of overtly partisan argument.

Board" that Clark ought to resign. The Board, with one dissent, approved, and Clark was so notified. He had not attended the meeting and protested his "trial" in his absence. He questioned the Board's authority to remove him. A new correspondence ensued between Clark and James H. Southgate, who had succeeded Alspaugh as chairman. When the story was leaked to one of the state papers, Clark was angry and he himself turned to the press. From this point, June 25, 1898, the controversy began to be well aired publicly and soon got out of hand. In one letter Clark wrote Southgate that he could have provided evidence of his charges against Kilgo if he had attended the Board meeting, and he added some more: he cited Kilgo's "sycophancy" toward Washington Duke in June of that year in a speech of appreciation for the second gift of $100,000. He added the insinuation that Kilgo had received a "personal gratuity" from the Dukes. He said Kilgo's reputation in South Carolina, and in North Carolina, was that of "a wirepuller of the ward politician type." He had heard suspicions of him in Tennessee. Kilgo was unworthy to be president of the college, and the Board's illegal trial of Clark had been the result of Kilgo's control.

Inevitably, Kilgo insisted that his character had been defamed and demanded an investigation to permit him to clear his name. One was duly scheduled for July 18, and "charges" were prepared. All parties were present, and Kilgo said he was prepared to defend himself. Clark stated that he required more time to collect the evidence to support his statements, and he was given until August 30. There was some uncertainty as to just what sort of investigation the trustees were to conduct. Clark naturally pressed for legal procedures, and some Board members agreed. Others, the ministers especially, preferred the machinery of the ecclesiastical inquiries of character with which they were familiar. The matter was never settled, and Southgate, in July and August, struggled to give the hearings order and fairness. Kilgo decided to act in his own defense; Clark, shrewdly enough, refused to serve as prosecutor. Through it all each man clung grimly to the position that he was the injured party and that he was on trial. Each tried to occupy high ground. Clark, with assistance from Editor Webster and others, spoke darkly of the Dukes' influence on Trinity. Kilgo seemed to feel that his career was at stake but also saw the controversy as another attack against Trinity. He was especially eager to interpret it as a threat to free discussion and academic freedom.

The sessions of August 30-31 were quarrelsome and noisy. Kilgo was a suspicious, contentious advocate of his own case. Clark prefaced his comments with a disclaimer: The Board was already prejudiced and was unlikely to be impartial. He was probably right. An assortment of witnesses and depositions was presented by both sides; these defended or attacked Kilgo's reputation, especially in South Carolina. (The issue of his reputation in North Carolina somehow was dropped along the line, to Clark's great indignation.) The enduring item in the entire proceedings grew out of the suggestion that Clark had received the damning reports of Kilgo's character from one Thomas Jefferson Gattis. Gattis was an elderly minister who for some years had been the Church book agent and who traveled the circuits. In his summation Kilgo was in good form, and he demolished Gattis as "the original slanderer." He delivered his famous characterization of the old man: "Behind a pious smile, a religious walk, and a solemn twitch of the coat tail, many men carry a spirit unworthy of them." This phrase and similar comments were to take Kilgo, Ben Duke, and others into the state courts for the next several years.[59]

The result of the investigation was that Kilgo was sustained on all counts. Clark had asked to deliver a summation himself but was refused unless he agreed that it would not be made public. He in turn refused, and the committee that deliberated that matter reported sarcastically that it hoped he "would not be tortured as a martyr." In the bitter aftermath Bassett and Flowers got out for the college a stenographic account of the proceedings that was widely distributed. Clark's friends followed with a pamphlet containing "suppressions and omissions" in the college report, including Clark's speech. The violence of the struggle lingered for years, and the epithets endured. Clark's description of Kilgo as a "preacher-demagog" was matched by Trinity supporters' description of him as "The Great Injustice." The legality of the affair received much lay analysis, although

59. In January, 1899, Gattis initiated suit for slander against Kilgo, B. N. Duke, and two other wealthy trustees and was twice awarded damages in lower courts. There were three trials and three appeals to the State Supreme Court. Finally the case was dismissed, and the dismissal upheld in November, 1905. It was in one of the trials that a prosecution attorney contrived a mocking enlargement of the Trinity motto, from "*Eruditio et Religio*," to "*Eruditio et Religio et Sugario et Cigarro et Cherooto et Cigaretto et Kilgo.*"

Trinity's Library Building, formally dedicated in February, 1903

his now seems irrelevant. Clark's charges were vague and hardy susceptible of proof, least of all in a trustee inquiry which could not serve as a court of law. Clark never did resign but allowed his term to run out in 1901.

What was the effect of the controversy on the college? Once again Trinity tightened its unity against those it believed to be its enemies. In the state observers could and did choose sides on the basis of early controversies: the university-denominational fight; East-West Methodism;[60] or Democrats vs. Republicans. The political issue was of particular significance and helped Clark and his supporters pin the innuendo of Republican "domination" on the college. Such charges, from Clark, Editor Webster, and others, were not accompanied by proof, but in the summer of 1898 proof was not necessary. A white supremacy campaign was in full flood, and the Democrats never had been more desperate to recapture the state from the fusion forces.

Was there Republican domination at Trinity College, then or later? If so, the record does not show it. As Republicans, the Dukes were in the minority in Durham and at Trinity as elsewhere. Ben Duke recalled "many petty persecutions and almost ostracism socially" in the early years in Durham.[61] Several members of the Trinity Executive Committee were active in the local Democratic organization (Bass, Ballard, Parrish; Southgate was Prohibitionist), as were some of the faculty and the Dukes' business associates, including their attorneys. As late as 1904 Ben Duke received complaints from Republicans that the Dukes' plant executives in Durham were influencing the employees to vote Democratic. He was asked "to make your bosses keep their hands off of your employees in the exercise of their political rights. . . ."[62]

However, Kilgo's public statements may have served to confirm Democrats in a belief that Trinity was subservient to its wealthy patrons. He was wont to refer to the "divine talent to accumulate property" and to observe that "the business genius is

60. Clark's knowledge of Methodist tensions was useful to him. He and his supporters could ring the changes on Craven and Old Trinity.
61. B. N. Duke, biographical sketch of his father, Jan. 6, 1897, B. N. Duke Letterbook.
62. Charles A. Reynolds to B. N. Duke, Sept. 6, 1904, B. N. Duke Papers. Washington Duke and Ben were firm Republicans, but not passionate about it. After the fusion victory of 1894, Ben wrote his brother that their father was happy over the election, "but says he fears it is too much of a good thing." B. N. Duke to J. B. Duke, Nov. 10, 1894, B. N. Duke Letterbook.

as much by divine appointment as the poetical genius."[63]   Kilgo refused to affiliate with any party, but he often sounded—to Bryan Democrats—very much like a Republican. Later when it was known that as a young man in South Carolina he had been a partisan Democrat, Walter Clark's reference to "sycophancy" fell on receptive ears. The tag of Republican domination at Trinity probably had no basis in fact, but facts were not wanted in the political torment of the time. Ben Duke was careful to assure inquirers that he had no control over appointments at Trinity. Sensitivity to the charge of domination may have insured that there would be none.

Perhaps the fruitless search, especially now, is for a "liberal-conservative" interpretation of the Clark-Kilgo controversy. If the words have meaning for today, they do not apply to the Clark-Kilgo issue. If Clark was "liberal" on some social and economic questions, his liberalism did not extend to protecting professors by tenure, to the Negro,[64] or to a disposition to tolerate minority political views. If Kilgo was "liberal" where Clark was not, his liberalism did not include sympathy for economic reform,[65] tolerance of human frailty, or professional good will to ward state educational institutions. The struggle was a personal conflict between two strong-willed men who were accustomed to being "right." Each represented various groups then contesting. Outsiders joined one or the other in accord with their most comfortable prejudice.

The College, 1898-1903

After the hectic summer of 1898, Trinity was able to turn again to its work and to look ahead. The spirit of the faculty consistently heavy gifts from the Dukes, and the unity gained in the recent battles were to make possible a new period of progress.

Washington Duke's second gift of $100,000 came in the spring of 1898. In the succeeding years he began to set his affairs in

63. Kilgo, Baccalaureate Address, published in the Raleigh *Morning Post*, June 6, 1899.
64. He believed the Republican victory in 1896 was a "reversal of the proper order of things which demands Anglo Saxon supremacy." *Clark Papers*, II, 29.
65. Kilgo was an admirer of Herbert Spencer and once told the students, "A sane, healthy pauper in America is a criminal." *Chapel Talks*.

order and to dispose of his estate. He was refusing appeals from other institutions, replying candidly that such gifts would require his taking money away from Trinity. He expected it would be necessary for him "to stand by it in a large measure in the future."[66] In October, 1900, he made a third gift of $100,000. Ben Duke's assistance also became more substantial. The profits of the American Tobacco Company were pyramiding, and in 1899 two old competitors, the Bull Durham and the Reynolds tobacco organizations, were brought into the combine. Ben still managed a large list of family charities and helped such institutions as the Oxford Orphanage Asylum, and Guilford, Elon, and Kittrell Colleges. There was even a gift of $1,000 to the University of North Carolina. Certainly there was more money to give, and Ben continued to put funds into grounds and buildings. In 1902 he agreed to underwrite new chairs in economics, German, Romance languages, and mathematics.

The result of this prosperity was that by 1903 Trinity could compete rather well, in the Southern area, in faculty salaries. In that year full professors were receiving $1,600, and most of them received housing as well.[67] A "fair estimate" of the average professor's salary in the South, excluding the weaker schools, was $1,000.[68]

Enrollments during the period 1895 to 1903 were never high. The total at the beginning of the Kilgo administration was 150, and in 1903 the figure was 197, the highest in the period.[69] Indeed, until 1902 the tendency was toward a decline, especially in the years after the tighter admissions procedures began. Many of the high schools and academies simply could not meet the new standard. Yet the dire warnings of those such as Judge Clark never came to pass. "The people" did keep sending boys to Trinity. One friend of the college thought that Kilgo's reputation in the newspapers probably was a good advertisement. In some areas of the state surely the reverse was true. Kilgo himself frequently assured the trustees that the enrollment was not in jeopardy, and he argued vigorously for indifference to size and "mere numbers." He resented being asked how many students

66. Washington Duke to W. F. Tillett (of Vanderbilt) June 3, 1899 and to Bishop O. P. Fitzgerald, June 3, 1899. B. N. Duke Letterbook.
67. *Minutes,* Executive Committee, Aug. 3, 1903.
68. *Proceedings,* Southern Association, 1902, pp. 48-55.
69. Trinity College catalogues, 1895-1903.

were at Trinity—"as though I were running a stock farm."[70] A wider geographical influence began to develop. In 1895 only a handful of students came from other states. By 1903 there were twenty-five outsiders and the beginnings of a clientele in South Carolina, Virginia, and Tennessee. More significant, and a source of pride to all, was the fact that 25 per cent of the graduates went on to advance work in the universities. The improvement in preparation was also producing dividends; 40 per cent more students than in 1894 were graduating.[71]

Fundamental to the new progress was the college's increasing security, via the endowment, from dependence upon tuition. Throughout the period fees remained the same. In 1898 there was even some sentiment, perhaps not seriously considered, to cut tuition to meet competition.[72] The significance of the new prosperity may be seen in the fact that by 1901 income from tuition amounted to little more than 10 per cent of the total income.[73] The floor of endowment income and heavy annual gifts from the Dukes persuaded Kilgo in 1900 to propose the establishment of fifty tuition scholarships. These awards were to be made in recognition of ability and character. At the same time a dozen graduate student awards were established.[74]

Increasingly Trinity sought a way to attract more well-prepared students. After a period of study, the solution came in 1898, when the college decided to open its own academy, the Trinity Park School. Southern Association rules against preparatory work in the colleges were designed to mark a distinction in training. The better colleges' need for able students still was not met. Thus, the Trinity Park School was organized without "organic" relation to the college, although the same trustees were in charge, and Kilgo was chief executive over a headmaster, J. F. Bivins.[75] The school opened in the fall of 1898 in a corner on the campus and soon had a small enclave of several buildings. Its students made use of the library and other college privileges but had their own faculty and pursued a program of studies specifically designed for entrance to Trinity, or to other colleges with similar admission requirements. Trinity Park was modeled after

70. *Chapel Talks.*
71. *Report of the President,* 1900-1901, pp. 8-9. This was Kilgo's "Sabbatical Report" and was his first printed one. Cited hereinafter as Sabbatical Report
72. N. M. Jurney to B. N. Duke, Aug. 1, 1898, Trinity College Papers.
73. Financial Report, *Minutes,* Board of Trustees, June 4, 1901.
74. *Minutes,* Executive Committee, June 8, 1900.
75. *Ibid.,* June 16, 1898.

the better Northern academies and was an immediate success. Between 1898 and 1903 its enrollments more than doubled (from 72 to 161), and there was always a sizable representation from Durham. Almost without exception its graduates went on to college, a large share of them to Trinity. In a few years the school prospered financially as well. Bivins reported in 1903 that he had a surplus of $2,500 and that deficits underwritten by Ben Duke would be paid back.[76]

In these years the changing character of Trinity College was passing Old Trinity by. After the move in 1892, the college trustees consistently declined to subsidize the high school left in Randolph County. Just as consistently the school fared poorly. A succession of college-appointed headmasters had to deal with friction in the little village, and always in every controversy Old Trinity became a symbol around which critics of the college might group themselves. Even mild Ben Duke wrote at one point: "If the Old Trinity people get down off of their stilts and meet us in the proper spirit, we will locate it [a college preparatory school] there; if not, we will go to Burlington and Old Trinity may go to pot."[77]

Plainly Old Trinity supporters, or Western Methodists who disliked Kilgo or the college on other grounds, felt left out. The college was getting better, and the school at the old site was not. The plaint for the "poor boy" was extended to the poorly prepared boy, and factions supported smaller Methodist schools in the West, such as Rutherford College. Of enduring importance was the fact that the move to Durham also had relocated the power. Trinity's Executive Committee continued to be composed of Durham men, and there were protests that the Western leaders were ill-informed about the college.[78] In the fall of 1898, after the Kilgo-Clark affair and upon the opening of the new Trinity Park School in Durham, a new dispute broke out. A group in the West again raised the tobacco question and asked that Washington Duke's last gift of $100,000 (in tobacco stock) be refused or the investment changed. A movement developed to withdraw the Western Conference from Trinity College altogether. At its height the Dukes duly arranged for

76. Headmaster's Reports, *Minutes*, Board of Trustees, 1899-1903; Catalogue, Trinity Park High School, 1898-1899.
77. B. N. Duke to N. M. Jurney, June 11, 1895, B. N. Duke Letterbook.
78. *North Carolina Christian Advocate*, especially 1896-1898, *passim; Minutes*, Board of Trustees, 1895-1899, *passim*.

the investment to be changed to stocks in the Virginia-Carolina Chemical Company.[79] When the Conference met in mid-November, the opposition was further mollified at a "peace conference" at which all prayed for harmony.[80] However, in succeeding years it was an uneasy peace. Editor L. W. Crawford's support of Trinity, and of Kilgo in particular, was lukewarm at best, and Kilgo himself was openly snobbish about the academic claims of the weaker Methodist schools. By 1903 the Trinity trustees were ready to dispose of the property at Old Trinity.[81]

Meanwhile the college was pressing for academic strength. The faculty, Few and Mims in particular, were active in the work of the Southern Association, Mims serving as its president in 1902. Admission requirements continued to rise, in some subjects beyond the association standard. By 1901 examination centers were established in a score of towns throughout the state.[82] The next year the Trinity faculty asked the association to enforce its rules more strictly. Mims complained in his presidential address that the association had faltered, that "we have scarcely held our ground." Kilgo rarely attended the association meetings, depending upon faculty representatives for reports. Apparently, he used his committee on courses of instruction as a working group and relied upon Few in particular to guide it. However, Kilgo was never passive about standards. He constantly held before the college a vision of its potential. Once he registered an "administrative protest" against granting a degree to a student whose work had been approved but which he felt was below standard.[83] In 1901 his ceaseless activity had worried his friends about his health, and the Board gave him a trip to Europe. During his absence his authority was divided among Pegram, who dealt with student problems, and Few and Flowers, who shared the remaining responsibilities. The next year Few was appointed dean, a post Kilgo wished created to "fill all the functions of what is ordinarily known as the vice-president of an organization."[84]

The development of the curriculum in the period to 1903 lay

79. *North Carolina Christian Advocate*, Aug.-Nov., 1898; Trinity College and B. N. Duke Papers.
80. *North Carolina Christian Advocate*, Nov. 23, 1898, p. 8.
81. *Minutes*, Board of Trustees, June 9, 1903.
82. *Proceedings*, Southern Association, 1898-1903; Trinity College catalogues, 1898-1903.
83. *Minutes*, Board of Trustees, June 3, 1903.
84. *Ibid.*, June 3, 1902.

in an expansion in the number of courses and in a return to a more liberal elective policy. From a total of fifty-four courses in 1894, the curriculum, and the catalogue, swelled to include 125. The increase, in the main, was due to the establishment of thirty-seven courses for graduate students only and fifteen more for undergraduates and graduates. Each member of the faculty could give at least one graduate course, although the expansion appeared to be greatest in English.[85] In 1901 sophomores in the "A" and "B" programs were granted a choice of one course from four designated fields. Two years earlier junior electives had been increased to six hours per term. By 1903 some 40 per cent of the work for the degree was elective. For the period, philosophy and economics received a strong place among the required subjects, to some extent at the expense of the sciences. When funds made possible a larger faculty, the modern languages began to prosper. In the "C," or science course, various experiments culminated in 1903 with the conversion of this program to an engineering degree. A heavier schedule of scientific and professional courses was established, at the sacrifice of the social studies and history. The languages gained the largest share of the required non-scientific work.

As the financial resources grew, it was possible to provide the personnel to implement the curricular changes described.[86] In 1900 Plato Durham, an alumnus who had been at the Union Theological Seminary, came to supplement Kilgo's Bible course with advanced work in religion such as Biblical criticism, including the tool languages, Hebrew and New Testament Greek. In English Few and Mims, with a growing graduate program, continued to depend upon assistants, one of whom was W. H. Wannamaker, a graduate student. History, under Bassett, for years enjoyed a favored position in the curriculum.[87] In 1898 a recent graduate, W. K. Boyd, assisted Bassett, and in 1902 Boyd became an "adjunct" (assistant) professor for one year. Yet, for most of the period Bassett was without regular assistance and was not relieved from extra work in economics until the fall of 1902, when W. H. Glasson, a Columbia Ph.D., came to assume that field and sociology as well. Glasson learned of Trinity through his ac-

85. Trinity College catalogues, 1898-1903; Kilgo, Sabbatical Report.
86. Trinity College catalogues, 1898-1903.
87. As early as 1898 Trinity required for the degree a greater amount of history, political science, and philosophy than did any other member of the Southern Association. *Proceedings*, 1898, pp. 25-38.

quaintance with Mims at Cornell and brought the college a new professional approach in economics.

In 1898 John I. Hamaker, a biologist with his doctorate from Harvard, joined the scientists and carried the additional work in physics until the arrival of Charles W. Edwards in 1900. Edwards had done graduate work at Columbia, and his coming permitted physics to gain separate status. Scientific equipment began to be collected in some quantity from this point, and in 1901 a Southern Association report concluded that the best science courses in the association were those of Vanderbilt and Trinity. The report bluntly noted that even this work was "sadly inferior" to that of the better Eastern colleges,[88] but Trinity must have been pleased anyway. Mims' earlier complaint clearly indicated the problem: the Southern schools were working against great odds. A few years earlier they had had far to go to match the best of their Northern colleagues. The best of them had come far, but others had not been marking time.

As suggested, for several years it had been difficult to assemble a full staff in the languages. For a time only the versatility of Bassett and Cranford had made it possible to offer French and Greek, and for a time Edwards taught German as well as physics. By 1902 for the first time there was a full complement of language professors. The ancient languages were divided. Meritt was in charge of Greek, and W. F. Gill (from Johns Hopkins) was teaching Latin. John C. Ransmeier, with a Ph.D. from Harvard, handled all of the work in German; and a visiting professor, Dr. George L. Hamilton of Columbia, taught French, Spanish, and Italian, which were now classified as Romance languages. A. M. Webb, from Yale, would replace Hamilton, and Wannamaker, who had switched to German, would replace Ransmeier, in 1902 and 1903. By the latter year there were twenty-three members of the faculty, where there had been nine in 1894. About half were Trinity alumni.

The new men, the new resources, and the receptivity to new ideas were wholly in accord with the optimism that greeted the new century. Kilgo fully shared this spirit. He congratulated the students on their good fortune in being at Trinity and in America at the time. It was a rich period, and all things were yielding their secrets. "It is a great thing to fall into the hands of this nation." In his Sabbatical Report he reviewed his first

88. *Ibid.*, 1901, pp. 43-47.

seven years and proudly reported the advances: a faculty with cosmopolitan interests, and trained in the major university centers; a strong and up-to-date curriculum; an enlarged and more attractive campus; nine new buildings (the Craven Memorial Hall, the Mary Duke [woman's] Building, a gymnasium, a home for the President, and five buildings for the Trinity Park School); and a 1600 per cent increase in endowment.[89] Most important was the attitude of the college community. Trinity's students loved their college "for its spirit of freedom, its generous feelings, its ceaseless energy, its patriotic bravery, its standards of education, and its aggressive positiveness."

An additional glow came with the first major benefaction of the wealthiest member of the Duke family, James B. Duke. The gift met Trinity's needs exactly. For years the pressure for library resources had been growing. "It is the one department," Kilgo repeatedly stated, "that measures the future development of the College."[90] Under Bassett the collections had been organized and enlarged. Breedlove, a trained librarian, was in residence. What was needed were more books and more space, and by the summer of 1900, James B. Duke was willing to provide both.[91] He agreed to build a library with a capacity of 100,000 volumes, and he added $10,000 for the purchase of books. Now Trinity might do what it had been hoping to do, build up the good collegiate library that the South lacked and needed. The building was completed and dedicated in February, 1903.

By 1902 Kilgo had concluded that the college organization was complete. There were no pressing building needs. The "heart and lungs," the faculty and equipment, were in good order. Now future development would lie in other directions.[92] He suggested two items for patient consideration: a step ahead in providing for women students; and a law school. The ideal arrangement for women should be an "annex" on the Radcliffe-Harvard model, in effect, the beginnings of a "co-ordinate" woman's college. Since 1896 the enrollment of women had risen from four to thirty-five. Over half had come from Durham. The new plan would make possible rapid increases and would permit

89. The endowment in 1894 was $22,500; in 1901, it was $333,750. Of the increase ($311,250), Washington Duke had given $309,000. Kilgo, Sabbatical Report. By 1903 the endowment had reached $440,000.

90. Kilgo, Sabbatical Report, p. 3.

91. O. M. Gates (architect) to J. B. Duke, Aug. 9, 1900, B. N. Duke Papers.

92. J. C. Kilgo, *The Lines of the Future Development of Trinity College* (Durham, 1902).

wider geographical distribution.[93] By 1903 the Greensboro Female College had closed, leaving open the field for Methodist women students. The G. F. C. trustees offered the property to Trinity if it would absorb the bonded debt. The college declined, citing among other reasons its own hopes for an annex.[94] Kilgo urged prompt action in formalizing the plan in order to "preempt the grounds" in female education, and he worked up an organization in some detail. He suggested to Ben Duke that a distinct college be established, perhaps to be named the Mary Duke College, in honor of Ben's late sister. The woman's college would operate under the Trinity charter and officers and would award Trinity degrees. The same faculty, admissions, and academic standards would prevail. In time a plant of several buildings would be required.[95] In July, 1903, the plan was approved, but its implementation awaited financial resources.[96]

The law school should be the first professional school, Kilgo said. Its opportunities for influence were obvious, it would stimulate undergraduate admissions, and it would provide a badly needed improvement in the profession. He believed that a faculty of five and an endowment of perhaps $100,000 would be required. The numbers would be kept small and expansion gradual.

At this time Kilgo counseled caution toward a growing sentiment for a medical school. The need was apparent all over the state, and it was recalled that Crowell had encouraged the idea. But Kilgo always was wary of the rapid multiplication of schools unless resources were in sight. In due time, he agreed, a two-year course in medicine and pharmacy might be a good idea.

Thus, at the turn of the century success seemed assured. Kilgo himself was the delight of his Board of Trustees, and they told him so. If he had made mistakes they were lost in the perspective of years of uninterrupted achievement. They liked his administrative ability, his patience about the future, and his skill in managing men. But most of all they liked his contagious "spirit of independence and of heroic devotion to the truth. . . ."[97]

To Kilgo only one fence needed mending. He never forgot the lesson of Crowell's trouble with the Church, and he had be-

93. *Ibid.*
94. *Minutes,* Board of Trustees, June 8, 1903.
95. John C. Kilgo to B. N. Duke, June 30, 1903, also containing a copy of the college plan; Trinity College Papers.
96. *Minutes,* Executive Committee, July 3, 1903.
97. Committee report printed with Sabbatical Report, 1901.

:ome intimately familiar with opposition from that source. He :ould not be certain that dissatisfaction with Trinity, especially n the West, might not provoke another movement against its)resident. Accordingly, he suggested in 1901 that the Board 'investigate the charter of the college, so as to better unify its)arts."⁹⁸ With a minimum of discussion, both Conferences ap->roved the appointment of a committee. A new charter was pre->ared, approved by the Executive Committee, and became law)n February 23, 1903. In June of that year the Board ratified it vithout recorded discussion.⁹⁹

The salient item, of course, was the Board's power to control ts membership. Crowell's charter of 1891 opened trustee selec-ion to "election" by the Conferences and the alumni. In the Old [rinity charter of 1859 the Board had been clearly self-perpetu-iting and held the additional powers of removal and filling ʳacancies. After 1891 the practice had developed whereby the 3oard "nominated" and the Conferences "elected" or "confirmed." [he new charter of 1903, which was not in the form of an amend-nent but a complete document in itself, marked a return to the ›riginal plan. There still would be thirty-six trustees, as in 1891, welve elected from each Conference and twelve elected by the ;raduates, but at this point the wording of 1859 was substituted ʳerbatim: *"Provided however,* That no person shall be elected a [rustee till he has first been recommended by a majority of the [rustees present at a regular meeting. . . ." The powers to remove .nd fill vacancies were also secured.¹⁰⁰

Kilgo did not publicly analyze this change at the time. In he Sabbatical Report of 1901 he merely observed that the col-ege was "under the care" of the Conferences and "under the

98. *Report of the President,* June, 1901. This and other recommendations ʳere presented at the meeting and not included in the printed report.

99. *Minutes,* Executive Committee, Jan. 15, 1903; *Journal,* Western Confer-nce, 1902, p. 46; *Journal,* N. C. Conference, 1902, p. 49; *Private Laws of North ;arolina,* 1903, pp. 408-410; *Minutes,* Board of Trustees, June 8, 1903.
The "committee" naturally would have been composed of Trinity trustees and ·erhaps representatives of both Conferences. Its membership is not recorded.

100. As early as 1896 the Board, by resolution, changed the method of electing lumni trustees to require that they first be nominated by the Board. *Minutes,* ·oard of Trustees, May 13, 1896. In 1897 the Trinity Park "municipality" ·eature was altered to delete any provision which limited the college's responsi-ility *in loco parentis.* Elections continued for some years (Kilgo was usually ιayor). *Private Laws,* 1895-1925. The "municipality" feature was dropped ʳhen the City of Durham extended its limits to include Trinity in 1901. Ap-endix, President's Report, 1905, Trustee Records. (The term "Trustee Records" ·fers to envelopes containing working papers of the various annual meetings. 'hey are deposited in the vault, Treasurer's Office, Duke University.)

general direction" of the entire Methodist Church. Several years later, in 1908, he believed it timely, in another context, to discuss Trinity's relationship with the Church.[101] He considered the role of an ecclesiastical body in the selection of trustees, and he concluded that if the role were unrestricted, it posed "a perpetual peril" to the institution. He said that the selection of trustees was a delicate matter, and leaving it in the hands of a religious body exposed the institution to too many hazards:

> Such a charter furnishes an opportunity for any number of an ecclesiastical body to attack the administration of the college and greatly hinder, if not utterly obstruct it. Any disaffected element in the synod or conference can make war on the college and, if they can secure a majority of representatives on the board of trustees, the college will become an agency for the promotion of their schemes and influences, and be degraded to all the purposes of warring factions that may arise in an ecclesiastical body. In such an unsettled state the administrator of the college would be constantly exposed to all sorts of opposition, and, if he should be a strong character, he would be kept in a constant contention with those who might oppose him. If, on the other hand, he should be a man who desires to avoid friction, the possibility of having conflicts with the synod or conference would naturally lead him to adopt an indefinite policy of administration, and this would amount to making the college serve the personal interests of its official head. All of these are possible evils which should be provided against in the charter of the institution.[102]

Therefore, he concluded, the ideal policy was to have a self perpetuating board. Obviously men of wealth preferred to give to colleges that were permanent and stable in their organization

Kilgo also raised the question of the public interest. He agreed that no college was really private and that the public had interests to be protected. At the same time the college must be protected from undue public interference, he said. The public at large was "wholly incompetent" to evaluate higher education Therefore, the Church organization might represent the public At Trinity under the charter of 1903, he believed that balance had been achieved. The Board's power protected the college and the Church's privilege of confirmation served the public. He paid tribute to the Conferences: what groups could better represent the public? Composed of laymen and preachers and dedi

101. *Report of the President,* May 1, 1908, pp. 8-21.
102. *Ibid.,* p. 10.

:ated to high moral standards, they were generally free of selfish aims, unlike political assemblies. They were permanent organizations and therefore stable. The analysis was perhaps Kilgo's most brilliant argument. It wedded tradition and sentiment to reality.

The charter of 1903 rounded out the strength of the college. Trinity now had resources in money, faculty, and equipment. The battles on Christian education, tobacco, with Old Trinity and the West had also hardened its self-consciousness. There was an attitude of independence, and there was confidence in new academic power. Perhaps there was even a tendency to swagger. All of these resources were to be needed in the fall of 1903.

Chapter IV

The Bassett Affair

"Eighteen—Seven, Thus They Voted"

In the 1890's and in the early years of the new century, an epidemic of professorial dismissals shook the college and university world. The act of taking a college teacher's scalp was not new; that so many were taken in these years was alarming. At private and state institutions alike, scholars who offended prevailing creeds, economic, political, or social, were likely to face the challenge of an irritated business community or a partisan political climate.[1]

The dismissals naturally followed the revolution in American scholarship and the ideological passions of the time. The force of "science" and the German influence had contributed to a professionalization of the college teacher. Now he was often a researcher, and with the rise of the social sciences, he was likely to be concerned with current issues in controversy. Indeed, men like Crowell had brought to North Carolina the dictum that a modern scholar was obliged to conquer his reticence and reach out with his learning to the people. In the reaching out, from one coast to the other, the articulate American professor was finding that he touched live wires.

From the rich native tradition of civil rights and from the German mystique of *Lehrfreiheit* (freedom of inquiry), scholars began to develop an ideological counterattack. At this time the professorial world at large could depend upon no national organization to manage a defense of its members, but increasingly dismissals were branded violations of academic freedom. There was a pitiful weakness in the tendency merely to repeat the word *Lehrfreiheit*, as though it had "a certain incantational value."[2] Aside from this professional attitude, there were few other resources in accepted theory or practice. The protection of even

1. This and summary on academic freedom from Richard Hofstadter and Walter P. Metzger, *The Development of Academic Freedom in the United States* (New York, 1955), especially chaps. viii and ix. Cited hereinafter as Hofstadter-Metzger, *Development of Freedom.*

2. *Ibid.*, p. 397.

limited tenure was still new. If an institution accepted the position that dismissal could only follow a clearly established "cause," the nature of the cause was far from clear. How did one define the extent of fair, reasoned comment? Should one defend a professor whose spirited advocacy of, say, economic reform seemed hopelessly intermixed with his sober analysis of economic ills? Was there a difference between the classroom comment and the "extra-mural" speech? The answers are not entirely clear today. But in the period under review little of the subsequent accumulation of organization, safeguard, and tradition had developed. It seemed to be open season on the outspoken academic.

In the South there were fewer celebrated cases of abrupt dismissal than in the East or Midwest, perhaps because there was less criticism of prevailing ideas. Certainly there were fewer trained scholars. The professor in the South found himself in a region that had developed, at least since the days of the anti-slavery debates, a resistance to criticism of things "Southern." Reconstruction excesses had helped harden sectional solidarity. After the 1870's, when the Democratic parties recaptured state governments from Republican rule, the political benefits of cultivating the status quo were obvious.

Yet, the South was not immune to new influences, and in the late years of the nineteenth century a small group of native heretics developed.[3] Some were scholars who had partaken of the cosmopolitan influence of the new graduate schools in the North; some became Southern exiles when they found it impossible to remain comfortable and critical in the land of their birth. This latter group might content themselves with firing salvos from afar. Many thoughtful Southerners were active and influential at home, but they were conditioned by the need for patience and quiet persuasion. It is of the impatient ones that we speak.

One of the best known exiles was Walter Hines Page, a native of North Carolina and a former Trinity College student. Dissatisfied at Old Trinity, he had moved to Randolph-Macon College. Later he spent two years at Johns Hopkins and then began an itineracy of newspaper editing and writing in North Carolina and abroad, finally settling in the Northeast. Page had edited the influential *Forum* and *Atlantic Monthly* before establishing

3. See, for example, Howard W. Odum, *Southern Pioneers in Social Interpretation* (Chapel Hill, 1925), pp. 3-27. Cited hereinafter as Odum, *Pioneers*.

in 1900 an impressive monthly, *World's Work*. By this time he was also a partner in the publishing firm of Doubleday Page and Company. Page and Crowell had just missed each other in the North Carolina of the 1880's, but both spoke much the same message. Page, too, was on fire for educational reform, industrial and scientific development, academic influence on social problems, and a total modernization movement in the South.[4]

From New York Page kept in constant contact with his native state. He came home frequently to speak, and the *World's Work* contained a heavy budget of articles on Southern problems. Always there was cheerful nagging for new ideas, intellectual reform. His ties with the new Trinity developed over a period of years. He had known the Dukes as early as 1892 (as investors in the *Manufacturer's Record*, in which he was interested). When the new corps of scholars collected in Durham, there were other contacts. Page's publishing house handled one of Bassett's first volumes, and he was interested in the life of Jackson that Bassett was beginning in 1900. He knew Few, Mims, and others of the faculty. Page's attitudes were much in harmony with the ebullience at the college. His encouragement and his ability to open avenues toward publication made the alliance a natural one.[5]

By early 1900 the Trinity College atmosphere was attuned to the ambitions and attitudes of the world of modern scholarship. The research-minded Ph.D.'s on the faculty were acutely conscious of the professorial dismissals throughout the country. Most important, in Kilgo the young scholars had a champion who was increasingly disturbed about any restriction on Trinity's right to speak out. Kilgo had always equated Christian education with "truth" (because God was the source of truth), but after 1900 he became more specific. He held that the poverty of Southern colleges had made them dependent upon the whims of their constituencies.[6] His favorite target still was

4. Burton J. Hendrick, *The Training of an American: The Earlier Life and Letters of Walter H. Page, 1855-1913* (Boston and New York, 1928), *passim*. For evaluations of Page, see Robert D. W. Connor, "Walter Hines Page," in Odum, *Pioneers*, pp. 53-67; and Edwin Mims, "Walter Hines Page: Friend of the South," *South Atlantic Quarterly*, XVIII (April, 1919), 97-115.
Page was best known in later years as the United States Ambassador to Great Britain during the World War.
5. B. N. Duke Papers; John Spencer Bassett Papers (Milton, Mass.); and Walter Hines Page Papers, Letters, American Period (Houghton Library, Harvard University), *passim*.
6. Durham *Recorder*, April 16, 1900.

the politically dependent state college, although he tended to include the church college as well. In both cases, political partisanship or social tradition fettered the mind and limited the work of the scholar. "We have built State Colleges for our States and typed them after the ideals of State habits and aims. . . . The church has taken its educational conceptions from the State, and has built conference colleges, synod colleges and conventional colleges."[7] In contrast, he pointed to the new business strength of the country that cut sectional lines and promoted a new spirit resistant to narrowness in the church or in politics.

Kilgo told the alumni in 1902 that Trinity, with its leadership in academic standards and its contempt for numbers, had a mission to perform. "Trinity has set its life" against provincialism, whether found in the legislature, on the bench, in the pulpit, classroom, or editor's chair. Trinity, at whatever risk in popularity, would not trim its sails. "There is no investigation which it should dread to make. There is no sincere argument it should dread to hear. . . ." Warming to the message, he said (or shouted), "No dread of unpopularity, no fear of small attendance, no criticisms and even hatred can divert it" from its mission.[8]

Kilgo's readiness to resist intimidation is best seen in his reaction to the Sledd case at Emory College (Georgia) in the summer of 1902. Andrew Sledd, a professor of Latin, had written an article on the ever-present item of discussion, the Negro problem, for the *Atlantic Monthly*. Sledd produced a vigorous indictment of the Southern whites' violation of the Negro's rights, with special attention to the brutishness of lynching. There was criticism of Northern extremists as well, in particular the sentimentalists who, Sledd contended, sought to theorize the Negro into a higher state of culture than he had reached. But the burden of the article was on Southern shortcomings, especially the "dehumanizing" of the Negro for political gain.[9] Sledd's article provoked newspaper attack and the anger of one of Emory's patrons, Mrs. W. H. Felton. Amid the uproar and to spare the college, Sledd offered his resignation, and the trustees accepted it.

Sledd was the son-in-law of Bishop Candler, Kilgo's old friend,

7. Raleigh *Morning Post*, June 8, 1902.
8. *Ibid.*
9. Andrew Sledd, "The Negro: Another View," *Atlantic Monthly*, XC (July, 1902), 65-73.

and Candler wrote Kilgo about it, seeking help in placing Sledd elsewhere.[10] Kilgo did not let the letter grow cold. He had not read the article and did not know Sledd, but he would try to help him. "I will never desert a brave man, tho' I may have to differ from him at times." And then Kilgo set about saying some "very plain things" to Candler:

> Dr. Sledd made a mistake in resigning, tho' he is to be commended for the spirit of his resignation. I do not undertake to criticize his article, for as I have said, I have not read it. But there is a fixed design on the part of the lower elements of politicians in the South to either run the church out of education, or force our colleges to serve their vile ends of social bondage, which is the most infernal bondage that has ever appeared among men. I am not cursing, I am using sober words. The supreme question in the South is, shall we be a free people or shall we be the slaves of a vile partizanship? The blow is being struck at the colleges first, because they are the critical point. The state schools have been bound hand and foot and are the vassals of this bondage. You recall the acts of Kansas University, Texas University, A. & M. College of N. C. and other state institutions.
>
> The only hope of freedom is in the colleges of the church, and these have been marked for the slaughter. I know what I am now saying, for I have stood in the severest place for seven long years. I am pained to see our Methodist colleges, one after another, yield to this crowd of freedom-haters. Now old Emory, the home of Pierce, Haygood and Candler falls down before this set, and surrenders forever the old College into their hands. It is enough to make the Angels weep. Trinity stands alone now in this conflict, and the struggle deepens.
>
> It is a shame, but it is true, that some in high church places have joined in the war, and I am hated and denounced because I will not yield, and by the eternal I will never do so. T'were better to die and wait on the slow run of centuries to vindicate me than purchase an easy popularity at the price of right. Fifty years hence Emory's deed will be quoted to show the un-Christian partizanship of the church in this generation. Then will be the time for weeping. Your sons will be called on to explain and deny the act of your Trustees. Georgia Methodist[s] trying to show why their fathers thought it a crime to write in the interest of a poor down trodden people at our doors, while they shouted over the idea of helping Chinamen ten thousand miles away, and all this in the name of Christ!
>
> No, I say Dr. Sledd should have stood his place, for he has

10. W. A. Candler to J. C. Kilgo, Aug. 13, 1902, Trinity College Papers.

done Emory greater hurt by going out than he could have done
by staying in, and the hurt will be lasting. He should have forced
the College to take the aggressive, but he has made it easy for it
to do the wrong, and now it has passed into the hands of Mrs.
Felton and her kind, and this is modern Methodism, and Methodist colleges to which we must send our boys. Well, there are
some of us who will not do it at any cost and the church will do
well to learn this. Men will not give money to put Louis XIV on
the throne of Southern Methodism, and thank the good Lord,
money is going very slowly into these schools. It should be so.
Methodism needs courage to run colleges as well as money, and
at this time she needs the first worse than she needs the latter.
When she gets brave enough to do her duty and separate herself
from the herd of slave-makers, she will get money and until then
she should not get it.

Pray, tell me for what does Christian Education stand if it
does not stand for the ideas of Christ? Is slavery one of these
ideas? The time has come for our Bishops to speak out, for
preachers are surrendering to this herd in ways they never dream
of. You cannot sit still and see the hands of your college bound in
such a manner. Where are Emory's sons? Are they all dead? Are
they willing to see this herd sit down in the chairs once filled by
royal men? I tremble for your new President, if he commits his
destiny to the popularity he may get among this crowd.

Well, Trinity shall be free tho' all the Bishops, preachers,
politicians, and wild women on earth decree otherwise, and I will
get out only when whipped out, and then I will leave the church
on record for a crime, the stench of which will never cease to
rise to heaven.[11]

The Trinity College community might well look at the Sledd
case with special interest and feel encouraged to believe that it
"would not have taken place in some Southern institutions."[12]
A student, writing in the *Archive,* thought the Emory authorities
"too easily frightened." It is possible to suggest that by the year
1903 a number of interwoven factors combined to make the college ripe for a test of academic freedom.

First, there was the prestige of Kilgo himself. For at least
five years his friends in the Church had kept him in mind as a
candidate for bishop. In 1902 there had been the beginnings of

---

11. J. C. Kilgo to W. A. Candler, Aug. 14, 1902, *ibid.* (Paragraphing supplied).

12. Edwin Mims, "The University in the South," *Annals,* American Academy
of Political Science, XXII (Sept., 1903), 264. Cited hereinafter as Mims, "University."

a definite campaign;[13] at the General Conference he received a token vote that looked well on the record. Moreover, Kilgo was clearly speaking the voice of the faculty, especially with regard to freedom at Trinity. He was now but forty-two years old himself and presided over a faculty of fifteen professors whose average age was thirty-four. Only Pegram, at fifty-seven, was over forty, and there were three not yet thirty. It was not a sedate group, nor was it provincial. The seven Ph.D.'s held their doctorates from Hopkins, Columbia, Yale, Cornell, and Harvard (three). Five others had done graduate work at Leipzig, Oxford, or one of the aforementioned institutions. The majority were native Southerners, although there were four Yankees. Six were native North Carolinians and six were alumni of Trinity—in short, a young group peculiarly susceptible by age and background to the spirit of derring-do which Kilgo encouraged.[14]

Second, the college felt encouraged in its preoccupation with standards. In higher education, Mims thought, there was much bigotry and conservatism to conquer, but brave scholars could do something about it—and there would be honor to those who did.[15] Bassett's friend, William E. Dodd, another intellectual heretic, then teaching history at Randolph-Macon, envied Bassett his place "in such a wide-awake institution. You can shape things and set the pace. . . ."[16]

Third, the Dukes's pride in the little college was enormous; it had come so far in a few years. Ben Duke wrote friends that he believed Trinity had reached the point "to warrant the claim that it is the best institution of learning in the South."[17] He thought the college stood for "the new forces working now very rapidly for the upbuilding of the whole South and tending to break up the sectional isolation and make the South a part of our common country."[18] In 1903 both his son and daughter were attending Trinity.

13. J. H. Southgate to B. N. Duke, March 1, 1902, Trinity College Papers; Garber, *Kilgo*, pp. 318-319.
14. The prestige of the Ph.D. may be seen in the fact that in 1900 only 342 such degrees were conferred by American institutions. Walter C. John, *Graduate Study in Universities and Colleges in the United States* (Washington, D. C., 1935), p. 19.
15. Mims, "University," pp. 261-265.
16. William E. Dodd to J. S. Bassett, Nov. 1, 1901, Bassett Papers. Dodd was later to make his reputation at the University of Chicago. He was United States Ambassador to Germany from 1933-1937.
17. B. N. Duke to E. J. Parrish (Tokyo, Japan), Feb. 4, 1902, B. N. Duke Letterbook.
18. B. N. Duke to Senator J. C. Pritchard, May 8, 1902, *ibid.*

Finally, though unrecorded, there may have been a nagging sensitivity to the frequent charge from critics such as Editor Webster and Judge Walter Clark that the college was the creature of the plutocrats. In spite of Kilgo's emphasis upon the vagaries of the state institutions, celebrated dismissal cases also had occurred at new universities created by capitalists such as Rockefeller or Stanford. There was a growing suspicion that the trust magnates, satiated by money power, now sought new fields to conquer and ruled their philanthropies by edict.[19] The taunt came more frequently as the tobacco trust grew and as the college became financially more secure. Bassett once queried Dodd on this matter and was told that "educated and thoughtful men" did not believe it, but Dodd conceded that Trinity suffered from the association in men's minds of the college with the trust.[20] Perhaps a move in rebuttal came in the spring of 1903 when Washington Duke removed the condition of his earlier gift regarding the admission of women. He was still interested in training women, he said, but the gift had been the only one "which in any way affects your policies in the management of the College." He wished to "remove the necessary restraints which it imposes on your Board, and to leave you free to adopt such a policy as may, in your judgment, seem wisest." He hoped that his action would relieve the Board "of any possible embarrassment."[21]

All of these strengths and attitudes, not forgetting the new charter that limited the Church's control, would indicate that if there were to be a test of academic liberty at Trinity College, it might well come in 1903.

It did come, and the man who was to provoke it was probably the college's strongest scholar. In the fall of 1903, John Spencer Bassett was thirty-six years old and was beginning his tenth year on the faculty. He was an alumnus and a member of the first class to graduate under Crowell. He was a Methodist and a native of Tarboro, North Carolina. His father, a contractor, had

19. This "thesis of conspiracy" is discussed in Hofstadter-Metzger, *Development of Freedom*, and in Walter P. Metzger, "College Professors and Big Business Men: A Study of American Ideologies, 1880-1915" (doctoral dissertation, State University of Iowa, June, 1950).

20. William E. Dodd to J. S. Bassett, Feb. 5, 1903, Bassett Papers.

21. Washington Duke to Board of Trustees of Trinity College, April 20, 1903, Trustee Records, 1903.

directed some of the building operations after the move to Durham.[22]

Bassett had been inspired by Crowell's vision of graduate work and had been one of the first Trinity men to seek it. He took his doctorate in history at the Johns Hopkins in 1894, and his name had been among those considered as successors to Crowell. When he came back to Trinity that year, he brought from Herbert Adams' seminars perspective and ambition. On the campus these qualities led to the reviving of the Trinity College Historical Society and inaugurating a series of historical publications. Both students and faculty contributed. He preached a doctrine of reason versus emotion in dealing with Southern history and scorn for the "pale skim of dilettantism" which so long had characterized it. He was hard on the Confederate Brigadier as historian: "Men who have fought bravely with the sword are thus tempted to make asses of themselves with the pen."[23]

Bassett's personal dedication to research was firmly established. He was a prodigious worker, and his light burning late was always a silent challenge to his colleagues. Certainly he found few daylight hours for his writing. His weekly teaching load was at least fifteen hours; after 1900 he was put in charge of the library and often worked three hours per day organizing and building its collections. At the same time he brought historical zeal to the state. As perhaps the only trained historian in North Carolina, he was a bureau of advice and information to school teachers and others of scholarly bent.

In spite of low pay and hard work, Bassett received steady encouragement from Kilgo. The president trusted his advice and cheered him on during his summer research expeditions.[24] Bassett in turn was helpful during the strenuous days of the Christian education campaign, writing frequently for the *Educator* and the Church papers. Indeed, in view of later events, it is ironic that Bassett should have written one piece that implied

22. See W. K. Boyd on Bassett in *Dictionary of American Biography*, II, 38 39. There are of course many details in the Bassett Papers. On Bassett as his torian, see Wendell H. Stephenson, "John Spencer Bassett as a Historian of the South," *North Carolina Historical Review*, XXV (July, Oct., 1948).

23. *Christian Educator*, March, 1898.

24. "You have been good to me at all times, and I can never repay you. want to help you to as large success as possible. No man is more in my confidenc and esteem than you." J. C. Kilgo to J. S. Bassett (Washington, D. C.), Aug. 1 1901, Bassett Papers.

that he would accept with equanimity the dismissal of a professor from a state institution if he were "tainted with skepticism."[25]

From Adams Bassett received constant support and advice
that carried him through the early days of low salaries and a
heavy teaching load. Adams told him he was "the most productive Hopkins graduate of our time,"[26] and once reminded him,
"You are transforming the historic consciousness of your people
and your State. . . . You are dispelling illusions and bringing the
truth to light."[27] By 1898 Bassett was caught up in the excitement of seeing Kilgo in battle. He told Adams that "as long as
the foolkilling is to go on" at Trinity, he would stay to see the fun.

The foolkilling that was to interest him most would have to
do with the Negro problem. Much of his research had been on
the Negro, in slavery and since the Civil War, and he believed
he had acquired knowledge and detachment as a native Southerner that the South needed. He admired the work of Bishop
Atticus G. Haygood, onetime president of Emory College, who
in 1881 had recommended a spirit of Christian charity for the
Negro and had urged educational and economic opportunities.
Haygood had been villified for his candor, but Bassett felt in
1895 that times had changed and that race relations were improving.[28]

If race relations were improving, the political struggles in
North Carolina in the late 1890's soon altered the situation.
Agrarian discontent had brought forth a militant challenge to the
long powerful Democrats—the Populist party. Its strength was
such that by an easy calculation one could predict that if the
Populists were to join with the Republicans they could outvote
the Democrats. This "fusion" took place in 1894 and gave the
union a majority in the legislature. Two years later the victory

25. "Shall A Church Have A College?," *Christian Educator*, May, 1897. This
suggests a piety that Bassett probably did not possess. At about the same time
he confided to Herbert Adams that he feared he might one day "clash with the
authorities here on the question of orthodoxy." Bassett to Adams, Jan. 24, 1898,
Adams Letters. In later years Bassett's views on religion approached agnosticism.
Interview with Richard Bassett, Milton, Mass., Sept. 26-27, 1960.
   Before he left Trinity Bassett had concluded that Kilgo's Christian education
campaign was useless. He later explained that he had felt the "ardor of combat"
most keenly because, like Crowell, he resented the state university's pretensions
and its "patronizing" attitude toward Trinity's scholars. Bassett to Edwin Mims,
April 18, 1909, Bassett Papers.
26. Adams to Bassett, Oct. 24, 1896, Bassett Papers.
27. Adams to Bassett, May 14, 1898, *ibid.*
28. J. S. Bassett, "Bishop Haygood and the Negro Problem," manuscript in
Bassett Papers, *ca.* 1895.

was complete, and North Carolina had its first Republican governor since Reconstruction. During the next four years the counterattack was violent, and it tended to center on the Negro, who voted Republican and received some political offices. The Negro thus could be used as a brand of association with which to mark both fusion parties, the Populists in particular. In white supremacy campaigns in 1898 and 1900 Democrats of all persuasions taunted the Populists with their Negro tie and built up a storm of racial animosity.[29] In 1898 the party leader, Furnifold M. Simmons (a Trinity alumnus and trustee), made secret agreements with business interests to keep taxes low and legislation "right" and with denominational college leaders to keep down appropriations for the competing state colleges.[30] In short, various elements of self-interest were enlisted in a campaign to ally all white men against the presumed threat of "Negro Rule." After 1900, campaign promises that there would be no disfranchisement were broken, and amendments that had the effect of removing the Negro from office and from politics by removing him from the ballot box were passed. A literacy qualification was itself sufficient to remove many Negroes; that it also might disqualify illiterate whites was an embarrassment that became an asset. It permitted the launching of a useful educational campaign for better schools—and more of them. Yet in politics, then and later, the cry of "nigger" worked. Its harsh accents somehow made the brutalization of the state's people seem defensible to those who used it. The electorate was confirmed in a belief that the end justified the means, and the "settlement" insured the supremacy of the Democratic party in North Carolina. Later the victors contrived the pious rationalization that their campaign had brought "peace" and "good government" to North Carolina.[31]

29. Two excellent studies of the period are Helen G. Edmonds, *The Negro and Fusion Politics in North Carolina, 1894-1901* (Chapel Hill, 1951); and Oliver H. Orr, Jr., *Charles Brantley Aycock* (Chapel Hill, 1961). Both emphasize the lengths to which white men were willing to go in their desire for power.

It is also clear that, for their part, the fusion parties, especially the Populists, did not seek reform in the Negro's interest but also used him for political gain. However, Orr points out that the fusion represented a "daring experiment. It was, and is, the only major such experiment of indigenous origin ever attempted in the South." P. 106.

30. J. Fred Rippy (ed.), *F. M. Simmons: Statesman of the New South, Memoirs and Addresses* (Durham, 1936), p. 29.

31. Orr's investigations raise serious doubts about the validity of the mythology, although few have been willing to challenge it before. P. 188.

A perceptive observer of the Southern attitude of the period has dramatized the prevailing attitude: "Here was that mighty frame the Democratic Party, as potent an instrument of regimentation as any totemic society that ever

Bassett watched the campaigns of 1898 and 1900 with disgust and sadness, and he frequently wrote Herbert Adams about what was going on. He did "not have the honor to agree with my fellow Anglo-Saxons on the negro question," and he was convinced that the crowing about settling the issue was merely a postponement.[32] Bassett had his share of Southern race feeling. The Negro in politics was a "nauseating" dose to take, but he could not swallow the appeals to passion or what he believed to be fraud in the elections. He favored an educational qualification for the suffrage if "honestly administered." He scoffed after the famous Wilmington Riot of 1898 when the white leader of a mob, later as mayor, appealed against violence. He was itching to try to modify racial sentiment. From Baltimore, Adams urged caution: "Men who disagree with you are quite capable nowadays of destroying your reputation and public influence by malignant accusations. . . . The tyranny of public opinion in N. C. at the present time must be frightful. The idea that there can be but one political party, only one sort of newspaper, only one way of looking at the negro problem!"[33] In spite of repeated hints from Adams, Bassett wanted to "set a limit to this wildfire of prejudice." It would be delicate, but he felt that Southern whites would respond to a gentle approach. He urged Adams to tell the Northern philanthropists that "the way to help the Negro in the South is to educate the white man."[34]

By 1899 the suffrage amendment had been drafted, and Bassett saw it at best as "an enamelled lie." The device, with the new Jim Crow laws, was simply "one more step in the educating of our people that it is right to lie, to steal & to defy all honesty in order to keep a certain party in power." He predicted accurately that the Democrats were assured indefinite tenure in office.[35] Now he was working up a series of lectures on the Negro for delivery in Baltimore, and again Adams was getting a little edgy. The best audience would be the Hopkins' seminar, not the Baltimore public, which was "rather cranky on the Negro ques-

existed. . . . Tolerance, in sum, was pretty well extinguished all along the line and conformity made a nearly universal law. Criticism, analysis, detachment, all those activities and attitudes so necessary to the healthy development of any civilization, every one of them took on the aspect of high and aggravated treason." W. J. Cash, *The Mind of the South* (New York, 1941), p. 135.

32. Bassett to Adams, Nov. 15, 1898, Adams Letters.
33. Adams to Bassett, Dec. 15, 1898, Bassett Papers.
34. Bassett to Adams, Dec. 16, 1898, Adams Letters.
35. *Ibid.*, Feb. 18, 1899.

tion."[36] Bassett explained his interest in tracing the Roman
parallel in slavery in order to analyze the development of a servile
population into responsible citizenship. Adams was more explicit.
Clearly the lectures would be best suited for Hopkins: "You
know this town as well as I do."[37]

But Adams' restraint was counterbalanced by the atmosphere
around the college. As early as 1896, Kilgo had invited the Negro
leader Booker T. Washington to speak at Trinity, and the boys
had cheered him as he left. Kilgo himself, though practical
enough to see merit in the campaign of 1898, cautioned the students against an excess of prejudice that would limit the Negro's
rights.[38] Later he insisted that the question could not be solved
politically, and he warned that when men were without the ballot
the nation was without a safety valve. Kilgo seemed particularly
concerned about the new emphasis upon race separation at all
levels. He could not reconcile concern for the dark peoples who
were coming into the American imperial orbit (e.g., in the Philip-
pines) with the decision to "ostracize a white man in North Carolina if he preaches the gospel to them [the Negroes] or teaches
them in their schools."[39]

The orthodox Southern position on the Negro was merely one
of many faults the young faculty thought needed attention. One
way to deal with them was to reach a literate, thoughtful audience. The opportunity came in 1902 when Bassett persuaded
"9019," the student scholarship group, to sponsor a literary journal, the *South Atlantic Quarterly.* Later the venture needed dependable financing, and a publishing company was organized and
stock issued.[40] In reality, the shareholders were simply donors,
and they came from the faculty and from sympathetic friends in
Durham.[41] The first issue appeared in January, 1902. Finally
Bassett, the editor, had the journal he had long wanted, and the

36. Adams to Bassett, June 22, 1899, Bassett Papers.
37. *Ibid.*, Dec. 16, 1899.
38. There is no record linking Kilgo to Simmons' secret agreements, but surely
he favored them. The Christian education campaign was still going on, and
Simmons was a member of his Board of Trustees. In the chapel talk cited here,
Kilgo said, "While you may work hard to put the negro out of office, and while
I think he is incompetent to govern, do not let those prejudices go so far that
you would work the negro out of a good character, an honest living, his rights,
and out of an opportunity to come to all that God may wish him to be."
Manuscript, chapel talk, Oct. 28, 1898, Kilgo Papers.
39. Baccalaureate address, Raleigh *Morning Post,* June 6, 1899.
40. William B. Hamilton (ed.), *Fifty Years of The South Atlantic Quarterly*
(Durham, 1952), pp. 4-7. Cited hereinafter as Hamilton, *Fifty Years of S. A. Q.*
41. *Ibid.*

faculty had the opportunity to discipline their thoughts for publication. The aim, Bassett said in the opening issue, was to stimulate a demand and a capacity for literature in the South. After so many years of cultural poverty, now, he believed, the region was ready for it. There would be a commitment to encourage "every honest literary effort" and a devotion to truth "in the spirit of honest tolerance." Contending points of view would receive equal treatment; the editor would offer "a fair field and a respectful consideration" to all.[42] He wrote Ben Duke privately that his hope was to collect "a fearless set of writers who shall lead this part of the nation into a sound intellectual life."

The *Quarterly* began with vigor. The lead article of the first issue carried an attack on lynching by Kilgo and on the political habit of educating the people to violence and resentment. In this and succeeding issues the Negro problem received steady consideration, including articles from men who spoke in defense of white supremacy and in criticism of Negro laziness and undependability. But the emphasis was on general social reform. Dowd wrote on the evils of child labor, "a refined form of cannibalism"; Mims linked the New England "Renaissance" to what might come to pass in the South; Henry Snyder of Wofford sniped at an overworked parochialism, the word "Southern"; Kilgo challenged the emotionalism, false standards, and claims of Southern education; and W. L. Poteat of Wake Forest offered a plea for the new prestige of science. There was a disposition to speak candidly in the book review section. Immediately there was heartening praise from a wide circle of academics, North and South.

Bassett himself established the practice of writing an editorial for each issue, and he wrote many of the reviews. He made practical suggestions to increase book sales in the South, and he lamented the plight of the Southern author who had to write under the shadow of poverty and intolerance and who found too few like minds with whom he could communicate. Yet it is fair to state that there was a drumming cadence on the Negro question. Bassett dismissed a popular novel on the subject by a native of the state as "an unscientific and impossible piece of social quackery." The "greatness" of Booker T. Washington and his Christian spirit were noted, and there were sideswipes at the

42. This and following from the *Quarterly*, I-II (January 1902-Oct., 1903).

sweet mists that poured from the pen of Thomas Nelson Page, whose novels built a vision of graceful days and loving slaves before The War. In one editorial Bassett dilated on "The Reign of Passion," his phrase for the political exploitation of the Negro. He outlined the historical development of political leadership from ante bellum days to the present, noting the change that had made the Negro question "the only vital" question in determining Southern votes since 1875. He paid due tribute to the good intentions of men who had led the Democratic party and gave credit for their interest in Negro education. But he found the net result injurious. The choice of the Negro issue in politics "has accustomed the citizen to party hatred" and "pauperized the intellects" of Southern statesmen. It had subverted the ideals of a republican form of government. Bassett opened the analysis with an indictment of the "contemptuous vituperation" with which an unnamed newspaper had covered a recent Republican state meeting. He asked, "To what have we come when the organ of a great body of American citizens ceases to meet its opponent in the fair field of argument and hails them with the taunts of the denizens of the garrets and the gutters?"[43] To many of Bassett's readers the anonymous newspaper was easily recognizable. It was the Raleigh *News and Observer,* and its editor and publisher was Josephus Daniels.

The Political Editor

Daniels was a Methodist and an alumnus of the University of North Carolina. He was an editor, and he was a politician. These loyalties and interests at the turn of the century contained many points of conflict. In recognizing Daniels' dilemma in reconciling them, much may be understood about his behavior in these years.[44]

As a Methodist, Daniels was friendly to the Church and to its institutions. He was one of the early group of subscribers who pledged money in the attempt to take Trinity to Raleigh in 1889. For a period he carried a Durham page in the *News and Observer*

43. *Ibid.,* II (Oct., 1902), 301-309.
44. The details of Daniels' career may be found in his multi-volume autobiography. For this period, see *Editor in Politics* (Chapel Hill, 1941). However, Daniels' memory was sometimes unreliable. The best source and the one used for the following is the Raleigh *News and Observer,* 1895-1903.

and gave special attention to Trinity College. Through the years he had a few ties with the Dukes. He and Ben Duke were interested in the Oxford Orphanage, and, as an editor with the ever-present need to build a successful business, Daniels frequently solicited and received advertising from the Duke tobacco companies.

As a university man and as a firm supporter of education at all levels, Daniels probably did not begin to break with Trinity College until the time of the Christian education campaign. Further, Kilgo was a pronounced critic of the university's shortcomings, cool to politicians, and unimpressed by newspapers. Increasingly through the years it probably became more difficult for Kilgo and Daniels to find, had they wished, common grounds. Moreover, Daniels always insisted that he was against "privilege" in any form. He applied this to the machinations of the railroads in North Carolina politics—or to any special group that he felt threatened the great majority. On the other hand, Trinity's habit of feeling alone tended to reinforce the college in its belief that majorities could be wrong.

Daniels' position on the tobacco trust requires cautious generalization. At an early date the *News and Observer* was suspicious of the combination and willing to accept the common opinion that the trust kept prices down in the markets. But, unlike the tireless Webster, Daniels waged intermittent war against the American Tobacco Company. He wrote rather regularly about trusts in general, in particular during William Jennings Bryan's campaigns for the presidency. It is not necessary to question Daniels' convictions to observe that his position on the trusts was profitable politically. The Dukes were Republicans, and Daniels was a Democrat. When tobacco prices fell, especially in an election year, one might honestly believe the trust to blame and at the same time see the political necessity of pointing that out to North Carolina farmers.[45]

45. The foremost student of the industry stresses the correlation between low prices and the role of the speculator. But she also makes it clear that the farmers were taught to blame the trust by the speculators, politicians, and others. Plainly, at the time the facts were hard to come by, and a large number of people believed the trust guilty. She suggests that Daniels and Walter Clark were both motivated, in part at least, by political interest. Nannie May Tilley, *The Bright-Tobacco Industry, 1860-1929*, pp. ix, 415-426. A scholar who lived through the period wrote: "Denunciation of the American Tobacco Company has been in North Carolina a popular political war cry for many years. . . ." R. D. W. Connor to Edward Channing, April 3, 1911, Henry Groves Connor Papers (University of North Carolina Library).

Daniels' background and his role as Democratic editor made him a steadfast defender of North Carolina achievements. This pride (or provincialism, as Bassett would have called it) made it natural for him to balance his criticism of the tobacco trust with praise of the Dukes' business success. In 1895 he wrote Ben Duke for help in getting out a special tobacco edition, explaining that it would include "an appreciative sketch of the life and business success of your brother in New York." He promised "such an edition as will make you and every other tobacco man, and every patriotic North Carolinian, proud of the industry and what it has achieved."[46]

Thus, during the years 1895-1903 there is no clear pattern of hostility to Trinity College in the *News and Observer*. Daniels always commented favorably, sometimes glowingly, on the Dukes' recurrent gifts to Trinity. He voiced opposition to Kilgo on specific issues occasionally but did not gratuitously attack him. Yet with Kilgo it was rarely possible to be neutral. When he spoke loosely, and dogmatically, of Jefferson as a "religious monster" and when he seemed unreliable on the current Democratic idols, Bryan and free silver, it was doubly difficult. One supported or fought the Trinity president; his tactic of linking his critics with "the enemies of Trinity College" was hard to combat. Daniels resented this, as did the Western Methodists, and in time both became to some extent opponents of the college. It was an evolutionary development among Kilgo's antagonists. Trinity was succeeding famously, and Kilgo remained there. It was frustrating to disagree with his management in the face of his success.

As to Daniels as an editor, one may be more specific and less uncertain as to motives. In 1894 he became editor and manager of the *News and Observer*. By early 1895 he announced his return from absentee direction in Washington (he held a federal post in the Cleveland administration) to join in the fight for "the redemption of the State,"[47] i.e., from the fusion forces. Swiftly in the years that followed he built the *News and Observer* into a readable, lively journal. Circulation grew, the paper was enlarged to eight pages, and soon Daniels was pioneering in the issuance

46. Josephus Daniels to B. N. Duke, Dec. 5, 1895, B. N. Duke Papers.
47. *News and Observer*, Jan. 25, 1895. In an earlier statement of intent, Daniels wrote that the paper would be "earnestly and aggressively Democratic," but promised that "honest difference of opinion will be recognized and respected." *News and Observer*, Aug. 12, 1894.

of profitable special editions celebrating state industries and activities. The paper quickly assumed the attitude and the reputation of *the* organ of the Democratic party in North Carolina.

For the most part, the *News and Observer* in the years 1895-1903 was not a newspaper at all. It was a vehicle of political persuasion, and its resources, headlines, news columns, news reporting techniques, as well as the editorial page, were turned to the service of the Democratic party. In these years Daniels was more the politician and less the journalist. The restraint and detachment of modern papers, common to some in that era, was hard to find in the *News and Observer*.

The immediate cause, of course, was the shock of the fusion victories, and the reliable weapon was racism. Years before the party leaders launched the white supremacy campaigns, Daniels was leading the way.[48] He quickly attacked the legislature of 1895 for a tribute to "a mulatto miscegenationist," Fred Douglass, and branded the assembly "The Douglass Legislature." The paper carried frequent references to Negroes as "coons." He attacked a fusion-appointed school official who reportedly sent his children to mixed schools. His paper recorded the convening of the North Carolina Republicans in 1896 with this jingle: "White men, small men, some a little bigger/All mixed up with the coal black nigger."[49] He early asked the question that was to be popular later, "Shall One Negro Rule Two White Men in North Carolina?" He carried an abundance of alleged Negro attacks on white women, many from areas all over the South, and customarily prominently displayed. As early as 1895 he was suggesting editorially that North Carolina might do well to learn from its neighbor, South Carolina, and agree on "white unity for white supremacy."[50]

After the complete fusion victory of 1896, Daniels had an executive as well as a legislature to work against, and from the fall of 1897 the *News and Observer* began to emphasize the "indignities" suffered by whites at the hands of Negroes who held public office. By the summer of 1898 the party had decided to make white voters aware of the hazards of "Negro Rule," and among the state press the *News and Observer* enthusiastically led the fight for white supremacy. A former cartoonist was brought back from New York for a three-month stint and soon

48. Following from *News and Observer*, Feb. 22, 1895–June 21, 1895.
49. *Ibid.*, May 14, 1896.
50. *Ibid.*, Feb. 22, 1895.

provided lurid pictures to match the headlines. The aim was to discredit the fusion forces by linking them with the Negro voter and officeholder. A Daniels reporter began early with a news story of the Republican convention: "It was only here and there that a bald white cranium glistened among a sea of black, wooly noggins." The scene was "nauseating, it is polluting, it is revolting, it is bitter. It is dirty, it is altogether too bad." It was a "great black mass of kinky-headed ignorance and prejudice."[51] In contrast, a few weeks later a series of Democratic mass meetings was reported as opening "gloriously."

It would be unfair to suggest that only the *News and Observer* whetted race prejudice; it was simply the most violent. Daniels had more space and stronger typography than smaller papers, and he had a greater appetite for the "crusade." A sample of campaign oratory is suggestive of what the people were hearing as well as reading: "This is a white man's government, and we intend it shall be. When unscrupulous politicians seek to lead them on, we say, 'All coons look alike to us.'"[52]

As noted, this approach worked. The Democratic victory was complete in the fall of 1898, although the Republican governor still had two years to serve. Daniels had joined other party leaders in branding as a "fusion lie" the claim that the Democrats aimed to disfranchise illiterate voters; two weeks after the ballots were in he was coolly analyzing the best means of disfranchisement.[53] In the next two years *News and Observer* subscribers had much the same diet as before. Nor did it end with a complete Democratic victory in 1900. As late as 1903 readers of the *News and Observer* might read with their coffee: "Gashed and Bleeding She Fought for Honor Against a Negro's Brutal and Merciless Might." It was appropriate that the paper often carried a large advertisement for a product to relieve nervous women. Daniels' position on lynching was somewhat equivocal. He was inclined to repudiate it on the editorial page and sensationalize it in the news columns. However, he frequently stated even editorially that the real cause was the horrible crime for which lynching was the punishment.

Apart from their effect on the reading public, were the reports of indignities and atrocities true? Apparently it did not matter. Years later Daniels conceded that his partisanship was

51. *Ibid.*, July 17, 1898.
52. Aubrey Lee Brooks, running for solicitor, Durham *Daily Sun*, Nov. 2, 1898.
53. *News and Observer*, Oct. 25, Nov. 5, and Dec. 20, 1898.

East Duke Building

"open, fierce and sometimes vindictive" and that in the campaign of 1898 many reports were not winnowed out for accuracy. Looking back, Daniels was somewhat amazed at his editorial violence in those years. After the elections the party leaders were startled to discover that they could not easily control the race passion they had unleashed. But Daniels had no regrets. He liked to see it as a contest between "progress" and "reaction." He was proud of his leadership, and he believed himself to have been on the side of progress.[54]

In many ways, then, Daniels was opposed, by habit and behavior, to those values held highest in an academic community—the rational, the cosmopolitan, the non-partisan. Certainly some of the *South Atlantic Quarterly*'s dissatisfactions were registered with Daniels, or others like him, in mind. The difference was heightened by Daniels' reiterated impatience with other critics of the South—such as Walter Hines Page—who, he felt, were moving away "step by step" from the wisdom of their ancestors and becoming traitors to the land of their birth.

Provocation and Attack

There is no evidence of pique in the *News and Observer* at the early fulminations of the *Quarterly*. The literary editor greeted the first issue graciously and frequently announced the contents as subsequent issues appeared. However, the paper and the *Quarterly* continued to deal with popular issues in different ways. Daniels was inclined to pay judicious tribute to Booker T. Washington, although after President Roosevelt's celebrated dinner with Washington in 1901, which aroused many Southerners, he and other editors agreed that the Negro leader was becoming something of a "fad." For his part, Bassett later was in contact with a man close to Roosevelt and was asked to try to get the President's views on race relations into the state papers.[55] When

54. Daniels, *Editor*, pp. 147, 284-296, 623-624. See also Orr, *Aycock*, pp. 136-137. Daniels did not agree with the common definition of "independent journalism," which he believed to be "irresponsible, counting house, dollar mark, corporation-dominated journalism." He preferred a partisan press like Horace Greeley's that "made and unmade party leaders . . . created a healthy public sentiment . . . dictated to the party." *News and Observer*, Feb. 22, 1903.

55. Gaillard Hunt to Bassett, Feb. 26, March 5, 1903, Bassett Papers. Hunt was an historian and an official in the State Department.
Bassett once said that he was voting Democratic locally and Republican

the Sledd case at Emory was reported, Daniels dealt with it light-ly, though conceding the article was a "slander" of the South. Significantly, he sought to dismiss Sledd as an impractical pro-fessor: "Whenever a scholar, who lives in the atmosphere of books and college life, begins to discuss the Negro problem, the chances are nine of ten that he will put his foot in it."[56]

Perhaps the Booker T. Washington incident at Hamlet, North Carolina, was a catalyst in creating open conflict between Daniels and the *South Atlantic Quarterly*. In August, 1903, Washington and a large party of Negroes traveling by train wired ahead for dining arrangements at a hotel in Hamlet. In order to care for them the hotel officials placed a group of whites in a side room. There was a storm of protest and conflicting reports about the behavior of the Negroes. (They were variously described as chortling over the affair and as having behaved in a dignified manner.) The *News and Observer* asked, "Did Booker Crowd Out Whites?" and later traced the incident to President Roose-velt's dinner invitation. Such things, said Daniels, excited Ne-groes about the elimination of social barriers. He did not think it was a small matter. Social barriers already were too low. Ne-groes, behavior recently had not been satisfactory, and "in conse-quence, more of them have dangled at the end of ropes."[57] The time to stop such mistakes as the one at Hamlet was right now, he insisted.

At Trinity College, Bassett did not approve of Daniels' hand-ling of the Hamlet incident, nor, as noted, of much that Daniels did as a political partisan. He was preparing another editorial for the October *Quarterly*, and the Hamlet incident was worked into the copy. The finished product, entitled, "Stirring Up the Fires of Race Antipathy," was a closely reasoned, coldly stated view of the total Negro problem. Bassett had been working to-ward such an analysis for years. In the summer of 1903 he had sounded out some friends about his speaking out and had re-ceived encouragement. His old friend Herbert Adams had died, but W. A. Dunning of Columbia urged him "by all means" to

nationally at that time. Bassett to Hunt, March 29, 1909, Bassett Papers. Later Bassett supported Woodrow Wilson.

56. *News and Observer*, Aug. 6, 1902.
Daniels did not much care for the scholar in public affairs. He once scolded Crowell for commenting on a railroad commission plan: " 'Mr. Crowell: Run your College and let the people decide about a railroad commission.' " Chaffin, *Beginnings*, pp. 402-403.

57. *News and Observer*, Aug. 25, Sept. 3, 1903.

treat the question in the *Quarterly*: "The sane men of the South must not hide away and say nothing at such a time as this." Earlier, one of the older scholars in exile had offered the same advice: "Stay there and do it. The Negro question is the biggest you all have to deal with and you need to be both brave and wise in handling it. . . . You young leaders of thought will have much to do in putting movements on foot."[58] The result was the editorial of October, 1903.

Bassett began by noting that in the past five years there had been, North and South, increasing opposition to the Negro. Why? For three reasons: "inherent race antipathy," as old as the arrival of the Negro in America; the progress of the race in recent years, progress both up and down; and finally, "the fact that the negro problem is, and has been for a long time, a political matter."[59]

The antipathy, he said, was not mutual. Negroes did not resent social contact with whites. The essence lay in the reaction of the superior against the inferior race. Indeed, "it is doubtful if the average Southern white farmer would admit that the highest negro in America is superior to the Southern hired man who is white." The antipathy was also related to the Negro's progress, whether up or down. Clearly, some ex-slaves without the restraining hand of the master "are more worthless than any negroes in slavery." Indeed, this was to be expected: "The typical ante bellum negro was the field hand. . . . Nine-tenths of the negroes now in America are descended from this part of the old slave population." Therefore it was natural that there would be many Negroes whose morals were loose, who were inattentive to sanitation and lazy in employment. These individuals aroused white contempt.

But there was a small group at the other extreme who had made "remarkable progress." Such persons sought greater comforts and now "are too intelligent and too refined" to be content with inferior public accommodations. This Negro "demands a better place" and rebels against "a mark of intolerance which he will some day seek to wipe out."

Bassett sought to make a distinction from this analysis:

> Neither of these two classes, the upper and the lower, are all the negroes; and in forgetting this fact some well intentioned

58. W. A. Dunning to Bassett, Sept. 6, 1903; and Charles Forster Smith to Bassett, July 18, 1903, Bassett Papers.
59. This and summary from *South Atlantic Quarterly*, II (Oct., 1903), 297-05.

people have fallen into serious error. A man whose mind runs away into baseless optimism is apt to point to Booker T. Washington as a product of the negro race. Now Washington is a great and good man, a Christian statesman, and take him all in all the greatest man, save General Lee, born in the South in a hundred years; but he is not a typical negro. He does not even represent the better class of negroes. He is an exceptional man; and, endowed as he is, it is probable that he would have remained uneducated but for the philanthropic intervention of white men. The race, even the best of them, are so far behind him that we cannot in reason look for his reproduction in the present generation. It is, therefore, too much to hope for a continued appearance of such men in the near future. It is also too much to set his development up as a standard for his race. To expect it is to insure disappointment.

In making the point, Bassett took occasion again to pay his respects to the current sentimental literature which he thought distorted discussion of the entire problem. Thomas Nelson Page and those who wrote of the old South "ought to know what it was before they talk about it." Page's "castles in Virginia are also castles in the air." There was a brief exposition on the "place of the Negro and the desire of many Americans to see that he occupied his proper place. The idea in general, Bassett declared "is neither scientific nor charitable. The 'place' of every man in our American life is such a one as his virtues and his capacities may enable him to take. Not even a black skin and a flat nose justify caste in this country."

Then Bassett came to the heart of the matter—the role of the Negro in politics. He traced the issue back to the arrival of the first slaves, through the Civil War and Reconstruction, noting its perennial usefulness to the politician. Concentrating on the recent turmoil, he stated that the Negro issue was "selected" by the Democratic party. There was "an opportunity to cry 'Negro domination.'" In fact, "raising the cry by the one side produced irritation on the other side, and the very denunciation of negroes for 'outrages' produced a continuation of the 'outrages.'" He observed that the success of the tactic had led to its repetition, and incidents such as the Roosevelt-Washington dinner were welcomed and sought by "some political editors." He told of the Hamlet incident and concluded that it had been distorted by the partisan press. Indeed, "a certain emotional and 'yellow' newspaper was conspicuous in its lurid descriptions," and lesser sheets had followed its example.

Bassett concluded that the total effect of such agitation "unquestionably tends to make votes." With the Negro removed from politics, the dominant party was keeping him alive for political capital. But more serious dangers existed; the agitation was "awaking a demon in the South. There is today more hatred of whites for blacks and of blacks for whites than ever before." The passion was leading "to an end which I dare not name." He saw no easy solution except "the adoption of these children of Africa into our American life. In spite of our race feeling, of which the writer has his share, they will win equality at some time." The race was weak but would grow stronger, and he predicted an undefined conflict yet to come. As the Negro developed he would have strong leaders; Bassett could only hope that they would be brave and Christian leaders.

Finally, he ended with a plea for understanding. The conflict would become worse and would be waged with greater intensity so long as one race "contends for the absolute inferiority of the other." He appealed for a "spirit of conciliation" in the hearts of white men. Should white men "also be beasts, like the dull-faced black men who stand over against them?" Is not the white man, he challenged, superior enough, "superior in mind, superior in opportunity, superior in obligation to do acts of charity?"

There has been a disposition to suggest that the explosion that followed merely reflected the heated emotions of the time. However, the article contained many of the attitudes of accusation against which the South had been building rationalizations since ante bellum days: Bassett's suspicions of Southern sincerity as to good intent toward the Negro; his use of the word "caste"; his pricking of guilty consciences about the Negro exploitation in politics. These criticisms, when mixed with praise for the Negro—especially the Negro "too intelligent and too refined" to accept his place—were deadly comparisons. When Bassett topped off the exposition with portentous warnings of a great, indefinable conflict to come, he was probing deep into the complex Southern defense of its "way of life"—a defense traditionally brought forth in reply to Yankee slurs. This is not to suggest that Bassett was wrong; his analysis was prescient. It is important to recognize how far removed in capacity for analysis he was from the mass of Southerners—indeed, how wide was the gulf between the new scholarship and the old emotionalism. Was the article deliberately provocative? Clearly, Bassett was determined that the race issue should receive "calm and intelligent discussion" in the South. There *were* fair-minded Southerners, he said, and he sought to convince some of them. His "Reign of Passion" and other comments on the Negro question had been discussed in the North, but not in the South. Then and later consistently he stated that the comparative phrase concerning Booker T. Washington and Robert E. Lee was inserted "to wake them up."[60] He said it was not a sudden thought, but that it was a sudden act and in later years conceded that perhaps he should not have given them "quite so big a dose." But he believed an "heroic" dose had been required. Yet scholars who were his best friends quickly condemned the statement, and he may have been embarrassed by his impulse. Certainly the superlative was indefensible on scholarly grounds and in the "calm and enlightened journal" he believed the *Quarterly* to be.

This, then, was the editorial that readers of the *Quarterly* saw on the first page as they opened their copies in late October. If they read further, they found immediately following an article by F. C. Woodward advocating wiser Northern policies in helping Southern education. But here too were nagging phrases: Woodward spoke of the Negro's "pseudo-freedom" and warned that no people can be kept down forever. He commented in passing on the "petty politicians" who kept power by "keeping alive the sentiment of race-hostility." Again, in the same issue, Edwin Mims offered a plea for a Southern attitude of criticism and a willingness among Southerners to ask themselves uncomfortable questions. Finally, the *Quarterly* presented a recent speech of Kilgo's on "Our Duty to the Negro." Kilgo challenged the excess emotion in discussions of the race issue and asked that disputants talk about the men involved, not "the problem." The white man must help the Negro, for Christian charity and for practical necessity, he said. To drag in fear of social equality was "political hocus pocus." Clearly, the October *Quarterly* contained an abundance

60. Bassett to Walter Hines Page, Dec. 3, 1903, Page Papers; Bassett to Edwin Mims, Jan. 1, 1909; Bassett to Prof. B. C. Wilder (Cornell), Dec. 9, 1909; Bassett to Charles Francis Adams, Nov. 3, 1911, Bassett Papers. Bassett wrote a narrative of the incident for Adams (photo-copy, John Spencer Bassett Papers, Duke University Library).

of material against which a sensitive defender of the South might rebel.

Such a defender was Josephus Daniels. Moreover, he had been personally stabbed. Bassett's themes directed at racist political editors could not have been misinterpreted. Copies of the *Quarterly* were reaching its three hundred subscribers during the last week in October, and by the end of the month Daniels had seen the magazine. The reaction came promptly and with assurance. The *News and Observer* of Sunday, November 1, had the extra space to deal with special matters. Bassett's article was printed in full, and the headlines descending the page reflected Daniels' view of the relative importance of its contents. First, "PROF. BASSETT SAYS NEGRO WILL WIN EQUALITY"; second, "He Also says Booker Washington Is 'The Greatest Man save General Lee, Born in the South in a Hundred Years'"; next, "SOUTHERN LEADERS SLAN-DERED"; and finally, "Dire Predictions of a Coming Conflict Between the Races—Struggle Will Go On as Long as One Race Contends for Absolute Inferiority of the Other. 'Dares Not Name the End.'"

Throughout the article a dozen of the more provocative phrases were lifted up for readers' attention by reproduction in capitals, with special attention to those comments condemning politicians. On the editorial page Daniels used one of his two-column editorials, reserved for matters of importance.[61] Here he noted that Bassett's was the "most remarkable article of a decade." Yet, it was in the spirit of recent utterances of college professors and ministers who sought to foment strife. His mind turned to the "freaks" of another favorite target, the "trust-dominated" University of Chicago. True, he said, the South needs a broad magazine, and the views of all honest men should be tolerated, but there should always be "at least a common respect for the attitude of nine-tenths of the Southern people." Bassett had shown contempt for this attitude. Then, Daniels turned to specifics, to the political arraignment in particular. The idea of a "'cry'" of the Negro issue was an insult to every Southern leader since the 1870's and followed the Republican line. Bassett was ignorant in not understanding that the race issue in politics was created by Republicans. Daniels offered the

61. Following summary from *News and Observer*, Nov. 1, 1903.

explanation that was to become standard Democratic fare for many years: the white supremacy campaigns had constituted a "revolution" and had restored good government and peace to North Carolina after the orgy of "Negro Rule."

Only then did he deal with the Booker T. Washington comment. When he first read it, he said, he could not believe his eyes. He cited a roll of illustrious Southerners who might be said to be "great," and rather effectively he attacked Bassett's superlative. He asked for the scholar's evidence for the statement and suggested that such comparisons did neither Washington nor the Negro any good. He tended to ignore the reservations which surrounded the statement, and he wondered if the author prayed "with his face toward Tuskegee." Yet, he said, Bassett might be forgiven this "enthusiastic ecstasy," but what could one say of the prediction of coming equality, which Daniels could only interpret as social equality, and of the coming conflict? Bassett was "the first white man in the South to hold these sentiments." Perhaps he would repudiate them. "Otherwise," he warned, "—but let us not anticipate the feeling that Southern people must entertain for a man who can give utterance to such opinions."

In the succeeding weeks Daniels dealt with the Bassett article in a manner he had learned to master. He did not hammer away every day as in the heat of a political campaign. This was a fire to be tended with care. After the initial blast, he waited. By November 3 he was able to report a "flame of indignation" over the state and soon to print, in increasing quantity, a number of expressions from other papers, generally in the vein of his own original reaction. Daniels did not interpret these comments except to offer a hint that Bassett's name might well be spelled "B. Assette." With few exceptions, the smaller dailies and weeklies followed his lead and some of his phrases. Bassett was "a fungeous growth," "the greatest ass since Balaam," and a "slobbering negropolist." The sentiments ranged from polite horror to frenzied denunciation. Even the two Methodist newspapers could not support the article, although both tried to preach moderation to others.[62] In time a few editors cooled off, and it is uncertain which intimidation was stronger, the loud abuse or the cynicism

62. The state press is well summarized in the *News and Observer*, Nov. 3 ff., 1903. The various comments are dealt with in detail in Garber, *Kilgo*, pp. 239-286.

of one editor who advised against making Bassett a martyr. The lesson had been learned by now, he said, "and we predict that the next issue of the *South Atlantic Quarterly* will read like the Twenty-third Psalm."[63]

By Sunday, November 8, there was space in the *News and Observer* for more of the "exchanges," including a prominent place for *Webster's Weekly* and the expected conclusion that the article was the logical outcome of the trust influence on Trinity College. The next day Daniels brushed aside the suggestion that the storm now brewing had any relation to freedom of thought. When an "explanation" came from Bassett, it was found wanting. The only possible explanation would be to state, " 'I have sinned.' " At this point, Daniels, for perhaps the first time, directly linked Trinity with the evil influences of the trust magnates who supported it. This association now could account for the departure of Trinity "step by step" from Southern tradition.

By mid-November Daniels may have seen signs that the campaign might pall. There was a rumor that Kilgo would stand by Bassett, but otherwise Trinity College was silent. The *News and Observer* began to ask what Trinity was going to do; it was "a question that is on every tongue." An interview with "a prominent Methodist" of Eastern North Carolina contained suggestions.[64] The anonymous commentator reported deep dissatisfaction with Kilgo in the East and a desire for his retirement. The reporter (presumably Daniels) agreed but could see no movement to that end. "Is anything going to be done?" he asked. The prominent Methodist did not know. The Board might support Kilgo in backing Bassett, but if so, there would be no students. And Kilgo would have to give way sooner or later to a "broad, loving man," and then Trinity would flourish. The reporter saw this as a "glowing prophecy" and wondered how long North Carolina must wait. By November 19 Daniels was getting impatient. It had been three weeks "since the State was aroused." Were the trustees going to be silent? One of them was Furnifold Simmons, the leader of the Democratic party and in 1903 president of the Trinity College Alumni Association. Daniels ran a list of all the Board members for the convenience of his readers.

63. From the Charlotte *News,* reprinted in the Raleigh *Morning Post,* Nov. 24, 1903.
64. *News and Observer,* Nov. 15, 1903. It is possible of course that Daniels interviewed himself; he qualified as a prominent Methodist.

Tactics and Ideals

What was happening at Trinity? The college's reaction falls rather naturally into two phases, a few days of watching the state to see if the campaign would blow over and some temporizing; and finally a definite decision to take the offensive and manage the problem.

The waiting period was short. Incoming letters did not encourage the notion that the storm would be brief. A family friend wrote Bassett how disappointed he was in him. A trustee, N. M. Jurney, certain the article was unwise and that the result would be bad, prayed, "May God save Trinity from any more such unwise utterances."[65] Governor Aycock, a strong friend of Trinity's, wrote Mims not to be a martyr for Bassett and reminded him of the perennial dangers in getting too far ahead of the people. Aycock believed Bassett to be wholly wrong on the race issue, which politics had not made; "politics merely seized it for its purposes."[66] Soon Bassett was receiving many angry letters, some from cranks and some placed under his door at night, for example:

> You ought to be run out of N. C. and if things don't change you will. A mob should lynch you for your contempt. You better go to Booker Washington College, you son of a bitch. You better get out of Durham at once. Fair *waring* [*sic*]. L. A. C.[67]

Bassett also was hearing from his friends out of state. Historian Frederic Bancroft, with whom he had spent the previous summer researching, had talked to Dunning, and to W. K. Boyd, Bassett's old student. None could endorse "that deadly yet really unmanly sentence" about Booker Washington and General Lee. Bancroft liked the substance of the article but thought the execution "crude." He and Dunning were sorry Bassett had

65. W. H. Borden and N. M. Jurney to Bassett, both Nov. 2, 1903, Bassett Papers.
66. Charles B. Aycock to Mims, Nov. 6, 1903, quoted in Edwin Mims, "Early Years of the *South Atlantic Quarterly*," *South Atlantic Quarterly*, LI (Jan. 1952), 40-41. Aycock was one of the attorneys who defended Kilgo and Ben Duke in the Kilgo-Gattis suits.
67. Nov. 3, 1903, Bassett Papers. At the height of the uproar Bassett also heard from Booker T. Washington, who sent him an article for the *Quarterly*. Bassett politely rejected it: "We have had so much recently on the negro question. . . ." Bassett to Booker T. Washington, Nov. 21, 1903, Booker T. Washington Papers (Library of Congress).

played with fire "in so careless a way." But all were for him and advised him to laugh it off. "*Feel* innocent, but don't do it again, or even mention the subject, I should say," wrote Bancroft.[68]

Bassett found laughter hard to come by. He was feeling the nakedness of an unwelcome reputation. The ugly face of intimidation made it clear that "foolkilling" could be grim business, and he lacked the toughness of Kilgo. The problem lay, he wrote Walter Page, with "this large mass of angered men whose leaders are politicians," and he wished he could "run off to some quiet and unobserved haven" where he could write and do research. "I cannot believe that nature made me to wage war."[69] But he was heartened on two counts. Kilgo and the faculty "stand like a rock on the question of liberty of thought. They have treated me like men and brothers, and I have no doubt that they will do all they can do." Second, the *Quarterly* was being helped; he had one hundred orders for copies of the October number. As to what would happen, he did not know. He had agreed to an interview on the advice of his friends "in order to put me before the public in a way fair to myself and safe for them [his friends] as a fighting ground."[70]

Clearly, then, to the surprise of no one who knew Kilgo, there was going to be a fight. The interview was duly given, with Kilgo serving as the reporter, and was published around the state on November 8.[71] It was conciliatory but not contrite. By "equality" Bassett explained that he did not mean social equality, but economic opportunity. By "greatness" in regard to Washington, he meant the capacity to overcome great handicaps. As editor of the *Quarterly* he was entirely responsible. He would not answer the criticism he had received but was glad to try to set aright "the extreme interpretation which some have very much wished to make of my article." This was the explanation Daniels found wanting.

On November 10 Southgate, chairman of the Board, called a meeting of the Executive Committee for the following day. A few trustees had asked for a meeting of the full Board. The Executive Committee disagreed and so informed its one member

68. "F. B." to Bassett, Nov. 8, Nov. 11, 1903, Bassett Papers.
69. Bassett to W. H. Page, Nov. 7, 1903, Page Papers.
70. *Ibid.*
71. Original copy of the interview, Trinity College Papers. It contains editorial changes in Kilgo's handwriting, and a note by William K. Boyd (June 1, 1910) attributing to Flowers the statement that "the reporter was Dr. Kilgo."

from out of Durham who had not been present, John F. Bruton, a banker from Wilson, North Carolina. Bruton accepted the decision but insisted that Bassett's resignation should be secured immediately. He told Southgate that sentiment in the East was strong, and "we cannot afford to jeopardize the College in our efforts to save him."[72]

A resignation might be put to good use by Bassett's friends, as well as his opponents. So Bassett wrote one, not an "offer" to resign, but as Josephus Daniels later said, a "you-may-have-it-if-you-insist-upon-it" resignation. Bassett wrote the letter on November 16:

> In view of the agitation growing out of my article in the October, 1903 number of the *South Atlantic Quarterly* and—in view of the report that some members of the Bd. of Trustees of Trinity College think that I should no longer hold a place in the faculty of the college, I wish to assure the Board that should they decide to request my resignation I shall not hesitate to comply with their wishes. When they shall have concluded that I should be displaced from the faculty, I request you to tender them my resignation. In an interview published in some of the papers of the State on Nov. 8, 1903, I undertook to explain my article. That explanation was offered in sincerity and truth.[73]

By November 20 Southgate had agreed to a meeting of the full Board, and he (or Kilgo) decided to present the letter as an offer, but it hardly removed Bassett from Trinity. It did not, as in the Sledd case, make it easy for the college "to do the wrong." The Board was not presented with a clear cut resignation; technically, it would be necessary to ask for one. In the meantime an "offer" might be used to build up sympathy for a professor, and an alumnus, whose love of Trinity was so evident. Indeed, it might carry the suggestion of apology and thus soften Bassett's "offense."

Personal connections were probably of great value in the unlucky circumstance that both Methodist Conferences were meeting during the month of November. By an opposing stroke of fortune, the Western Conference (meeting November 11-16) was presided over by Kilgo's old friend and adviser, Bishop Coke Smith, and the Eastern Conference by Kilgo's even greater old friend, Bishop W. A. Candler. The records of neither meeting

72. J. F. Bruton to J. H. Southgate, Nov. 14, 1903, Trinity College Papers.
73. Bassett to Southgate, Nov. 16, 1903, *ibid.*

betray a sign of unrest. The bishop's power to control a Conference was strong.[74] Daniels attended the Eastern Conference, which met November 25-30, and picked up many rumors but complained at the lack of information. He did hear that the entire Trinity faculty might resign if Bassett were cast away and that under the same circumstances the students might leave. Daniels also heard much dissatisfaction with the management of Trinity, and he recommended that the Board fire Kilgo too.[75]

In the meantime, at Trinity the managers of the affair were developing their plans. At a faculty meeting on November 19, Kilgo praised Bassett and his work at the college and spoke of how much he had meant to him personally.[76] On the following day it was announced that there would be a meeting of the full Board of Trustees in ten days. At the same time the student body handed Bassett a resolution begging him not to resign and declaring that "a large number, at least, of the student body" in defense of freedom of opinion would leave the college if "those in authority take upon themselves to force your withdrawal." The students declined to consider the accuracy of Bassett's article and asked that their remarks be read to the faculty.[77]

During the final week before the Board meeting additional pressure was forthcoming. A flurry of letters came to Southgate from academic sources. A group of alumni in New York, many studying at Columbia (including Boyd), warned of the value to Trinity of a good reputation at the graduate centers. A similar sentiment came from Harvard (from Ralph M. Odell, the son of a trustee) and from Yale (from Mims's younger brother). From out of the past came word from Crowell, who wrote Southgate and Bassett—and Ben Duke as well.[78] All sounded the call to a defense of academic freedom. Friendly newspapers began to carry some of the counterattack. Letters appealed to readers to study the article thoughtfully and to take note of its general con-

74. Commenting later, one minister said that resolutions condemning Bassett were drawn up but that Bishop Candler advised against any "hurtful" discussion and suggested a petition instead. The petition was not prepared until too late for the Conference to act. Letter by M. H. Tuttle in the *News and Observer*, Jan. 12, 1904. Tuttle also stated that a "prominent" trustee said resolutions were not necessary since the Board would accept Bassett's resignation. There was no chicanery, he added; the trustee did vote as he spoke. On the last day of the Conference Bishop Candler wrote Southgate in support of Bassett. Candler to Southgate, Nov. 30, 1903, Trinity College Papers.
75. *News and Observer*, Nov. 29, 1903.
76. Bassett to "My dear friend" (Kilgo), Nov. 19, 1903, Trinity College Papers.
77. Original in Bassett Papers, dated Nov. 20, 1903.
78. The letters are in the Trinity College Papers.

text. Some of Bassett's friends presented a lengthy tribute to his scholarly reputation and historical work for the state.[79]

A most intense observer from afar was Walter Hines Page. Since November 13 Page had been writing Ben Duke and was taking it "for granted" that no harm would come to Bassett. A defense of Bassett would be a "splendid vindication" of the freedom at Trinity and would give the college a world-wide reputation. "God help us all to a little courage—don't you say so?" he asked.[80] But Page wanted more details. He wired Mims for a confidential report, and Mims appears to have told him all he knew. The incident, he wrote, had put weapons in the hands of Trinity's enemies, and it was understandable that even the college's friends might see the need to let Bassett go. But those "in vital touch" were going to make "the fight of their lives for a declaration of independence on the part of the Trustees." The Executive Committee, he said, "notably Mr. B. N. Duke— are thoroughly committed to the policy of retaining Bassett at any cost." Mims remembered Page's message from J. B. Duke a few months before and thought that alone should stiffen the faculty,[81] although most of them thought the article "unwise or inexpedient." By this time (November 24), he wrote, there was "a spirit of dedication to a great and worthy ideal that is in every sense sublime." What remained was to give the trustees from outside Durham this point of view, which they had not yet heard. When Kilgo spoke at the meeting there would be, he felt confident, a "declaration for freedom of thought in institutions of learning that will be most satisfactory. This is the consummation most devoutly wished for."

However, Mims thought the odds were great. The sensitivity on race was deep. He had heard from many academic friends elsewhere, but "not a college man in the state has lifted his voice."[82] He pointed out that the group at Trinity was con-

79. Charlotte *Daily Observer*, Nov. 28 and Nov. 30, 1903, and Raleigh *Morning Post*, Dec. 1, 1903.
80. Page to B. N. Duke, Nov. 13 and Nov. 23, 1903; Trinity College Papers.
81. Page made the dedicatory speech at the opening of the new library in February and brought a message from Duke, the gist of which was to "think for yourself." *Formal Opening of the Trinity College Library*, Feb. 23, 1903 (Durham, N. C.), p. 23.
82. Mims to Page, Nov. 24, 1903, Page Papers. This was not strictly true. Bassett received a word of encouragement from Charles Raper, a Trinity man then at the University of North Carolina, in a note of Nov. 27, 1903. However, the point was well taken. Unhappily, two professors at state schools replied to Daniels' customary call for a brief Thanksgiving Day message by scornful refer-

sidered by some as "alien" and was misunderstood. Page com-
missioned Mims to wire him the result after the Board met and
to write it all up for *World's Work* later. He wanted "the most
spirited compact account . . . how they tried to throttle free
speech. . . ."[83] On the same day, just in case, Page wrote Ben
Duke another letter. It was such a *"great* chance" to speak out
for freedom and would help Trinity so much. The issue was
squarely drawn now and the cry against Bassett "a blind howl by
those who think they can rule North Carolina." After all, what
harm could they do if Bassett were supported?

> What if the fools criticize it? What if even some good men
> criticize it? What if half the boys are withdrawn? Nothing better
> could happen. What is a great college for? Isn't its main purpose
> to be a place for absolute freedom of thought and speech? For
> every boy that may be withdrawn, the college will get a dozen
> a few years hence, when men come to their senses. For every
> man who takes offense, a hundred better men will be pleased
> and will rally to you.[84]

Page closed by congratulating Duke "in advance" on the wonder-
ful victory that soon would be forthcoming.

His own brother was less optimistic at this time. Henry A.
Page had been on the Trinity Board only a few months. He was
not uncertain about his own position but guessed he was in the
minority. He had written Bassett earlier asking him not to resign
because he wanted the issue to be, not the acceptance of a
resignation, but whether or not to ask for one. Henry Page too
had read of the faculty threat to resign, and he planned to see
Kilgo at the Eastern Conference and advise him to hold that in
reserve; there should be no threat before the Board had debated.
He wrote his brother, it was "the very same old intolerance and
bigotry and narrowness. There is nothing new in it." His course
had been settled from the first. A local minister had tried to
induce him "to keep quiet and go along with the crowd, but I
don't want to have to kick myself out of bed, and I will be
hanged if I am willing to sleep with a coward." He was prepared to fight at the coming meeting, but he did not know that
he would have any help.[85]

---

ences; one was thankful that he had no "Jackassett friends." *News and Observer,*
Nov. 22, 1903.
83. Page to Mims, Nov. 26, 1903, Page Papers.
84. Page to B. N. Duke, Nov. 26, 1903, Trinity College Papers.
85. Henry A. Page to "Wat," Nov. 26, 1903, Page Papers.

Apparently Trinity was going to be able to depend upon the Dukes as well. Later it was a common notion on the campus that Ben Duke had been opposed to the article in the beginning, but that Kilgo had persuaded him to back Bassett.[86] Ben had known and liked Bassett for many years, and in 1902 he had personally underwritten a salary increase for him which the college had been unable to pay. His views on the incident are unrecorded. At this time he had established a home in New York and was spending only about half of his time in Durham. About November 5 he returned from New York. In the days before the faculty meeting and the announcement that there would be a meeting of the Board, James B. Duke was also in Durham. It is unthinkable that he was not consulted, but he returned to New York before November 20. As for Washington Duke, he was now quite feeble, and his family was not troubling him with any worries. As in the past, Ben Duke represented the family. During the week of November 23, he canceled engagements in New York to remain in Durham until the meeting. At this time Mims was able to write with confidence that Ben was committed to supporting Bassett.

In Raleigh during the last week before the meeting, the *New and Observer*'s optimism, which rose on a rumor that Bassett would resign, had been shaken by various reports of a counterattack. Daniels was restive about the lack of information and warned about "Star Chamber Proceedings." He believed that men in charge of "public institutions" could not defy just public sentiment or public interest in important matters. In his last editorial before the meeting, he warned the trustees that the eyes of the state were upon them.[87]

It is probable that most observers, North and South, expected to see another professor feel the weight of disapproval.[88] The plans at Trinity were hardly known, except as local rumors, and the people of North Carolina were accustomed to seeing Daniels win his battles, especially on the race issue. Bassett himself was asking his friends to be alert to help him find an opening elsewhere. Certainly, he received little comfort from his friend Ban croft:

86. Interviews with Gilbert T. Rowe, Sept. 14, 1959, and with A. M. Webb Sept. 21, 1959. Webb recalled that the general feeling on the campus was on of caution and restraint; that Kilgo had the situation in hand and it must be left with him.

87. *News and Observer*, Nov. 29, 1903.

88. Walter Page's words of optimism to Duke may be easily read as persuasion

. . . my guess is that your President & the Faculty will bend as the wind blows. Academic independence is a dream; & freedom, North as well as South, means liberty to say whatever will not arouse the ire of the benefactors or patrons of the college. Which Northern College would tolerate an advocate of socialism or of free thought in religion? None would harbor an advocate of free silver.[89]

By the day of the meeting, December 1, the managers at Trinity were ready. William Garrott Brown, a successful writer, a Southerner, and a friend from Few's Harvard days, had been on the campus for several weeks. He had helped a committee of professors prepare a faculty statement,[90] and he and Few had drafted the statement it was hoped the Board would adopt.[91] Every member of the faculty had written his resignation and dropped it by the president's office.[92] Kilgo had written one himself and had it ready.[93] Trustees arriving in Durham could not assist inquiring reporters; no one knew how it would go. Of the thirty-six members of the Board, twenty-five attended the meeting.

The session opened at 8:00 P.M. in the Washington Duke Building, and from an adjoining room a number of intensely interested students heard portions of the proceedings.[94] Southgate as chairman led off with the business of the meeting, Bassett's letter, which was read aloud. Next, Kilgo was called in and spoke for an hour. No one can say how many were swayed, but the old stirring manner was in evidence.[95] In the grand tradition there was a nugget of the practical in a mixture of the idealistic —and, indeed, a bit of bathos. He said the debate was not over Bassett's ability or character, but merely over some "words" he had written. Admittedly, they were offensive and could not be defended. Personally he did not think Bassett meant them to have the interpretation they had received; and the explanation he had made satisfied Kilgo. Then he pointed to the source of the college's discomfiture, the ancient enemies among the press, in particular, the *News and Observer*. He ridiculed Daniels with

89. Frederic Bancroft to Bassett, "Friday," n.d. (perhaps Nov. 20, 1903), Bassett Papers.
90. Autobiography, W. H. Glasson, manuscript, *ca.* July, 1938, W. H. Glasson Papers (Duke University Library).
91. Garber, *Kilgo*, p. 276.
92. Interview, A. M. Webb.
93. Garber, *Kilgo*, pp. 273-275.
94. *Minutes*, Board of Trustees, Trinity College Papers; interview, B. S. Womble, March 15, 1961.
95. Garber, *Kilgo*, pp. 269-273.

editorials written some years before, protesting the dismissal o
President Andrews of Brown University.[96] He insisted the motiv
now was "to compass the ruin of Trinity College." In the fac
of this, would the trustees cast aside the great dreams all share
for Trinity? He called for a supreme act of faith in the future
in defiance of the hazards. He pictured the college in shado
if the wrong decision were made, and in "the night of slaver
and bondage," he painted an image of Bassett, his wife, and littl
children passing from the campus, "exiled and banished." It wa
a supreme flight of oratory.

It was not idle rhetoric. There was loyal tribute to Southers
ideals, due recognition of Christian principles and the moral forc
of the Church. Most important, Kilgo saw with precision th
significance of the case at hand. A defense of Bassett would b
a victory for Trinity and would "settle forever" Trinity's polic
on academic freedom. More important, he said, the questio
would be decided for other Southern colleges.

When Kilgo finished and left the meeting, Southgate rea
the faculty statement, which was devoted almost exclusively t
the principle of academic freedom. The faculty explained tha
they felt free to defend Bassett because they disagreed with hin
At issue were a professor's "rights" which could not be invadec
A scholar must always accept criticism, but Bassett was bein
persecuted in an attempt to deprive him of his "means of livel
hood." Following Kilgo, there was an appeal to Southern an
state ideals and to the welfare of Trinity and its reputation. I
the face of clamor from "the open enemies of the college," woul
the trustees give in, or would they follow Jefferson and defen
the "illimitable freedom of the human mind"?[97]

Southgate topped these opening moves by reading several c
the letters he had received. They were heavily in favor of kee
ing Bassett. Next, a committee was appointed, with Southga
as chairman, to which Bassett's letter was referred. Then th
debate was on, and it lasted for hours. The minutes merely sho
that eleven trustees spoke. One was Furnifold Simmons, wh
reportedly said he had come to the meeting to win his "last fig

96. Reportedly, Andrews had resigned under pressure because of his fr
silver views. At the time and later, Daniels referred to the incident as a "mode
inquisition" and spoke of "intolerant bigotry" toward men who would not ada
their views to suit those with money and power. For example, *News and O
server,* July 24, 1897.
97. Faculty statement is part of the *Minutes.*

for white supremacy."[98] But the final three speakers were for Bassett, with Southgate in the anchor position. The committee retired, and in fifteen minutes brought in the Few-Brown statement and recommended its adoption. There were parliamentary moves to block it, a motion to ignore the committee report and ask for Bassett's resignation, and a motion to recommit. Both failed, and, about three o'clock in the morning, the fateful ballot was taken. The trustees voted eighteen to seven to support Bassett.

The minority was heavily clerical. There were twelve ministers on the Board. The nine who attended the meeting split, five voting against Bassett and four with him. Of the sixteen laymen at the meeting, only two, Simmons and Bruton, voted with the minority. On the other hand, the majority was largely composed of Methodists from the business community in Durham and throughout the state. Most of them at that time or in the past had business associations with the Dukes.

Perhaps in deference to the minority and with a view to harmony all around, the Board agreed to add a final, equivocal sentence to the Few-Brown statement: "We state as a fact that Professor Bassett does not believe in, nor does he teach social equality, and we have confidence in him, both as a man and as a teacher."[99] Finally, in a thrust at Daniels *et al.*, the trustees unanimously, and "gladly," reiterated their confidence in Kilgo and their "abundant satisfaction" in his administration.

The measured sentences of the trustee statement contained an enduring glow—and followed the direction of Kilgo's speech and the faculty statement. The college disclaimed responsibility for what Bassett had written and in fact disagreed with his words. But "coercion of thought and private judgment" were at stake here. Trinity was committed (in the recent statement of Aims) to "cherish a sincere spirit of tolerance" and could not be a party to anything that encouraged intellectual intimidation. There had been "some conspicuous instances" of this in recent years, and the Board was "particularly unwilling to lend ourselves to any tendency to destroy or limit academic liberty." Indeed, "we cannot lend countenance to the degrading notion that professors in American

98. Mims to Page, Dec. 4, 1903, Page Papers.
99. The trustee statement is part of the *Minutes*. Throughout the original copy, references to Bassett's resignation were edited to read "offer to resign." For the full text of the faculty and trustee statements, and an editorial from the *Archive*, see the Appendix.

colleges have not an equal liberty of thought and speech with all other Americans."

There was an appeal to patience as opposed to resentment. "The evils of intolerance and suppression are infinitely worse than those of folly." And finally, the changes were rung on Southern and state pride and on the spirit and teaching of "the great church" with which Trinity was affiliated. In short, then, "duty" required that Bassett be retained. "It were better that Trinity should suffer than that it should enter upon a policy of coercion and intolerance."

In the glorious aftermath of the Board meeting, the students rang the college bell and built a bonfire. A crowd descended on Bassett's house, woke him up, and demanded a speech. A group contrived two effigies of Daniels and hanged them from a persimmon tree and an electric wire near the Memorial Hall. The comic sequel came two days later when the North Carolina Press Association solemnly resolved to condemn the students' action as a threat to freedom of the press. A minority of the publishers sought to condemn the Trinity trustees for their vote but was defeated. Daniels was grateful to the "brave editors" for the resolution.[100]

Meanwhile, the news covered the country, and soon the college was compiling a scrapbook, "an immortal volume," of its press notices. Predictably, the Northern press was surprised and delighted; Walter Page wrote Mims that "Trinity stock keeps soaring on the market."[101] After the meeting, Ben Duke had wired his brother the decision, and in the following weeks was proudly sending clippings and copies of the *Quarterly* to his friends. When the Northern papers reached Southern eyes, the reaction was angry. The Board's statement was said by some to be platitudinous. Others warned that it had "dynamite" in it.

At the end of the long strain, Bassett broke down with an attack of a chronic ailment, rheumatism, his convalescence warmed by congratulations from colleagues throughout the country—and there was an invitation to speak on academic freedom. His friend Dodd, who at first had not agreed with parts of the article, now disliked even the tendency to deprecate the utterance about Booker T. Washington.[102] Inevitably, there was a disposition to make Bassett the darling of the crusaders for the

100. Raleigh *Morning Post* and the *News and Observer*, Dec. 4, 1903.
101. Page to Mims, Dec. 6, 1903, Page Papers.
102. William E. Dodd to Bassett, Jan. 26, 1904, Bassett Papers.

Negro. He was invited to go to Boston to help raise money for a Negro school, and the son of the great abolitionist William Lloyd Garrison made him a gift of the four-volume life of his father.

As for Daniels, he was wholly unconvinced. Stung by the hanging and perhaps more deeply touched by Kilgo's use of his old editorials on Andrews, he did not give up. Trinity's "liberal" spirit was apparent in the effigy incident. Simmons had made a "masterful" speech. And there was no analogy between the Brown and Trinity cases. The difference, he insisted, was this: President Andrews had dealt with a financial question. Bassett had touched on matters affecting "the mudsills of civilization" in the South. In Rhode Island good men honestly differed about bimetallism. But Bassett's "spirit is alien; his words incendiary." The professor had dishonored "a wise and necessary policy" regarding the Negro. "He has committed the only unpardonable sin." Daniels summed it up: "Freedom of speech is important and must be preserved, but there is one thing dearer to the Southern people, to wit: the preservation of its civilization, and the purity of the white blood, the supremacy of Anglo-Saxon ideals and white government."[103]

In later weeks Daniels was encouraged by similar comment in many Southern papers and irritated by Northern praise of Trinity. He vowed "to wage eternal warfare upon the false teaching of history and the perversion of the minds of the youth." In time, he spoke of Bassett's offense as that of teaching "social and racial anarchy," and he continued to demand Kilgo's head.[104]

Trinity's friends sought to get the story well recorded and in useful perspective. Mims wrote it up for *World's Work,* and William Garrott Brown took occasion to straighten out a misconception. The trustees, he said, did not find Bassett guilty and then let him off because the punishment proposed was too heavy. On the contrary, "they decided that they had no right to try him or to punish him. . . ." It was one of several important distinctions, and Brown also pointed out another. Bassett's words were deemed "incendiary," yet were given wide publicity. "Here we have been for weeks debating freely, violently, passionately, a

103. *News and Observer,* Dec. 3, 1903. His headline announcing the action of the Board was "Eighteen—Seven, Thus They Voted."
104. *Ibid.,* Dec. 10, Dec. 17, Dec. 27, 1903.

subject which we were told must not be discussed at all unless we all sustained the prevailing view of it."[105]

Another friend, perhaps Walter Page, wrote an "inside story" of the affair for the Boston *Transcript*. The writer vigorously attacked the white supremacist Democrats and attributed the attack on Bassett to political motives, e.g., hostility to the Republican Dukes. He was hard on the Southern clergy when he noted the number of ministers who had voted against Bassett. "Timid to the point of cowardice, they can be driven to any cruel action if they are made to think that the pillars of society are about to be pulled down. . . ." At Trinity, therefore, "the preachers were simply scared into submission."[106] This judgment was itself a bit cruel; after all, four ministers had voted with Bassett. The article merely restoked the fire. In the *News and Observer* Daniels reprinted some of the comments and sought to use them to rally Methodism to his position.

In the college and on the Board, satisfaction in the victory was tempered by knowledge of the sharp division the incident had caused. At least one who had voted with the minority, John Bruton, was willing to work for unity and wrote Ben Duke that "there should now be 'no other side.'" Indeed, Bruton felt, "if it had not been for the malicious attacks of the *News and Observer*, I believe the minority would have shown decidedly more strength—in my weak moments this paper actually caused me to question my own judgment as expressed at the meeting of the Trustees."[107]

What of the political editor who had led the attack? It was not the kind of battle to cause the vanquished to concede error easily, and Daniels never did make such a concession. However, thirty years later in the perspective of old age, there was a hint that he had come to understand the pathology of racism. In 1936 he counseled his son (who was then editor of the *News and Observer*) against the hazards of making an "incident" into an "issue." He was reminded of the Bassett Affair, and he remembered it this way:

105. W. G. Brown, letter in Charlotte *Daily Observer*, Dec. 8, 1903.
106. Boston *Transcript*, Dec. 9, 1903. The article was unsigned, but Bassett had reason to believe Page wrote it. Bassett to Page, Dec. 11, 1903, Page Papers. Certainly Brown, who was doing a series for the *Transcript*, did not write it. Later he wrote an article in protest of the criticism of the clergy. Boston *Transcript*, March 12, 1904.
107. John F. Bruton to B. N. Duke, Dec. 12, 1903, B. N. Duke Papers.

Public opinion and letters, in the imperfected [?] days, overwhelmed me and when I spelled his [?] name bASSett floods were
opened. It had gotten out of bounds and if I had wished to stop
it (as I did wildly but helplessly) I could not have done so. . . . I
was caught in irrepressible flames which I had kindled.[108]

. . .

The Bassett Affair has been presented in detail because it is
n important episode not given such treatment heretofore. It
as been a legend in the history of Trinity and Duke. Yet, even
fter exhaustive description, the story has an unfinished quality,
ich in opportunity for speculation. A variety of alternatives was
vailable to the leading players; why did they make the choices
hey did? The answers rest on personal motives unrecorded and
bscure in any case.

Were the several contestants helpless in the grip of "too many
olitical passions, prejudices and emotions for unalloyed reason
o have prevailed"?[109] Where then does an individual's responsi-
ility for his actions lie? Years later Daniels vigorously supported
he University of North Carolina in an academic freedom issue.
s consistency to be expected and how far may a principle be
tretched? Had he learned something from the Bassett incident,
r with Daniels did it depend upon whose ox was gored? For
he historian, the decision to move through time, identifying
nonolithic groups and "forces," can prove unreliable. In a given
nstance, one is driven to consider individuals, united and divided
y shades of agreement on many issues; one man's crusade is
nother's heresy, one man's reformer another's tyrant.

Was the Dukes' support a reflex against Trinity's enemies or
devotion to principle? Would Ben have voted as he did if the
ssue had been a different one? What would have happened if
e had decided to keep out of it entirely? Within the Trinity
3oard, was the verdict the result of the influence of the patron?
Most of the laymen had been involved in profitable business
entures with the Dukes. If such considerations were involved,

108. Josephus Daniels to Jonathan Daniels, Nov. 4, 1936, Jonathan Daniels
apers, University of North Carolina Library.
109. For a defense of Daniels on this ground, see Joseph L. Morrison, "Jo-
ephus Daniels and the Bassett Academic Freedom Case," *Journalism Quarterly*,
XXIX (Spring, 1962), 187-195.
For studies of Bassett as a scholar, and in his role of leadership in the South,
ee Wendell H. Stephenson, "John Spencer Bassett as a Historian of the South,"
Vorth Carolina Historical Review, XXV (July, 1948), 289-317; and "The Negro
n the Thinking and Writing of John Spencer Bassett," *North Carolina Historical
Review*, XXV (Oct., 1948), 427-441.

the minority, especially the ministers, did not respond to them, although scarcely a Methodist clergyman or church in North Carolina had not benefited from Duke charity.

What can be said of Bassett and the provocative edge of his pen? Where is the line between scholarly analysis and impatience for social reform? Or was it deeper than that? To a rational man with a sense of humanity, was it Daniels and his political colleagues who had committed the unpardonable sin? Is the essence entirely as Learned Hand suggests?

> You may take Martin Luther or Erasmus for your model, but you cannot play both roles at once; you may not carry a sword beneath a scholar's gown, or lead flaming causes from a cloister. Luther cannot be domesticated in a university. You cannot raise the standards against oppression, or leap into the breach to relieve injustice, and still keep an open mind to every disconcerting fact, or an open ear to the cold voice of doubt.[110]

The tactics by which Trinity won are themselves productive of rumination. On the whole the defenders clung to an unassailable rampart. But there are some contradictions. Are academic freedom and truth best defended when a community of scholars rejects the substance of an offending commentary (with which many agreed) as a maneuver to defeat reprisals against its author? What of some of the rhetoric? Who can say that "all other Americans" in fact enjoy the freedom claimed for Bassett? Are the cause and the truth ultimately better served by openly demanding for scholars the special treatment that is really sought —a claim based upon the best possible grounds, the desirability of truth and the fragility of the human personality that must be protected in the search for it?

Then there is the role of Kilgo, who managed the defense. Principle was important to Kilgo but best when useful. Daniels' great error may have been in swinging so wildly that he struck both the president and the college. For Kilgo, the joys of combat may be assumed, including the exquisite relish of a victory over Daniels. In any case, the triumph was his and the effect of his leadership has been well-stated:

> He gave them [the faculty] the moral support without which few would have dared to be bold; he urged no strategy of com-

110. In Irving Dilliard (ed.), *The Spirit of Liberty: Papers and Addresses of Learned Hand* (New York, 1960), p. 136.

promise to tempt them with safer options; he spared them the need to conspire. . . .[111]

With all of its convolutions, the defeat of irrationality remains; the heart of the legend is intact. The phrases of the trustees' statement have been described as "notable additions to the *belles-lettres* of academic freedom,"[112] and so they are. More important is the grant of power as a statement of policy. Conviction, tradition, and the heat of battle produced a working document that left few loopholes for "the slightest measure" of coercion in the years to come. The Bassett case permitted the erection of a platform upon which all might stand. There was a clear warning against outside influences. From within, if an administrator needed corrective advice, he would find it here. If he needed support, he would find it here. On other campuses the example was available for use. Lesser institutions might follow it; Trinity's competitors and betters would be uncomfortable in admitting to less. It was something to remember.

111. Hofstadter-Metzger, *Development of Freedom*, p. 448.
112. *Ibid.*, p. 449.

Chapter V

The Aftermath

1904-1910

In the aftermath of the Bassett incident, the college enjoyed a warmth of well-being and confidence. The threatened boycott by students did not take place. Mims wrote Walter Page that only one student failed to come back after Christmas because of the affair and possibly only one or two in the Trinity Park School.[1] Kilgo told Ben Duke that enthusiasm was at a high pitch and that "the hardest kind of work is being done."[2]

Kilgo himself added a new laurel to his reputation in the spring of 1904. He was asked to deliver the "fraternal message" from the Southern Methodist Church to its Northern counterpart. From all accounts he scored heavily. Flowers accompanied him to Los Angeles for the address and reported that he "completely captured them. . . . He took them by storm."[3] Perhaps the chance for the bishopric in 1906 had never looked better. At the end of the year the faculty called on him in a body to celebrate the tenth year of his presidency and to pay him tribute.

How fared Bassett and the *South Atlantic Quarterly?* Immediately after the trustee meeting Bassett was shaken and uncertain. The intimidation had, of course, made a difference. He believed that he had best move "as cautiously as possible, but without hesitancy." He wanted to continue his plan for a series of articles on social life in the South, and he did not want to abandon the critical spirit. Yet he was reluctant "to give them a chance at me on more details." The difficulty would lie with Trinity's friends who counseled moderation. Bassett stood, he felt, "like a donkey between three bundles of straw": one, "timid whispering friends (some of them in the faculty)"; two, "the pack"; and three, "partial friends who say, 'sic 'em again.' " He told Walter Page to warn his friends in the North not to expect too much. It was his personal opinion that the college would do

1. Mims to Page, Jan. 8, 1904, Page Papers.
2. Kilgo to B. N. Duke, April 6, 1904, Trinity College Papers.
3. R. L. Flowers to B. N. Duke, May 11, 1904, *ibid.*

well to "ride out the swell of the storm we have passed through."[4]
Yet he was certain the administration would not like to see a
back-down, and a few days later he reported that he had spoken
to Kilgo and that the president did not belong among the timid
friends.[5]

Certainly, the *Quarterly* did not back down. In succeeding
issues the earlier laments were repeated. U. B. Phillips complained of that Southern "misfortune," the "fealty" to the Democratic party, and William E. Dodd wrote caustically of the plight
of the Southern history teacher who had to deal with the prejudices of the Confederate veteran. There was continued analysis,
by Bassett and others, of the Negro race and of its future and
continued concern for the intellectual shortcomings of the South.
When Dodd's article aroused some editors, Bassett replied in
"The Task of the Critic," pleading for a willingness to hear and
discuss criticism. The critic is born to wage war on the conservative, he explained, and, right or wrong, should be met with
answering argument, not personal abuse. He may be uncon-
ventional, may be ahead of his time; he may think erroneously,
or he may be wise. "How is he to know what he is?" The point
was, "Rail as we may, we cannot avoid our critics. . . . No unification of public opinion can destroy them." The Southern attitude
toward its critics, he felt, would be the measure of its greatness
or its littleness.[6]

With the *Quarterly* of January, 1905, Bassett retired from the
editorship. He had been offered an opportunity to do a volume
for A. B. Hart's *American Nation* series in American history, and
the deadline was a close one.[7] He explained that the decision
to retire was taken "reluctantly and solely because of an accumulation of other labors which cannot be declined."[8] Perhaps he
had become disillusioned about the power of any journal to alter
Southern parochialism. In any event, he was always ambitious
to publish, and the *Quarterly* took much of his free time.

For the next four years Mims and Glasson directed the
Quarterly as co-editors, and, after Mims's departure in 1909,
Glasson and Few shared the task. The emphasis on reform con-

4. Bassett to Page, Dec. 8, 1903, Page Papers.
5. *Ibid.*, postscript, dated Dec. 11, 1903.
6. *South Atlantic Quarterly*, III (Oct., 1904), 297-301.
7. Bassett Papers. Another scholar had undertaken to do the volume, but had
withdrawn, and Hart needed the manuscript, 70,000 words, in nine months.
Bassett's contribution, Volume XI in the series, was *The Federalist System* (1905).
8. *South Atlantic Quarterly*, IV (Jan., 1905), p. 91.

tinued, with a new attention to Southern education. The editors leaned toward their own fields, and there were more literary and economic studies than in the past. The Negro and lynching were repeated items for analysis, and increasingly, the *Quarterly* reported the shifting industrial scene of the South. Glasson spoke for railroad regulation and for the Australian ballot, and W. F. Tillett of Vanderbilt assaulted the orthodox position on that new scholarly tool, Biblical criticism, with the comment, "Belief without evidence is credulity." Gradually the journal spread its net to include a wider circle of contributors, although it remained the ready means to publication for Trinity's scholars.[9]

Bassett and the faculty were anxious to get full value from the incident of 1903, and the opportunity came two years later. President Roosevelt planned a Southern tour, and it was arranged that Trinity College would be on the itinerary in North Carolina. Bassett suggested in advance that Roosevelt might well remark on the academic freedom case, and he forwarded background material to Washington. He said that a comment from the President "would greatly strengthen our hands in a contest we are waging, and it would have a good influence with our people of the South." He was anxious to make the suggestion because Roosevelt's hosts in North Carolina would be "the dominant political group, and from that source, I fear, he will get nothing of our side of the question."[10]

The President was willing, and Bassett was asked to join the entourage at Raleigh.[11] At Trinity, Roosevelt spoke to some 15,000 people in front of the campus. The whistles of the Durham mills greeted his train, and the town declared a holiday.[12] Roosevelt did Trinity proud. He read aloud the Aims of the college, "with significant emphasis" upon the phrases defending scholarship and the spirit of tolerance. He addressed himself in particular to the college audience, and he told them:

> You stand for all those things for which the scholar must stand if he is to render real and lasting service to the State. You stand for Academic Freedom, for the right of private judgment, for a duty more incumbent upon the scholar than upon any other man,

9. *Ibid.*, April, 1905–April, 1910.
10. Bassett to Alfred W. Cooley (U. S. Civil Service Commissioner), Oct. 12, 1905, Bassett Papers.
11. Telegram, William Loeb, Jr. (Roosevelt's secretary) to Bassett, Oct. 16, 1905, Bassett Papers.
12. Raleigh *Morning Post*, Oct. 20, Oct. 21, 1905.

to tell the truth as he sees it, to claim for himself and to give to others the largest liberty in seeking after the truth.[13]

Bassett was particularly pleased. The speech "gave satisfaction to all parties. It cannot fail to hearten the colleges of the whole South, and it gives this one a stronger grasp on the public, as well as a better appreciation of its own duty."[14]

In the meantime, Kilgo returned to the two items that had interested him in 1902, the law school and the woman's "annex." The first was in line with a recent national trend. There had been a rapid increase in the number of law schools since 1890, but there had hardly been uniformity in standards. Kilgo was determined that Trinity's should be impeccable. By the spring of 1904 he had broached the subject to Ben Duke and his brother and soon thereafter received their promise of $6,000 per year as a joint "annuity" to support a law school. By late summer the plan was ready for implementation in the fall. There would be a faculty of professional lawyers whose work would be supplemented by instruction in history and economics. The admission requirements would be high, uniquely so in the South. Two years of college work would be necessary for admission, and three years' study in law would be required before a Bachelor of Law degree could be conferred.[15] There were at this time many schools, North and South, which required only high school training for admission, or even less. As late as 1921 only six American schools required three years of college and only three others a college degree.[16]

Kilgo clearly anticipated a small school and a slow growth. Nor did he expect to confer many degrees in law. Across the nation the state bar associations lagged behind in the rigidity of their examinations and were "blind to all distinctions" as to varying methods of instruction.[17] North Carolina was no exception, and therefore the Trinity course was designed primarily to prepare men in two years for the state bar. Only twice in its history did Trinity confer the LL.B. degree.[18] However, the standard

13. Text, Trinity College Papers.
14. Bassett to Theodore Roosevelt, Oct. 24, 1905, Bassett Papers.
15. *Minutes*, Executive Committee, Aug. 16, 1904.
16. Alfred Z. Reed, "Training for the Public Profession of the Law," Carnegie Foundation *Bulletin No. 15* (New York, 1921), pp. 434-441. Cited hereinafter as Reed, "Training for the Law."
17. *Ibid.*, pp. 392 ff.
18. Graduates of the two-year program received a certificate. The two LL.B.'s were conferred, by special arrangement, for additional work completed at Har-

was never relaxed. No improvement could be expected, Kilgo said, "unless some college assumes the responsibility. . . ."[19]

Originally, the plan was to find a man of wide reputation to head the new school and to give the faculty separate status Former Governor Thomas J. Jarvis was one of those approached who declined to serve as dean. Finally Kilgo decided to get "strong teachers and bring them into the Trinity faculty."[20] He began with three, Samuel Fox Mordecai as senior professor and dean; and R. P. Reade and A. C. McIntosh as professors. When one of the new men raised the question of his religion (he was not a Methodist; Mordecai called himself an "Episcopal Jew") Kilgo's reply was prompt, "I am not hunting for a churchman but for a lawyer."[21]

With the acquisition of Mordecai, the college acquired a fresh new personality, a wit, perhaps something of an eccentric, and withal a first-rate legal scholar who loved to teach.[22] He came to Trinity at the age of fifty-one with almost thirty years' experience in legal practice, especially in legal scholarship and in the writing of briefs. His admirers spoke of his "cutting mind" and its service in piercing technicalities to arrive at the essence of the law. Reputedly, his knowledge was near-encyclopedic, and he became a one-man research bureau for many practicing attorneys His students, his "children-in-law," never tired of trying to put together his many-sided personality. He was given to the outrageous posture and to a contempt for pretense. He was a punster a collector of dogs, an untidy dresser, and the composer of execrable doggerel. His sallies and his anecdotes ranged from Rabelaisian earthiness to tears for homeless waifs. Essentially, he was a sentimentalist, "one of those soft persons, full of bluster," who had a tough legal mind. He had nine children, but he chose in mock fury to speak at Christmas of "Saint Herod of blessed memory who was the greatest nuisance abater who ever lived." He was generous with his money but insisted that he kept his dogs "as a protection against the Footpads of Worthy Causes."[23]

vard. Memorandum in *Record of Grades, Trinity Law School,* Dean's Office Duke University School of Law.

19. Raleigh *Morning Post,* Aug. 13, 1905.
20. Kilgo to B. N. Duke, Aug. 18, 1904, Trinity College Papers.
21. A. C. McIntosh in *Samuel Fox Mordecai,* memorial volume (n.p., privately printed, *ca.* 1932), pp. 32-33.
22. Following from memorial volume cited above; interviews, Charles E. Jordan; S. F. Mordecai, *Mordecai's Miscellanies* (Durham, 1927), *passim.*
23. *Mordecai's Miscellanies,* pp. 15, 20.

Mordecai became dean at Trinity in the fall of 1904 and in December visited the major law schools, seeking in particular a resolution of the issue between Harvard's "case system" of teaching and the older forms of teaching by lecture and text. He brought back a conviction that Trinity must adopt the case system even if gradually. He was aware of hazards in following Harvard; such a system was hard on the dull student, required better prepared teachers, and took more time. It pushed men into the law quickly, some before they could walk. But a bright man would be a better lawyer with this training, he concluded. Soon he worked out a combination, apparently somewhat on the Columbia pattern, with more emphasis upon conventional instruction in the first year and with concentration on cases in the second. The aim would be to adopt the case method completely as time went on.[24] In the meantime he busied himself acquiring the beginnings of a law library, and he and his faculty began writing some of the texts and references that their students would need.

Trinity's first law graduates, three in all, went out to practice in 1906. All passed the bar examination. Enrollments in the period followed Kilgo's expectations. Six were enrolled in 1904 and seventeen in 1910. The average enrollment per year was about twelve. One cannot prove the quality of their training. It is true that these and the generations that followed them assumed leading positions in the profession, and time itself proved the best test of the case system; increasingly many schools accepted it. An analysis later concluded that, when mixed with the fundamentals, it trained the students in intellectual independence. "For it really teaches the pupil to think in the way that any practical lawyer. . . . ought to and has to think."[25]

In its second year the Trinity Law School was taken into the new Association of American Law Schools. There were then thirty members, and among them only the University of Tennessee from the South. Slowly other Southern schools met the admission requirements, Texas in 1907 and Tulane and Vanderbilt in 1910. Most of the others came in in the 1920's.[26] Yet as late as 1921 only thirty American schools, including Trinity (about 20 per

24. Memorandum, Mordecai to Kilgo, Dec. 26, 1904, Trinity College Papers.
25. Josef Redlich, "The Common Law and the Case Method in American University Law Schools," Carnegie Foundation *Bulletin No. 8* (New York, 1914), p. viii.
26. *Proceedings*, Association of American Law Schools, 1900 ff.

cent of those in operation), had reached the "high-entrance" classification imposed by a Carnegie Foundation study.[27] In the little college's first venture into professional training, there was from the beginning a preoccupation with high standards and an indifference to numbers.

Less successful was the move for a woman's college, although it was renewed vigorously enough in the spring of 1904. Since 1897, Kilgo reported, women had made up about 10 per cent of the student body. There had not been more for two reasons, a lack of dormitory facilities and the lack of a concentrated effort to bring them to Trinity. He restated his plan of 1902, emphasizing that women should receive education "identical in standards, methods and spirit" with that given men. Other colleges, which sought to educate only women, could not, he said, draw the best faculty members. But he insisted that there should be a separation of the sexes in classes. Otherwise, men students would not come to Trinity.[28]

At the commencement of 1904, Ben and James B. Duke again made a conditional offer. They would provide land worth $50,000 and give $50,000 in cash for a woman's college if the Conferences would raise another $50,000. Preliminary discussions with an architect were begun, and a group of Durham citizens agreed to try to raise $20,000 of the sum needed, leaving the remainder to the Conferences.[29] In the fall the Eastern Conference pledged co-operation, but in the West there was warm praise of the idea, not the substance. The Western group had another problem at this time, the need to revive Greensboro Female College, which had closed. A campaign for endowment was under way, and Ben Duke gave rather heavily. He assured the trustees of G. F. C. that their plans did not interfere in any way with those of Trinity.[30]

Apparently the "annex" plan was stalled again. No extra sums were forthcoming, and Trinity's own funds were being husbanded to increase faculty salaries and to hire additional staff to meet rising enrollments. Again, gifts were harder to come by in the depression that followed the Panic of 1907. Kilgo did not discard his hopes, however, and in his final report as president, in 1910, said the time had come to establish the "coordinate college

27. Reed, "Training for the Law," p. 413.
28. *Report of the President*, 1904, pp. 9-11.
29. Durham *Daily Sun*, June 8, June 30, 1904.
30. B. N. Duke to C. A. Bray, March 29, 1904, B. N. Duke Letterbook.

for women." He suggested a site near the campus, left vacant by Watts Hospital (later the site of McPherson Hospital).[31]

Trinity's attention was being directed to other matters in the years after 1906, a period conspicuous in American higher education for the influence of the Carnegie Foundation for the Advancement of Teaching. The foundation was established by Andrew Carnegie to help college teachers retire by providing pensions, and it was administered by a board of educators. The group found its first task to be one of definition and standardization. In the welter of institutions then calling themselves colleges or universities, how did one determine which college professors were eligible? In the search for standards the Carnegie Foundation soon began to contribute to a revolution in college admissions requirements. First it accepted a definition that came to be called the "Carnegie unit," the measure of a course of study given in the secondary school five periods per week for a full year. Soon the board determined that the completion of fourteen such units should be the minimum requirement for admission to college. Those colleges which established the requirement were eligible for inclusion on the foundation's "accepted list," i.e., colleges whose professors might be awarded pensions from the fund.[32]

There were additional criteria by which one got "on the foundation," and they will be discussed later. But the admission standard itself was enough to spur many institutions, some in unseemly haste, to upgrade their requirements. In the South in 1906, only Vanderbilt and the Randolph-Macon Woman's College were then requiring the equivalent of the fourteen units. Trinity was next with twelve and one-half[33] and, with an ironic bow to Chapel Hill (eleven units), was inordinately proud of the distinction. But not too proud to improve it. The Southern Association of Colleges and Secondary Schools then required the equivalent of ten Carnegie units, a level which had remained the same since 1895. In 1908 the association agreed to accept the Carnegie standard, effective two years later.[34] Trinity was not content to wait, although as will be noted, from the beginning the college's denominational standing precluded its ever becoming eligible for

31. *Appendix*, President's Report, 1910, Trustee Records.
32. *Annual Report*, Carnegie Foundation for the Advancement of Teaching, 1906-1910, *passim*.
33. *Ibid.*, 1906, p. 25.
34. *Proceedings*, Southern Association, 1907, p. 6.

Carnegie pension benefits. In 1908 the new Trinity requirements were made effective, and they were as follows: two units of history; three of English; two of mathematics (one and one-half algebra, one-half geometry); four of Latin; and two of Greek. As in the past, one substituted French or German for Greek in the "B" and "C" programs. The remaining unit might come from further work in one of the required subjects or from among the sciences. A student could be admitted with four conditional units, all of which had to be made up by the end of the sophomore year and none of which could be counted toward graduation. As before, a student might be admitted without examination in any of the subjects mentioned if he came from one of Trinity's "certified" schools.

Trinity's pride in its modest standards can only be understood in its Southern context. The Southern Association was for years impressed and tempted by the standards of a few Eastern colleges, but, regretfully, could not apply them. Nor could even the best Southern colleges join the movement of the College Entrance Examination Board, to standardize admissions requirements.[35] There was a chronic fuzziness between secondary and "college" education. Some colleges accepted most of their students without examination, without certification, and in fact frequently reached down into the ninth and tenth grades to raid the high schools. The pattern was not wholly a Southern one. Hence, the Carnegie board's bewildered question, "What is a college?"

The situation described, which had obtained for many years, serves to emphasize the "gamble" Trinity undertook in the years after 1895 when it raised entrance requirements above the capacity of many high schools. Perhaps the college's greatest assets in later years were the Trinity Park School and the Durham city school system. As late as 1907 only eight secondary schools in the Carolinas even offered as much as fourteen units of work.[36] In the same year the college reported that 90 per cent of Trinity Park's graduates went on to college. Earlier E. C. Brooks, then connected with the North Carolina State Department of Public

35. The effort of the College Board to develop uniform requirements and examinations was a great step forward in "articulation" with secondary schools. However, most colleges in the Midwest, West, and South continued to depend upon certification. Cf. Claud M. Fuess, *The College Board: Its First Fifty Years* (New York, 1950); and Joseph Lindsey Henderson, *Admission to College by Certificate* (New York, 1912).
36. *Proceedings,* Southern Association, 1907, pp. 65-66.

Instruction, stated that the Durham system, with its eight-month term and other assets, was the best in North Carolina.[37] Surely there was a relationship between the two efforts, private and public, in the zeal for progress in Durham. The college's presence in the town was in no way limited to the challenge it offered local youth to seek advanced training.

In the period 1904-1910 the curriculum at Trinity underwent a minimum of changes. The earlier modernization, with its three paths to the degree, remained substantially unchanged. The first two years of the "A" and "B" courses were left precisely the same. The important change was a further concession to electives. In 1905 the junior year in "A" was made fully elective, as had been the senior year, with the exception of the mandatory course in Bible. This meant dropping required work in psychology and economics and the one-year requirement of French or German. The same changes were made in the "B" program, except that the modern languages requirement was retained. This meant that "A" graduates now finished at Trinity with two years each of Latin and Greek. The "B" graduate had to complete three years of a modern language for his degree. The "C" or engineering course became still more technical. The language requirement was cut from three years to one, and by 1910 electrical and mechanical engineering had become departmentalized.[38]

A handful of other curricular alterations took place in this period. As admissions standards were raised, there was upgrading in some departments. For example, in Latin students read Livy in the sophomore instead of the junior year. There was increased attention to an old problem, the need for more composition work in English. In history beginning study of the ancient world withered away as a new European emphasis appeared, especially with William K. Boyd's return in 1906. By 1910 courses in economics and political science were split, and the old term "political economy" was less commonly used. There were also a few special changes. In 1906 Wannamaker began offering scientific German for graduate students and for undergraduates interested in science, and in 1909 the young department of education was co-operating with the historians in a course on the history of European culture. Boyd in turn was readying a senior-graduate course in the teaching of history.[39]

37. *Ibid.*, 1903, p. 101.
38. Trinity College catalogues, 1904-1910.
39. *Ibid.*

Enrollments for the period increased by 40 per cent, from 245 to 356. The major increases came after 1907, by which time North Carolina was well embarked on the public school expansion promised in 1900. By the end of the first decade the program was producing more students with at least minimal high school training, and Trinity with other colleges was the beneficiary.

The representation from Durham tended to level out at 25 per cent of the student body. In almost every year half of the Durham students were women.[40] No explanation of enrollment can be precise, but one surmises that preparation at the Trinity Park School and the opportunity to go on to college at Trinity, in both cases within sight of home, made an attractive combination to Durham parents. Somewhat surprisingly, however, Trinity consistently drew a number of women from a wider area. For the period about one-third of the women, some twenty a year, came from cities throughout North Carolina and from a few other states.

Trinity's financial situation during these years was directly related to rising enrollments. There were no new windfalls from Washington Duke. He died on May 8, 1905,[41] having disposed of most of his fortune some years before. Probably he expected that his sons would continue the family support of Trinity. And so they did. In addition to the law school fund, Ben and James B. Duke each year gave sums which amounted to about one-third of the annual income.[42] Although the endowment did not increase for the period, the payments from the Dukes were welcome "annuities," and, as in the past, they made progress possible. The annual gifts became habitual with Ben Duke. He had long since learned that the material needs of the college could only increase, and he spoke frequently of "the burden of Trinity College" on his shoulders. "I am practically carrying that institution single handed. It needs more money than I feel able to give it."[43]

40. *Ibid.*
41. The college and his friends sought to perpetuate the memory of the "founder of the New Trinity." A movement developed to collect funds for an heroic seated statue for the college. The statue was unveiled on June 10, 1908. Among the tributes expressed were, from the trustees: "We have never seen him less than a man acting under the fear of God and under the inspiration of lofty purpose . . . there was no act of his life for which the College need make apology." *Minutes,* Board of Trustees, June 6, 1905. From the faculty: "Without the advantages of education himself, he gave liberally to build and establish this College. . . . He never hampered us with a small idea or a personal wish or preference." *In Memory of Mr. Washington Duke* (Durham, *ca.* 1905), p. 26.
42. Treasurer's Reports, 1903-1910, Trustee Records.
43. B. N. Duke to Richard Wilkinson, June 11, 1909, B. N. Duke Letterbook

In one of the rare tabulations of the Dukes' gifts, he agreed that by 1907 the family probably had given one million dollars to schools and other institutions.[44] Of this sum, perhaps $800,000 had gone to Trinity.

The urgent need of the college was to alleviate the faculty load and to meet the competition in salaries. If Trinity were to continue to bring in men with credentials in graduate training, she would do so only at the price of meeting offers elsewhere. For a while the pressure of larger enrollments could be met with graduate and undergraduate assistants, who helped with grading papers. The senior faculty, the corps of professors, was not enlarged quickly. Economies were directed to building up small annual surpluses toward future expansion in staff.

At the same time, the salary scale moved upward, and, in marked contrast with earlier years, a wider gap between the pay of older and younger professors began to develop. The range grew from a minimum of $1,200 to $1,500; and from a maximum of $1,700 to $2,500. In 1909, with the addition of "second men" in several departments, the minimum dropped to $1,000 for the new arrivals.[45] Among the new men were three who were to make significant contributions to the development of Duke University after 1924. They were W. T. Laprade in history; C. B. Markham in mathematics; and Frank C. Brown in English. One measure of the financial policy is seen in the share of the budget given to faculty salaries. In 1904 salaries made up 49 per cent of total expenditures. By 1910 the percentage had risen to more than 60.[46]

How did this compare with other institutions? A Carnegie foundation study of one hundred colleges and universities disclosed a broad range of $1,350 to $4,800 for professors and concluded that the average professor in the financially strongest institutions was receiving about $2,500.[47] Boyd's correspondence indicates that an associate professor might receive as much as $2,500 at the University of Chicago. Young men from Columbia with the Ph.D. were getting from $1,000 to $1,500 in their first

44. R. B. Arrington to J. E. Stagg, March 19, 1909, Trinity College Papers.
45. *Minutes*, Executive Committee, 1904-1910.
46. Treasurer's Reports, 1903-1910.
47. "The Financial Status of the Professor in America and in Germany," Carnegie *Bulletin No. 2* (New York, 1908). Cited hereinafter as Carnegie, "Financial Status."

jobs.[48] In the Carnegie survey, Trinity reported an average of $1,850 for its full professors, placing it somewhat higher than a group of colleges such as Kenyon ($1,600); Ohio Wesleyan ($1,800); Colgate ($1,740); and Earlham ($1,550). Actually, Trinity's average was higher than the one reported. From the arrival of the college in Durham, free faculty housing was available as a bonus to senior professors, and was uncharged in the accounts. In some cases younger men were accommodated in college-owned rooming houses, or in the Epworth Inn. Perhaps one may conservatively add $300 to the average salary for free rent.

Modest though it was, Trinity's pay scale came at the price of rather rigid economies in other directions, in particular in aid to students. For several years the college borrowed annually from its general loan fund, as well as from local banks, and the result was seen in the administration of student loans. A tougher repayment policy was vigorously pushed, and the sums loaned declined from $4,000 to $2,000. At the same time the new policy produced twice as much return in interest.[49] There was much carelessness in repayment. Since 1894 Ben Duke had made dozens of personal loans to students. He wrote one borrower who paid him back in full that it was "the first instance in which the money has ever been returned to me, nor have I ever received any reasonable excuse for the non-payment."[50]

In the period the number of new scholarships established was almost negligible, and students turned increasingly to part-time jobs. The location in Durham was favorable to this end. In one year 50 per cent of the students, presumably men only, were working their way through Trinity. In Durham one might clerk in a store, keep books, sell newspapers, or find employment in the hotels, printing offices, or restaurants. By 1910 the Durham alumni and the college Y. M. C. A. each operated employment agencies for students.[51]

The Methodist Conferences continued to help with annual appropriations but in varying degrees. The Eastern Conference gifts leveled out at $5,000 per year. From the West, the annual sum

48. William E. Dodd to Boyd, May 10, 1909; James T. Shotwell to Boyd, March 13, 1909, Boyd Papers.
49. Treasurer's Reports, 1904-1910.
50. B. N. Duke to E. C. Perrow, Aug. 30, 1909, Trinity College Papers.
51. Raleigh *Morning Post*, Aug. 13, 1905; *North Carolina Christian Advocate*, March 24, 1910.

was more likely to be about $1,700. As the money came in, Trinity sought to earmark it for specific purposes. For a time it was agreed that Church collections would be used to pay the interest on the mortgage of 1893. Again, insurance premiums might be met with such funds. In time part of the Eastern Conference appropriation underwrote a professorship in Bible. By 1909 a single goal had been agreed upon, and both Conferences accepted the plan. Each would contribute to a sinking fund with which to retire the mortgage bonds.[52] They would come due in 1913, and unity in this objective was encouraging. The $2,400 interest was an annual drain on the budget; such a sum would easily support an extra professor.

The addition of second men in several departments was of great service in reducing teaching loads. Before 1908 a load of fifteen to perhaps eighteen hours per week was routine. There were variations, of course. However, after an enlarged staff was assembled, twelve hours per man was more generally possible,[53] although some professors in the languages and English undoubtedly continued to teach more. In this regard Trinity compared with other institutions much as it did in salaries. In the stronger universities a full professor's teaching stint averaged from six to twelve hours. In the "better smaller universities and colleges" the figure was twelve to fifteen hours. In some institutions the load ran as high as twenty-five hours per week.[54]

It cannot be said that the management of the college made aggressive moves toward increased "faculty power." In the absence of printed by-laws, the catalogue of 1902 simply stated that the president had the right to veto any faculty action "which he may deem hurtful to the policy of the College." The faculty, another statement noted, transacted at faculty meetings "such business as refers to the work in the various departments." The faculty had the additional right to determine the awarding of degrees, and, perhaps with Crowell's quarrel with the faculty in mind, the following appeared: "Each professor and adjunct [assistant] professor may arrange his courses of study and determine his plans of work in so far as these courses and plans do not interfere with other departments and policies."

A more definite statement of responsibility came after the new

52. *Journals*, Western Conference and N. C. Conference, 1904-1910.
53. Trinity College catalogue; interviews, A. M. Webb, Sept. 21, 1959, and W. T. Laprade, Dec. 9, 1960.
54. Carnegie, "Financial Status," p. 62.

charter of 1903. At that time a constitution and by-laws were drawn up, accepted, and thereafter printed in the catalogue. The document contained a statement of the Aims of the college (written by Kilgo and identical with those of Duke University later) and sought to state in legal form what had been recent practice. Details of choosing officers of the Board of Trustees were included, and by now the Board was referred to as "the corporate body" of the college. Four "officers of the College" were named: the president, dean, treasurer, and registrar. The president's duties included presiding over the faculty, administering all regulations, and nominating all faculty to the Board. He retained the broad veto power but must give reasons for any veto. As to the faculty, "they shall have the right to enact such regulations as they may deem necessary to carry on the instruction of the College, advance its standards of work and otherwise develop the scholarly aims of the College." Again, all such actions were subject to presidential approval.

The important change lay in tenure. As noted earlier, Crowell had sought in 1893 to secure approval for "three-year" tenure but had been denied. Kilgo in 1897 had asked for four-year tenure and had been rejected by Judge Clark's committee. In June, 1906, the trustees passed a resolution stating that "officers and teachers" might be elected for terms of one, two, three, and four years, "and after six years' service, officers and teachers with the rank of Professor may be elected without time limit to serve at the will of the Board of Trustees."[55] The next year seven professors were elected without time limit and the remainder of the faculty for terms in accord with their service at Trinity.[56]

In the years before the quadrennial General Methodist Conference of 1906, the item of personal concern to Kilgo was his candidacy for a bishopric. Token votes at earlier Conferences had established his name, and his friends were working hard for his election. There was much optimism, and he received numerous warnings not to "hang" himself "by some hard remarks in some speech. . . ." A few weeks before the Conference, a close adviser said, "I think your call is coming" but urged him to direct his public statements "to the hearts more than the heads of men" and counseled "no unusual views or statements but strong and fresh presentations of the old paths. . . ."[57] Ben Duke took occasion

55. Trustee Records, June 4, 1906.
56. *Minutes*, Board of Trustees, June 3, 1907.
57. "J. O. W." (John O. Willson) to Kilgo, Feb. 1, 1906, Kilgo Papers.

o work for Kilgo, urging former Governor Jarvis (a member of he North Carolina delegation) to leave no stone unturned. He agreed "that his election would be a blow to Trinity College, but we could not let that stand in the way of his promotion."[58]

When the Conference met in Birmingham, Alabama, in May, Kilgo's supporters were ready. Soon it was evident that his opponents would not be idle. Three bishoprics were vacant, and he first two were quickly filled. Kilgo received 100 votes on the first ballot, and his support rose steadily. At the end of the seventh ballot he had 128 of the 136 votes needed. At that point, an adjournment for a recreational program was passed, although it required a division of the house. When the Conference reassembled, Kilgo's stock dropped quickly. On the twelfth ballot, James Atkins, another North Carolinian, was elected.[59] It is significant perhaps that Atkins was the leader from Western North Carolina who had been a candidate to replace Crowell in 1894 before the Board had turned to Kilgo.

As Kilgo's friends reconstructed the maneuvering, the adjournment had given his opponents time to work against him.[60] Reportedly, editor John R. Webster had circulated pamphlets hostile to Kilgo. There had been criticism of his smoking. Surely here was no shortage of ammunition with which to combat the controversial Trinity president. When Jarvis returned home, he was certain how it happened: "The adjournment, for the free street car ride and free ice cream treat, beat you."[61] Such was the admixture of Church politics and the simple life.

Kilgo's friends wired him their sympathy, Ben Duke expressing his disappointment, but assuring him, "we love you more than ever." All commented upon his public demeanor in the face of the blow. Since he had come so close, it was natural that some were embittered. There were many vows to elect him on the first ballot four years later.

Kilgo had received another piece of bad news in Birmingham. Bassett had written him there telling of an offer he had received from Smith College, one attractive enough to take seriously. The pay was moderately higher ($2,500 versus $2,100), but Bassett

58. B. N. Duke to Thomas T. Jarvis, Feb. 20, 1906, Trinity College Papers.
59. *Journal of the Fifteenth General Conference of the Methodist Episcopal Church, South* (Nashville and Dallas, 1906), pp. 178-191; Raleigh *Christian Advocate,* May 24, 1906.
60. Kilgo Papers, *passim*; Garber, *Kilgo,* pp. 320-321.
61. Jarvis to Kilgo, June 4, 1906, Kilgo Papers.

also would have a teaching load of ten hours per week, possibly less within a year. There was a library of 160,000 volumes (Trinity now had 40,000), as well as accessibility to the research libraries of the East. He would have a full professorship in a department of four men doing "highly specialized" work.[62] Bassett had written the departmental chairman at Smith: "Here I am safe from severe annoyances, but I do feel that the years of my life which ought to be productive are going away with little done which ought to be done."[63]

There had also been a hint from Yale, and Bassett, in writing Kilgo, conceded that he was tempted to move. "On the other hand," he wrote, "I wish I could live in the South, which I best understand and best love. It would also be a sore trial to break away from Trinity, which I have every reason to love and be grateful to." At the time he wrote, Kilgo's election seemed imminent, and Bassett freely observed that with Kilgo gone from Trinity, the college was less attractive to him. He hinted at personal difficulties with some members of the faculty (probably Flowers and possibly Few). "At all events," he said, "I know I shall never find a superior under whom I shall have a more satisfactory position, and I confess that nothing would so much reconcile me to a change as your own removal. . . ."[64]

The Yale position did not open up, but in late May Bassett accepted the Smith offer and assumed the new duties in the fall of 1906. Apparently in leaving Trinity, he had mixed feelings of hurt and guilt. Upon his return from the defeat in Birmingham, Kilgo had been unwilling to discuss Bassett's leaving.[65] Bassett himself had apologized to Walter Page for departing the South. He reminded Page that he too had left some twenty years before. It would be another generation, he said, before the South would be ready for "the scholar or the writer of serious books. When you left . . . it was not ready for a good newspaper editor." He asked Page, "Can I do the world any good by sitting down waiting for the procession to come? And haven't I done about all I can do to hasten the arrival of the procession? I say nothing of eating out one's heart in the meantime, because I am willing to do that if any good may come of it." He explained, "The thing

62. Bassett to Kilgo (Birmingham, Ala.), May 12, 1906, Bassett Papers.
63. Bassett to Charles D. Hazen, May 3, 1906, Bassett Papers.
64. Bassett to Kilgo, May 12, 1906.
65. Undated note in Bassett's hand on the back of Bassett's copy of the May 12 letter cited.

in my profession which I like best is the writing of history; it is impossible to do that with success where there is no good library; probably it is impossible to do it in the South. . . ."[66] A few weeks earlier he had complained to a friend in Cambridge that he was discouraged in the work of the North Carolina Literary and Historical Association. Its secretary and his friend, R. D. W. Connor, had the right aims, he said, but Connor was hampered by the attitudes of some of the directors of the association (e.g., Josephus Daniels, Walter Clark, R. W. Winston, and W. J. Peele), who, Bassett believed, "think that it would be best to print history from the standpoint of present political necessity."[67]

Finally, Bassett told Page of his regret in leaving Trinity and hoped it would be understood, because, "if someone should say in the future that when my own interests called me I forgot the time when the college befriended me, why that would pain me deeply."

Kilgo's coolness to discussing Bassett's departure may have come from the lost bishopric and the reaction that set in after his return, or he may have felt that Bassett, of all men, owed Trinity too much to leave her. But Kilgo tended always to give a grudging farewell to a good man. His fierce sense of loyalty was quickly touched. There had been strain a few years before when Jerome Dowd went to the University of Wisconsin, and in 1909 when Mims left for the University of North Carolina there was a minimum of cordiality.[68]

However, Bassett left in the wake of tribute from the trustees and faculty and from scholars and friends over the South. Soon he and Kilgo were on friendly terms, and their correspondence continued until Kilgo's death in 1922. In Massachusetts Bassett developed a feeling of homesickness and nostalgia which never

66. Bassett to Page, May 29, 1906, Bassett Papers. He began, "I will tell you my reasons because I want to stand well in your eyes, and you may scold me as much as you choose after it is all over." Later Bassett hoped Ben Duke had understood; "I fear he feels I did badly." Bassett to Boyd, Jan. 2, 1912, Boyd Papers.

67. Bassett to Gilbert T. Stephenson, March 30, 1906, Bassett Papers.
He was not alone in feeling the pressure. From Chapel Hill a fellow historian had written that he himself was "too scientific and too little sentimental to do much in history in this place." Charles Lee Raper to Bassett, April 11, 1905, Bassett Papers.

68. At the trustee meeting in June of 1909, a prepared word of praise for Mims was discarded, Trustee Records, June 8, 1909. Later, Kilgo could manage only a left-handed tribute: "Good wishes go with Dr. Mims, but the Department of English at Trinity will begin next year with larger plans, revised policies, new aims, and greater strength." Raleigh *Christian Advocate*, July 22, 1909.

left him. He subscribed to North Carolina newspapers and followed Trinity's affairs closely and fondly. He contributed to the college's alumni fund and was intensely interested in the plans for Duke University. In 1916 Trinity gave him an honorary degree, and in 1926 he was serving as vice-president of the alumni association.[69] His old student, William K. Boyd, came back to replace him at Trinity, and the two maintained a correspondence through the years. As late as 1922, Bassett was writing another friend: "In that old time at Trinity . . . I spent the happiest days I have lived. It was not altogether the effect of youth. . . ."[70]

Bassett went on to a career of productive scholarship at Smith. The hours were ideal, and he could indulge his love for writing history. He once confided to Boyd "in the depths of secrecy" that "my first inclination and desire is to write, and after that to teach. . . . That has ever been my feeling."[71] As the number of his books grew, so did his reputation. At one time he toyed with the idea of running for the Senate against Henry Cabot Lodge. In 1919 he became secretary of the American Historical Association.

Hard as he tried, he never shook off the hurt of Josephus Daniels' attack of 1903. Daniels liked to remember that Bassett changed after leaving the "pro-trust and anti-Jefferson policy" at Trinity.[72] But Daniels did not leave him entirely alone. He occasionally referred to "Bassettism," and when Bassett spoke at an inter-racial meeting in New York, there was comment in the *News and Observer,* as well as when Bassett in his life of Andrew Jackson could not defend North Carolina's claim as Jackson's birthplace.[73] As late as 1917 when both men were strong supporters of Woodrow Wilson and when Daniels was serving in Wilson's cabinet, Bassett wrote: "I know a wicked and narrow man served to accomplish his selfish ends at the expense of my happiness, and I know that he knows that he acted as he would not have been acted by."[74]

69. Bassett Papers, *passim.*
70. Bassett to Charles F. Lambeth, April 8, 1922, Bassett Papers.
71. Bassett to W. K. Boyd, June 10, 1917, Bassett Papers.
72. Daniels, *Editor in Politics,* pp. 434-435.
73. Daniels' reactions scarcely resembled the attack of 1903. He merely printed the criticism of others, but Bassett had made up his mind about Daniels. He composed several verses of doggerel for the private amusement of a friend in Raleigh. For example, Bassett to Mary S. Smith, Nov. 5, 1911, Bassett Papers:

"Lord keep the dear Josephus   "And if he wants to know the truth
From men of bad intent,   As several times he's meant,
He ain't the man to argue   He always looks to see if it
Against a monument.   Is on a monument."

74. Bassett to Thurston T. Hicks, Jan. 20, 1917, Bassett Papers.

In the long years before the next General Conference of the Church, Kilgo himself suffered a letdown.[75] He was ill for a period, suffering from what he called "torpid liver." As secular schools boomed, he became discouraged about Christian education. In his depression, he wondered if his freedom of thought (in regard to his chances for the bishopric in 1910) were going to be restricted. His friend Bishop Candler conceded that this was probably so and warned him if he went out on any "intellectual jaunts, do you be sure *to think*. Don't mistake an abdominal disturbance for a cerebral movement."[76] If this referred to a rising issue, unification of the Southern and Northern Churches, Kilgo disregarded the warning. In the *South Atlantic Quarterly* of July, 1906, he delivered an eloquent plea in favor of unification—a view he was later to renounce.

One may merely suggest that Kilgo was changing in those years. Motives are of course always obscure. Everyone at Trinity was getting a little older; perhaps some of the glow was gone. If so, there was resilience, and there was alertness to new opportunities. The state of North Carolina was equipping itself with the beginnings of a complete public school system. There was a rash of consolidation of school districts. Hundreds of new buildings were built, and the school term was extended. New tax laws were passed, and a system of state loans was established. There was emphasis upon rural libraries and uniform courses of study. In 1907 the legislature appropriated money for rural high schools, and soon the need for teachers became acute. Here was a new opening for Trinity, and Kilgo was not slow to see it. He moved swiftly to establish a teacher training program.

How did this square with the Christian education philosophy? It probably did not have to, although Kilgo did not discuss that point. He and Bailey always claimed for the Christian educators a share of credit for the public schools, even though it was sometimes hard for Kilgo to concede that secular education was all that it might be. By 1907, however, the handwriting was on the wall, and there were practical considerations. Trinity, like other colleges, would be served if her alumni were well placed in the

75. He was writing gloomy letters to close friends, and they were worried about his health. Bassett, Kilgo, and Trinity College Papers. Mims, after deciding to leave the college, wrote of "the general let down we have been having for two or three years. Dr. Kilgo seems to be more and more out of sympathy with his position." Mims to Bassett, April 11, 1909, Bassett Papers.
76. W. A. Candler to Kilgo, June 1, 1906, Kilgo Papers.

new schools as teachers, principals, and superintendents. Moreover, there was an ample tradition linking Trinity with public education, from Craven's normal school and Crowell's vigorous school campaign, to Kilgo's own definite role in helping secondary education by improving college standards. The rural high school movement may have had special appeal; Kilgo frequently observed that comparatively few ministers came from the city school systems.

Whatever his reasons, Kilgo lost little time in putting Trinity into close relationship with the public schools. In May, 1907, he was writing an alumnus, Eugene C. Brooks, to offer him a new chair at Trinity as professor of the history of education.[77] Brooks was an ideal choice. In 1907 he was superintendent of schools at Goldsboro. In previous years he had been a teacher, a principal, and a leader in the state Teachers' Assembly. When J. Y. Joyner, as state superintendent of education, had led the school campaign of 1902-1905, Brooks had been his chief aide. The Goldsboro system was thought to be a model. In 1906 he began editing the *North Carolina Journal of Education.* Plainly, in Brooks Trinity would have its own resident expert on schools and a man with years of close association with teachers and public educators.[78] Brooks said he would come to Trinity for $2,000, his present salary, and Kilgo agreed.

The new department of education was tailored for the preparation of teachers. There were background courses in education, and there was attention to current problems, especially those in North Carolina. Related work was arranged in history, psychology, and sociology. Soon the number of courses was increased to provide, in addition to "methods," some analysis of the school curriculum and school management. At the same time Brooks, who possessed great energy and personal charm, developed programs for teachers in service. Durham teachers took courses on Saturday at the college, and county teachers began extension work under Brooks's direction, the first of its kind in the state. Brooks himself, operating from his platform as editor of the teachers' magazine, was a peripatetic ambassador for Trinity. He conducted summer institutes for teachers throughout North Carolina and was a constant speaker in the meetings of various educational associations. He quickly became a leader in the Southern

77. E. C. Brooks to Kilgo, May 27, 1907, Trinity College Papers.
78. Willard B. Gatewood, Jr., *Eugene Clyde Brooks: Educator and Public Servant* (Durham, 1960), *passim.* Cited hereinafter as Gatewood, *Brooks.*

Association of Colleges and Secondary Schools.[79] Enrollment in
education courses at Trinity rose, especially in extension work,
and soon the college was sending out its products for employment. Brooks's biographer observes that his tenure at Trinity,
which lasted until 1919, "gave the institution a pre-eminence
throughout North Carolina in teacher training."[80]

By 1910 Brooks was ready with a plan for enlarging the effort,
a scheme that was accepted and given the prestige of a big title, a
"School of Education." The program was designed for the many
working teachers who had only a high school education or less
and who were not likely to begin a conventional college course
toward a degree. Some were teaching in high schools; others
could be expected to do so. In the two-year course the school
would provide technical courses and practice teaching in the
Trinity Park School. The students would have to choose a major
and two minors in the academic subjects they were expected to
teach. Advanced work was available for those who could stay
longer. In his proposal Brooks cited appealing considerations.
The time was ripe for the program, and "the institution that sup-
plies this, the greatest educational need, will control public education in North Carolina." The high school, he noted, was now
the strategic point in the school world. Here was a chance for
Trinity to plant its roots by training teachers, but also, by con-
necting its academic departments with the schools, to give the
subjects taught there academic respectability.[81] The new departure also marked the drift of the liberal arts professors away from
their old interests in secondary education. With the arrival of a
young discipline, education, the "subject matter" specialists would
turn more deeply into their specialties.

As Trinity's programs in public education produced teachers,
the Trinity Park School continued to emphasize college preparation; the existence of new public high schools did not insure
a general enthusiasm for college. Trinity Park had joined the
Southern Association in 1902 and was the only secondary school
in the state to do so until 1915. For the period to 1910, Trinity
Park enrollments dropped slightly, perhaps due as much to the

79. *Ibid.*, pp. 117-179. See also, William B. Hamilton, "Duke University and
the Schools: The First Century," *Duke University Centennial Conference on
Teacher Training*, Historical Papers of the Trinity College Historical Society,
Series XXX (1951), pp. 3-17.
80. Gatewood, *Brooks*, p. ii.
81. The plan is in the Eugene C. Brooks Papers (Duke University Library).
See also a bulletin, *The School of Education, Trinity College* (Durham, 1910).

building up of good high schools in Durham as to the existence of more high schools over North Carolina.

Finally, however, the public school movement marked the end of Old Trinity. Many of Crowell's old "feeder" schools had been converted or replaced by public schools.[82] They had never been of much use to the college, nor had the college ever really supported them. For years the trustees maintained a committee on Old Trinity and occasionally sent the school small sums of money. However, there were repeated admonitions not to expect major support. There was talk of transferring the property to the orphanage of the Western Conference, but apparently the plan was still-born. In 1909 the college agreed to sell the property to the Randolph County Board of Education.[83] Eventually, Old Trinity ended much as it had begun, as part of a popular school movement.

Carnegie and Church "Control"

Another movement of vital interest to Trinity came from the creation of the Carnegie Foundation in 1906. The aim was to reward "the least rewarded of all professions," that of the college professor, by providing him security in his old age. The Carnegie board also hoped to freshen college work by removing the infirm from the classroom and by making room for younger men. Although the funds were limited, the foundation soon provided pensions averaging more than $1,500 per year.[84] Hence there was an understandable excitement among American colleges to get "on the foundation." The stimulus was increased when academic standards were linked with eligibility. Prestige became involved when the foundation began publishing its Accepted List of institutions.

As we have seen, the Carnegie board encountered great difficulty in deciding about academic standards. Greater still was the need to determine the nature of control of American colleges. Andrew Carnegie expressly excluded from foundation benefits state-controlled and "sectarian" institutions. His words regard-

82. Kilgo writing in the Raleigh *Christian Advocate*, Sept. 5, 1907.
83. *Minutes*, Board and Executive Committee. For the decision to sell, see *Minutes*, Executive Committee, July 7, 1909. In the fall of 1924 the old building was condemned to make way for a modern high school building.
84. *Annual Report*, Carnegie Foundation, 1906.

ng the latter were: "Only such as are under the control of a sect
or require Trustees (or a majority thereof), Officers, Faculty or
Students, to belong to any specific sect, or which impose any
theological test, are to be excluded."[85]

When they learned the network of organic law by which
American colleges had been created, the officers of the foundation saw a dilemma. What constituted "control"? Comparatively
few colleges required sectarian tests of trustees or faculty, and
hardly any required them of students. Yet the energy of American churches in founding colleges had by 1906 produced a variety of charters. Trustees might be "appointed," "confirmed," or
"elected" by church bodies. In some cases, especially in the
North, the relevant statement was a curiosity of history. In others,
especially in the South, the degree of church involvement had
real significance.

The foundation board was led by Henry S. Pritchett, a scientist and former president of the Massachusetts Institute of
Technology. Pritchett and his colleagues soon decided on a strict
interpretation of Carnegie's words. In the need to make the
necessary distinctions, they could hardly do otherwise. Rules
were developed, and lengthy interpretations of them were prepared. It was necessary to avoid a war of semantics. For example,
a college president might truthfully protest that in practice, *he*
determined the membership of his board, that the church group
approved the choices merely as a formality.

The foundation decided to rule out all institutions "owned
or controlled by a religious organization" or whose charters required any of the denominational tests cited. The board decided
on the one hand that the power to nominate trustees was the
power to control. On the other hand, if nomination came from
the trustees themselves (as at Trinity), the church's power to
elect was also interpreted as control. The limitation at Trinity,
whereby the Conferences could elect no trustee whom the Board
had not nominated, was not discussed. Few contended that, if
the Conferences failed to confirm, the Board could proceed with
one vacancy until it could be filled for the unexpired term by the
Board itself. In all likelihood the role of the Conferences would
have been interpreted as real power to elect. The Carnegie board

85. *Ibid.*, pp. 7-8. The summary following is from the foundation reports
of 1906-1910. See also, Howard J. Savage, *Fruit of an Impulse: Forty-Five Years
of the Carnegie Foundation, 1905-1950* (New York, 1953).

held the line rigidly. If a college merely reported to a church body, even voluntarily, the foundation ruled it out.

In their deliberations Pritchett and his board quickly found the heart of the problem. Many colleges, some of indisputable academic quality, long had felt themselves independent of church control. Yet, in the struggle for support, for students, or money, traditionally they had appealed to their denominational heritage. As Pritchett said, "Each college desires a constituency." The foundation understood this and counseled against abrupt severances of useful denominational alliances. At the same time, Pritchett did not conceal his belief that "a great university" probably could not exist with religious restrictions. Such ties were "in direct contravention" of the larger spirit of intellectual freedom which a university must have, he said.

When the state institutions in their turn challenged the limitation that excluded them, the foundation yielded, but with great caution. The foundation's resources were far too limited for it to undertake the task set for it; this fact necessarily influenced its policies. In 1906 there were fifty colleges on the Accepted List. In 1910 there were only seventy-one, and only two from the South, Tulane and the Central University of Kentucky.

The operation of the Carnegie Foundation may have constituted something of an assault on denominational education, especially in the South, but, if so, it met with determined opposition Vanderbilt, though perhaps pre-eminent in academic standards could not join the Accepted List. Indeed, for years it had been waging a long, violent war with the Church in an attempt to free itself of ecclesiastical demands for more control.[86] Another Methodist institution with high standards, the Randolph-Macon Woman's College, suffered an embarrassment in its interest in the Carnegie scheme. Randolph-Macon's trustees passed resolutions disclaiming Church control and satisfied the foundation as to their independence. Two years later, after a storm of protest, the trustees resolved themselves off the list and back into the Church.[87]

From Trinity College, Kilgo and Few surveyed these develop ments carefully and with mixed feelings. For years Trinity had been among those institutions that claimed to yield to no one in academic integrity or in its freedom from sectarianism. Trinity

86. Edwin Mims, *History of Vanderbilt University* (Nashville, 1946), pp. 291 318. Cited hereinafter as Mims, *Vanderbilt*.
87. Roberta D. Cornelius, *History of Randolph-Macon Woman's College* (Chapel Hill, 1951), pp. 127-147.

would not disguise its Church tie but insisted that its trustees were "absolutely" free of outside control. With the Bassett incident in mind (with which Pritchett was familiar), Few told the Carnegie president that there was no college "less servile to what is bad in public opinion or that is more unyielding to its surrounding 'atmosphere.' I think that if any college in the United States has a right to be called autonomous, this college has earned that right." On the other hand, the Church tie produced students, some money, and was in accord with the sentiment of the president, dean, and perhaps most of the trustees. Moreover, North Carolina Methodists were aware of the Randolph-Macon incident and sharply condemned that college. T. N. Ivey of the Raleigh *Christian Advocate* may have been warning Kilgo when he praised him for his belief in the "absolute ownership" by the Church of its institutions.[88]

From the other side, Kilgo was hearing from a trustee, J. W. Alspaugh, the former chairman. Alspaugh thought that in Trinity's case the word "denominational" was "just a name. In all respects of service to the public, Trinity is as broad as any university. Nor does the church support the college financially, nor has it ever done so. Certainly not at Durham. Individual effort alone has made Trinity what it is." He urged Kilgo to try to secure President Roosevelt's influence with Andrew Carnegie to get Trinity on the Carnegie list.[89]

It was in this context that Kilgo sat down to write his annual report of 1908, the report cited earlier, in which he discussed Trinity's relationship to the Church. He chose to attack the premise that ecclesiastical "controls" in general were disadvantageous. He conceded the shortcomings, in duplication of institutions and competition. But he insisted that there was a vast difference between being sectarian and being denominational. At Trinity, an institution "owned" by the Church, there was no taint of sectarianism. Trinity, he said, catered to all classes and bestowed her benefits "without regard to religious creeds, political faiths, or social castes." Scholarships, remissions of tuition, and loan funds were granted upon the same terms to students of all faiths. Nor, he said, was there any attempt to tamper with one's faith; "no attempt to proselyte students would be tolerated for a moment."

88. Raleigh *Christian Advocate*, April 16, 1908.
89. J. W. Alspaugh to Kilgo, June 6, 1908, Kilgo Papers.

Written with one eye on the foundation and the other on the Church, Kilgo's arguments were carefully drawn. He plainly described the Trinity Board as "self-perpetuating." Yet, the Church "owned" the college. He devoted considerable space to the need for spiritual influence in any college and upon the inability of secular institutions to provide it. But he conceived the Church's primary role as that of representing the public in bringing to the college an awareness of the public interest. Finally, he criticized the Carnegie policy, which in effect discouraged church organizations in their educational work. "The conditions of the nation call for more, not for less, educational effort. . . ."[90]

Kilgo probably was not making a vigorous appeal for Trinity's inclusion in the pension plan, even if he sought to counter the Carnegie argument for exclusion. His remarks received the approbation of the Methodist papers in North Carolina. If the example of Randolph-Macon was not influential upon him, his own argument of Christian education provided no force for a move to separate Trinity and religion. Nor is it likely that he wanted another fight in the Church; there had been so many in recent years. To safeguard Trinity from the interference of the two Conferences was one thing; to remove the college from the Church was another. In its relations with education and religion, Trinity would wish to have the best of both worlds.

University Dreams—and a New President

If Trinity were ineligible for Carnegie pensions, the college received sufficient encouragement to dream rather vaguely of a future that might lie ahead. Pritchett and his staff encouraged Kilgo about Trinity's standards and praised its objectives, as did others who surveyed the national scene.[91] As early as 1906 Kilgo began to talk of Trinity's eventually becoming a university. At the General Conference in Birmingham he had discussed the idea with friends[92] and later asked T. N. Ivey to indicate in the Raleigh Christian Advocate "a wider field for Trinity." In 1908 the North

90. *Report of the President*, May 1, 1908, pp. 8-21.
91. See, for example, Lyman Abbott (editor, *The Outlook*) to Donald P Mackay, Jan. 2, 1907; H. S. Pritchett to Kilgo, June 25, 1907; John G. Bowman (secretary of the Carnegie Foundation) to Kilgo, July 22, 1909. Trinity College Papers.
92. James A. Duncan and William E. Thompson to Kilgo, both letters May 24, 1906, Kilgo Papers.

Carolina Conference chose to include Trinity with Vanderbilt under the classification of "universities." Aside from the desire for university status, hardly forgotten since the time of Crowell, there were pressures on the campus of which Kilgo was aware. His faculty was trained in the research tradition, but its time was given almost wholly to teaching. The library grew slowly, and there were few graduate students, only ten of them in 1910. Perhaps Boyd personified the university man as well as any of the faculty, and he complained frequently to Bassett and others of the handicaps to scholarly work. He liked both teaching and research, he said, but Trinity made possible very little of the latter.[93] It was a common problem across the country. At Columbia, historian James Harvey Robinson heard it "from every hand." Even at Columbia, he said, "most of us have to be teachers and little else, for that is as yet the generally accepted notion of the duties of a college professor."[94]

In another way the college was moving toward the attitudes that might characterize a more complex institution; it was becoming more organized itself.[95] By 1905 the officers named in the by-laws were being listed as "officers of administration." In 1907 Trinity was getting out news releases of important events, and student correspondents for various papers formed their own campus organization. By 1910 an advisory board of the faculty was dividing the freshmen into small groups to give them academic counseling. A few years earlier student health service was provided by an arrangement with Watts Hospital. And the number of faculty committees grew as the number of student organizations expanded. Soon there was a glee club touring the state and an orchestra for home concerts. There was still no intercollegiate football, but an active program in other sports, especially baseball, made an athletic council seem necessary. Clubs for students interested in German ("Deutscher Verein") or in literature ("The Fortnightly") were formed, and a decline in the role of the ancient literary societies led to a student newspaper under their sponsorship. The first issue of the *Trinity Chronicle,* a weekly, appeared in December, 1905. It was a sign of the times that one of the sorest needs of the college in 1907 was an administration building.

93. Boyd to Bassett, March 1, 1910, Bassett Papers.
94. J. H. Robinson to Boyd, June 24, 1908, Boyd Papers.
95. Summary from the Trinity College catalogues; the *Advocate*; and from the *Trinity Chronicle*, 1905-1910.

As the General Conference of 1910 neared, and as it was increasingly apparent that Kilgo would receive his bishopric, events seemed to accelerate the larger designs of the college. Architects were drawing up a campus plan that involved the realignment of some existing structures and the erection of new ones. The major alterations would be the removal of the old Washington Duke Building and the substitution of a new tower and cloister in its place. At the East and West ends of the cloister would be twin wings, one an "academic," the other an administration building (the present East and West Duke Buildings). By the time of Kilgo's last commencement work was underway on the first, the West, of the two wings. To meet increasing enrollments, additional dormitories were also in the planning stage.[96]

As 1909 was the fiftieth year of the college under its present name, discussions of the anniversary served to focus attention on institutional problems. The alumni association asked for a stronger organization to stimulate interest in Trinity.[97] Enrollments had boomed, especially in state institutions, and there were those who felt Trinity was being left behind. The college's public relations seemed to be ailing. The editor of the Raleigh *Christian Advocate* saw it as a "sad fact" that Trinity was not growing fast enough. He also observed in North Carolina "a spirit of indifference, and almost hostility" from some who should have been the college's friends. He detected floating rumors, "misconceptions as to [Trinity's] true character" and "false reports as to its management."[98]

A more specific analysis came from the trustee, John F. Bruton

> There is a feeling in the Church that Trinity College does not need help or support; that it is independently rich in funds and brains; that the high standard set for entrance precludes the many and therefore includes necessarily a limited number. While all these things are in a measure true, yet something must be done to prompt our people to accept and stand by their own, and the biggest thing to them, to wit: Trinity College.[99]

E. C. Brooks was asked to work up an alumni organization plan and soon presented his own analysis of Trinity's constituency. A roster of alumni was compiled, and county organization

96. *Minutes*, Executive Committee; B. N. Duke to Kilgo, Dec. 6, 1909 Appendix, Report of the President, June, 1910, Trustee Records.
97. Petition, June 9, 1908, Trustee Records.
98. Raleigh *Christian Advocate*, Aug. 6, 1908.
99. John F. Bruton to Kilgo, July 14, 1908, Trinity College Papers.

were developed. Particular attention was given to collecting information about outstanding alumni with the hope of preparing a biographical dictionary. At this time, Brooks reported, there were 3,000 living alumni. In all, there had been 5,000 Trinity students; 935 had taken degrees. He counted 220 alumni in Durham.

Brooks, too, was concerned about the public attitudes toward Trinity. He complained of a lack of understanding, some of it based on hostility, some on ignorance. The alumni, he said, should be informed of the college's academic standing. He said that the Carnegie report (of which the college had been so proud) had for the first time acquainted some alumni with the facts about "the strength of Trinity College." Unfortunately, in North Carolina, he said, people were confused about educational standards. Trinity also faced a dilemma in its denominational tie, Brooks said; some people believed the Church connection meant "Sunday school rules" on the campus. On the other hand, some churchmen saw the college drifting from righteousness. In the process, too many people wrongly believed Trinity to be a second-rate institution. An organized alumni body could deal with this. He asked:

> Is Trinity College a leader among the colleges of the state? Ask the elementary schools of the state what institution was first to advocate a six months public school term? Ask the high schools of the state what institution was the first to move up out of their way and lend them assistance long ago when it meant a loss of numbers; ask the Carnegie Foundation what institution takes the lead in scholarship in the state; ask other institutions of learning what is their standard of teaching and compare the methods of reaching the student body. . . .[100]

By 1910 Brooks could report the establishment of "educational days" in the Church districts, reminiscent of Crowell's mass meetings. The aim was to provide a forum through the Church organization for the spreading of the word about Trinity.[101] The trustees directed Kilgo to prepare a lengthy brochure. It contained highly favorable estimates of Trinity's work by various leaders in North Carolina.[102] Finally, the phrase "Greater Trinity" came into vogue by 1910, and the students organized a Greater

100. Notes and manuscript, "The Constituency of Trinity College," 1909, Brooks Papers.
101. *North Carolina Christian Advocate*, March 24, 1910.
102. *Bulletin of Important Facts* (Durham, 1909).

Trinity Club to promote a larger enrollment and to advertise the college in general.[103]

How did the local estimates compare with outside professional judgment? At this time one of the first serious attempts was made, by the federal Bureau of Education, to classify colleges on a qualitative basis, and the results were distributed "semi-confidentially."[104] Institutions were placed in one of four classes, depending upon an estimate of the additional preparation their graduates would need in order to earn master's degrees at the graduate centers. Fifty-nine institutions received a Class I rating; three Southern institutions, Vanderbilt, Texas and Virginia universities, made Class I. Trinity, and 160 others (25 of them Southern) were given Class II ratings, indicating that their graduates would need additional preparation, ranging from an extra course or two to as much as an additional quarter. The lower two ranks included 124 institutions thought to be one to two years below standard. Trinity would not have been happy with its classification, but there is no record of comment locally. Perhaps the college was unaware of the study. On some campuses, however, there were violent protests; ultimately, President Taft had to ask that the study be suppressed. As its author commented, " 'the bureau learned that there are no second and third and fourth class colleges; that it was an outrage and infamy so to designate institutions. . . .' "[105]

Simultaneously with the drive to promote the college came another suggestion that Trinity move into medical training. A physician from Durham, Dr. Joseph Graham, spearheaded a movement to secure from George Watts, the Dukes' partner, the old Watts Hospital property near the campus. He recommended training programs in medicine, dentistry, and pharmacy. The Executive Committee was willing, if an endowment of $300,000 could be obtained,[106] and there was a flurry of erroneous reports that Trinity had the money in hand. Like the woman's college, this venture lay on the shelf, awaiting resources.

The culmination of events and ambitions of these years made

103. Raleigh *Christian Advocate,* May 19, 1910.
104. Kendric C. Babcock (Specialist in Higher Education, United States Bureau of Education), *A Classification of Universities and Colleges with Reference to Bachelor's Degrees* (Washington, 1911).
105. William K. Selden, *Accreditation: A Struggle Over Standards in Higher Education* (New York, 1960), pp. 46-47.
106. Telegram, Joseph Graham to B. N. Duke, Sept. 20, 1909, Trinity College Papers; and *Minutes,* Executive Committee, Nov. 22, 1909.

a bold move forward essential. A more complex organization, some zeal for larger enrollments, and hopes for a woman's college and medical programs isolated the urgent need, more endowment. It was timely to turn to a foundation.

Since the Civil War Northern philanthropy had been available to Southern education. Funds started with a desire to stimulate Negro education later embraced all education, secondary and collegiate. There had been the Peabody Fund, the Slater Fund, and at the turn of the century, a group of conferences and funds known collectively as the Ogden movement. Robert Curtis Ogden, in consultation with men such as Walter Page and others, sought thereby to help stimulate the Southern educational revival.

By 1902 John D. Rockefeller had established his General Education Board, which had many charitable aims, not the least of which was to help Southern education. The G. E. B., with large resources, tended to sweep into its operation many of the men, including Ogden, and many of the objectives of the earlier, smaller agencies. By 1907 it was interested especially in colleges and universities and had assets of twenty million dollars. The G. E. B. developed a policy of making matching gifts to institutions in an effort to stimulate local initiative and to help insure the collection of sums far larger than its own initial gifts. The foundation believed firmly in institutional solicitation: "'People bleed more easily after a vein has been opened.'" Unlike the Carnegie board, the G. E. B. favored a hands-off policy as to college control and fostered "constant and sympathetic cooperation" with denominational organizations. The ultimate criterion was the promise of the individual institution.[107]

By 1909 Trinity's hopes had crystallized into a goal of one million dollars for endowment, and Kilgo turned to Wallace Buttrick, secretary of the G. E. B. The aim of the college was to pay higher salaries and increase the faculty, especially in the sciences. Trinity asked for $300,000. An additional $500,000 would then be forthcoming (from the Dukes), and the college would ask other friends for the remainder. Kilgo conceded that it was a large undertaking, but told Buttrick, "the conditions of Southern education demand that some colleges commit them-

107. *The General Education Board: An Account of Its Activities, 1902-1914* (New York, 1915), pp. 3-17, 103-159. See also Raymond B. Fosdick, *Adventure in Giving: The Story of the General Education Board* (New York, 1962).

selves to large enterprises." Trinity was turned down in 1909, but Buttrick was encouraging about the future. By early 1910 the Trinity application was on the G. E. B. docket, and Buttrick promised Kilgo it would be a special item in the fall.[108]

Trinity's president, however, was nearing the end of his tenure. The General Conference of the Church was held in Asheville in May, 1910, and this time Kilgo was not to be denied. Six bishops had died, and there were seven vacancies to be filled. Kilgo's vote at the previous Conference made him a front runner, and an honorary degree from Tulane a few weeks before did no harm. He was elected on the first ballot.[109]

Who would succeed him? The record provides little discussion on the subject, and it is probable that little was necessary. William Preston Few had been dean since 1902, a position Kilgo had looked upon as that of vice-president. Few had served as the perennial administrative head in Kilgo's frequent absences. He was Kilgo's choice, surely, and was thought to be Ben Duke's also.[110] In his fourteen years at Trinity, Few had come to know Ben Duke well, and perhaps the two shared similar personal traits. Through his position as dean, Few corresponded frequently with Duke, informing him of Trinity's progress and her hopes. He was not Kilgo, nor sought to be. He once thanked Ben for a gift to Trinity in this fashion: "You will not expect to get anything like moral or religious consolation from me, but it is one of the legitimate satisfactions of a successful man's life to feel that he has been able to set forces at work that will continue to bless men after he has ceased to work and will keep his memory green through countless generations."[111]

Few was less well known to the Trinity alumni than he might have been, but he had an academic reputation. Among his supporters was Wallace Buttrick of the G. E. B., who had recommended him for a university presidency in the Midwest. Since 1898 Few had been active in the work of the educational commission of the General Conference of the Church and later in that group's efforts to improve the standards of Methodist colleges. In recent years he probably had been the most frequent contributor to the *South Atlantic Quarterly*, writing, for the most part, on educational subjects.

108. Kilgo-Buttrick correspondence, April 9, 1909–May 6, 1910, Trinity College Papers.
109. *North Carolina Christian Advocate*, May 19, 1910.
110. See note 113 below.
111. W. P. Few to B. N. Duke, Dec. 24, 1898, Trinity College Papers.

In summation, there seems to have been no movement against Few's election, although he suffered badly in comparison with Kilgo as an orator—as did most everyone. A few of Brooks's friends hoped the professor of education might be elected,[112] but one trustee was quoted as saying that Ben Duke's preference was strong in this case and that Few was the man.[113] He became Trinity's fourth president on June 6, 1910, and made the earnest pledge "to do my level best to make the College serve in all possible ways the causes of men." At the same time Cranford was named dean to succeed him, and Flowers was elected to a new post, Secretary of the Corporation. Both men enjoyed great popularity with the students and the alumni.[114]

From the day of his election as bishop, Kilgo's friends in Durham insisted that he continue to live there, and the trustees decided to build a Bishop's Residence for him on the campus. There were similar overtures from Charlotte, but Kilgo chose Durham. The trustees also elected him to membership on the Board—and on the Executive Committee. After so many years of excitement and success, inseparable from the personality of the leader, it seemed hard to let him go altogether.

In his farewell to the college, Kilgo rejoiced in the years of progress and in the "high-minded, unselfish, sincere, wise and pure-souled men" who had made up the faculty. In all their deliberations, he said, there had been frank expression and free discussion. Nor could he recall a single instance of student disloyalty to him. He was grateful to the Board for its support and hoped the trustees understood Trinity's great opportunities. "Your college is the gateway to a greater South." He congratulated the faculty on the new leader just elected. The Board was reconciled to his leaving only by the belief that he would continue to serve the college.[115]

112. N. R. Reid and Harry Howell to Brooks, May 17, May 18, 1910, Brooks Papers.

113. A friend of Brooks quoted Dred Peacock, then a trustee, as having said that Few was the choice of the Dukes; that "anybody acquainted with things knows that the man whom the Dukes want will be elected." Harry Howell (superintendent of schools, High Point, N. C.) to Brooks, May 18, 1910, Brooks Papers. Some trustees went to the meeting to vote for Few "with reluctance," but when they learned that Kilgo and Duke both were strongly supporting him, their attitude changed. E. C. Register to Kilgo, June 11, 1910, Trinity College Papers.

114. Trustee Records, June, 1910; interview, B. S. Womble, March 15, 1960.

115. Letter to the Board, and the reply, June 3, 1910, Trustee Records; letter to the faculty, June 9, 1910, Trinity College Papers.

Chapter VI

Few: Patience and Tenacity

1910-1918

To sit in the president's chair at Trinity College from 1910 to the end of the World War was to preside over disappointment and uncertainty. Rising enrollments proved costly. With the former president in residence, and on the Board, the power structure was ambiguous. There was a crisis with the Church and a sorry period of personal bitterness. The years called for a chief executive with patience and tenacity, two enduring qualities in the character of the new president.

William Preston Few was born on December 28, 1867, in the rural community of Sandy Flat, South Carolina.[1] He was the son of a physician and grew up in "genteel poverty," in some contrast to the grinding need that had been Kilgo's lot. Few's was a boyhood marked by affectionate family ties, especially with his mother, by an early commitment to the Methodist Church, and by recurrent poor health. He attended local schools at Greer, whither the family moved when his father established a drug store there. He graduated from Wofford College in 1889, then taught school in an academy for a term and for the next two years returned to Wofford to teach in the college's preparatory school.

The young Few was a quiet, somewhat withdrawn youth. His frequent invalidism contributed to an early fondness for reading and to an almost precocious solemnity. He was introspective, analytical, sensitive to a certain social weakness, yet anxious to do something about it: "A man ought to try to be as symmetrical in character as he can. . . ." He seems early to have found within himself and his religion a capacity for accepting the pain in life. While a junior at Wofford he was advising his sister that he had adopted as his philosophy: "to bear is to conquer our fate."

1. Summary following from Robert H. Woody (ed.), *The Papers and Addresses of William Preston Few* (Durham, 1951), especially the editor's "Biographical Appreciation," pp. 3-18. Cited hereinafter as Woody, *Few*. Also, William Preston Few Papers (Duke University Library), *passim*.

Later he was fond of Carlyle's injunction to "learn to devour the chagrins of your life."

Inspired perhaps by one of his former high school teachers, Few decided to do graduate work in English and went to Harvard in 1892, receiving his Ph.D. in 1896. His chief mentors were F. J. Child and G. L. Kittredge. There was a strong emphasis upon the heavy Germanic approach to literature and modern languages, the fields Few studied. His thesis was "On the *-ing* Suffix in Middle English with Special Reference to Participles and *-ing* Verbals." He did well at Harvard, in spite of the cold winters and sporadic periods of eye trouble, but modern scholarship, as he found it in Cambridge, left him with dissatisfactions. Even at Wofford he had concluded that "not all, or even the best part, of our education is gotten from books." In later years he was steadfastly disenchanted about the absolute virtues of the training of the specialist. Few seems to have passed over the hurdles of scholarship without quite enjoying the exhilaration. Later as president his abiding concern about character in education supported his hesitancy about training that was "thinly speculative."

But Few was entirely aware of the need for educational reform and had played a major role in Trinity's demand for standards in the South. He came to the college in 1896 as the first "second man," joining Mims in the English department. When he became president in 1910 he had lived through fourteen years of Trinity's battles. As dean for eight years he had occupied a position of responsibility. With Kilgo standing out front, another public figure would have been superfluous, but there had been great need for attention to academic administration. This was a quiet labor for which Few was fitted, and it had long been his role at Trinity. When he became president at the age of forty-two, his ideas were already developed by time and experience.

The inauguration of the new president, on November 9, 1910, was a considerably more elaborate event than such occasions had been in earlier years.[2] The decision for ceremony was not Few's. It may have seemed necessary to introduce properly a new personality, especially since the former president was to continue to live on the grounds and to serve on the Board of Trustees. The mayor of Durham issued a proclamation heralding the occasion,

2. *The Inauguration of President William Preston Few, Trinity College, November 9, 1910* (Durham, 1910), *passim.* Cited hereinafter as Inaugural Volume.

and a special train was provided for the out-of-state guests. The little college drew an impressive assemblage. The presidents of Harvard, Chicago, and Clark were in attendance, as were the deans of Yale and Princeton, and the United States Commissioner of Education. The procession mounted the steps of Craven Memorial Hall to a chorus of "How Firm a Foundation." At the president's luncheon the guests ate oysters, filet, and squab and later attended a reception at the home of Mr. and Mrs. B. N. Duke. All of the dignitaries were photographed, and the entire program was done up in a handsome volume.[3]

When Few was inducted into office by Bishop Kilgo, the ceremony served to emphasize certain differences between the two men. Kilgo spoke for ten minutes. He congratulated Few upon "coming into the possession of such a large organ through which to express your thought and faith. . . ." He declared that there was now a devoted Trinity family and a spirit of unity, speaking with certainty "out of a good and somewhat vigorous experience."[4] In his inaugural address Few dwelt on a few basic themes, discussing ideas that he had slowly and carefully developed over a period of years and from which he was never to depart.[5] He was absorbed in ideals and universals, freedom and democracy, service and courage, religion and character. Always he found extremes unpalatable.

In one form or another much of the speech dealt with freedom and its necessary relation to democracy. Surely, "to contemplate human life with any degree of patience, one must believe that the people wish to do right and in the long run and in the main will do right. . . ." But the people cannot manage a college, and in a democracy they are susceptible to waves of hysteria and to alarmist leaders. The colleges must serve as bulwarks against which passions "beat in vain." For many years Trinity had been teaching this doctrine, he said, and now there was more freedom in the South, but always there would be a need to stand up and be counted. Trinity, then, as in the past, "will always throw itself unreservedly into the doing of the supreme duty of the hour." At the same time she shared with other colleges a major problem —how to lead and yet retain the sympathy of the people.

3. *Ibid.* Ben Duke thoroughly enjoyed the occasion: "The day was perfect and the exercises attractive. . . . I felt prouder of Trinity than ever before." B. N. Duke to R. B. Arrington, Nov. 11, 1910, Trinity College Papers.

4. Inaugural Volume, pp. 27-33.

5. *Ibid.*, pp. 47-56. The address also appears in the *South Atlantic Quarterly*, X (Jan., 1911), 1-8; and in Woody, *Few*, pp. 284-293.

Rather clearly, Few outlined his worries about rampant democracy and how it might endanger colleges. He was impatient with the "vicious doctrine of numbers," wherein colleges were tempted to court public favor by striving for bigness. He warned of another situation. College athletics "and equally irrelevant undergraduate absorptions" were coming under the tyranny of public opinion and were "tending to obscure the true ends of a college course." He was proud and hopeful of the new industrial strength of the South but concerned that materialism could obscure higher aims. "Greed is already perhaps our characteristic national vice, and it does not need the fostering of education."

He registered his reservations about the higher learning. Colleges do not need teachers who are experts so much as they need "men of ideas and power." He had respect for the search for truth, but it was not the main end of a college education. "An undergraduate ought not to be ever learning, and never able to come to the knowledge of truth," he suggested. "The thin air of high speculative knowledge cannot nourish hardy and robust manhood. . . . Some things, after all, are known, and there is no need for a man to stop and build his own bridge every time a bridged river crosses his path."

As to the church, the wise Southern college would work with the powerful forces of religion. At Trinity the union of religion and education was complete and inseparable. Yet Few spoke not of Christian education (the words did not appear in his speech), but of a "religion that comprehends the whole of life. . . ." The Southern college's duty was that "of mediation between the religious conservatism of this region and the great intellectual ferment of the age." Here, as in all things, the aim was to keep the good of the past and adapt it to the need of the present.

Essentially the message was one of service and balanced idealism. Trinity must devote herself to doing "the hard tasks of society." True education was a matter of character and efficiency. There was no impatience to become a university or even a big college, but, he concluded, "we are immensely concerned that [Trinity] shall be a shining place where high-minded youth may catch aspirations to true character and genuine excellence. . . ."

The speech represented no abrupt departure from what Trinity audiences had been accustomed to hearing. It was natural that this should be so. Kilgo and Few had worked together for many years; they would do so in their new relationship. Nor did

Few conceal his belief that Kilgo had long been a source of inspiration to him. He said once that only his father had more influence upon his life.[6]

The difference lay in the emphasis of Few's words. When Kilgo spoke of problems he was accustomed to exhort, to call for battle. His quick fluency often seemed just a phrase ahead of his thought. Few's remarks were carefully prepared, predigested. The effect was an invitation to reason and the delivery an apparent musing aloud.[7] The contrast reflected two personalities. Kilgo was volatile, aggressive, full of nervous energy. Few was ever quiet, slow to excitement, characteristically imperturbable. The distinction is well stated by his biographer.

> One cannot imagine him waving his arms and shouting to the crowd in a crisis some such phrase as 'we stand at the crossroads of destiny. . . .' He would more probably have thought that we stand always at the crossroads and should have with us constantly a strong faith and a steady courage—that never was the time for excitement.[8]

Whatever his poise and experience, it is doubtful if the new president felt complete self-assurance during his first years. As dean he had held a secondary role in over-all management, and financial matters and the problems of a building program were new and troublesome. He frequently complained of being overwhelmed, and he was slow to give leadership to his Board of Trustees.[9] Kilgo's experience and presence close at hand were reassuring. Moreover, Few would continue to deal with an experienced Executive Committee, also close at hand. Kilgo had replaced John F. Bruton; all the others were from Durham and had served for many years. In 1910 the membership was: Southgate, the chairman; Ben Duke; J. E. Stagg, a successful businessman and former aide to Duke; G. W. Flowers, father of Robert L. Flowers; and C. W. Toms, the first of a series of able Durham school officials whom the Dukes had brought into their enterprises. At this time Toms was managing the Durham branch of the American Tobacco Company. His interest in Trinity and his intimacy with the Dukes were to prove to be great assets to the college.

6. Unpublished statement, Dec. 14, 1914, prepared by Few following the "Buffalo" incident discussed below. Few Papers.
7. The generalization holds for most of Few's writings. Speeches, Few Papers.
8. Woody, *Few*, p. 110.
9. Few Papers, especially *ca.* 1911-1912.

Ruins of the Washington Duke Building ("Old Main"), January, 1911

"Ole' Marse," salvaged from the ruins of the Washington
Duke Building, in its bell tower near
Crowell Technological Building

In addition to relying on existing sources of support, Few ried to build an administrative organization which would permit 1im to delegate. By the end of his first year the duties of Flowers 1s secretary and Cranford as dean had been outlined. Flowers vas given charge of records, much institutional correspondence, 1dmission details, and soon, responsibility for business administra-ion. Cranford was in charge of student discipline and chairman of the faculty in Few's absence.[10] Few also asked Wannamaker, 1nce his student in the Wofford preparatory school, to assume 1xtra academic duties. Wannamaker assisted Cranford and was 1elpful in admissions but also immediately received appointments 10 the major faculty committees, those on courses of instruction, 1dmissions, and the executive committee of the faculty. By 1912 Few was assuring him that his services made him a *de facto* col-ege officer.[11]

Kilgo had referred to the unity of the Trinity family, and loubtless some of the old scars were beginning to heal. But Few vas aware that a great deal more could be done. He was ambi-ious to make it clear that Trinity was heartily in agreement with 1he growing educational movement, and he insisted that Trinity vas "as much a North Carolina institution as if it were supported 1y public taxation. . . ."[12] He worked hard for school legislation 1nd was untiring in efforts to place Trinity men in educational 10sts throughout the state—greatly aided in the total effort by 10th Brooks and Edgar W. Knight (Brooks's understudy whose listinguished career as the historian of Southern education was vell underway at this time). Moreover, Few made a point of get-ing to the Church Conferences and was quick to state Trinity's letermination to support Methodist aims. A related problem, 1lumni unity, was of particular concern after 1910 when fund rais-1g efforts were intensified. Few was pleased in 1915 when "a 1ermanent means of communication between the College and her 10ns," the *Trinity Alumni Register,* was established. There was 1ven a quiet gesture in the direction of Josephus Daniels; Few hanked him for his coverage of the 1911 commencement.[13] At

10. *Minutes,* Board of Trustees, June 5, 1911.
11. Few to Wannamaker, Sept. 26, 1912, Few Papers.
12. Few to Governor Locke Craig, Nov. 7, 1912, Few Papers.
13. Few to Josephus Daniels, June 12, 1911, Few Papers. Few also preserved 1nd strengthened Trinity's harmony with the Negro people. A leading colored 1ducator wrote him that friendly race relations in Durham and North Carolina

the end of his first year the new president was hearing voices of satisfaction from Trinity's friends.

The financial fortunes of the college after 1910 were erratic. Symbolic of the pattern was a fire that destroyed the old Washington Duke Building in the early morning of January 3, 1911. A recent rainfall prevented strong winds from igniting adjoining buildings.[14] The disaster left the old central tower standing. That edifice, which had fallen twenty years before, had been so well rebuilt that it took weeks of blasting finally to reduce it to rubble. The fire destroyed important records and worked a hardship on the current expense fund, but there were assets. Earlier the Executive Committee had decided to tear the building down to make way for the new East and West Duke Buildings. Fortuitously, now the job was done free of charge, and there was $40,000 worth of insurance. Immediately the college used the insurance to retire the bonds still outstanding from the mortgage of 1893.[15]

Meanwhile, the application to the General Education Board had been acted upon. Trinity was granted $150,000 (half of the request) if the college raised the remainder of the million dollar goal. Trinity had counted on a maximum of $500,000 from the Dukes and $200,000 from the Conferences; the reduction posed problems. Even the original proposal had been an ambitious one. Few and Buttrick negotiated for some months, eventually agreeing that about half of the college share might be counted in the value of the new buildings under construction, and the campaign was begun in the Church and among the alumni.[16] A complica-

---

were "due now more to the influence of Trinity than any other agency." James E. Shepard to Few, April 6, 1912, Few Papers.

A suggestion of how widespread was the rancor that Few inherited is seen in the following: "I sometimes think that my lot in life is to pour oil for Dr. Kilgo and Trinity College! When I was sent to Spring Garden Church, Greensboro, I had to follow in the tracks of Dr. [L. W.] Crawford. When I was sent to Walkertown, I found a constituency opposed to Dr. Kilgo, Trinity College and the American Tobacco Company. When I was sent to Winston, I had Mr. R. B. Crawford [L. W. Crawford's son] for my Sunday School Superintendent. When I was sent to Reidsville, I found that this is the home of Mr. John R. Webster's widow." W. A. Lambeth to Few, March 3, 1914, Few Papers.

14. *Trinity Chronicle*, Jan. 11, 1911.
15. *Minutes*, Executive Committee, Jan. 6, 1911.
16. Few-Buttrick correspondence, Oct. 27, 1910-June 10, 1911, Few Papers. The plan for a tower and cloister between the East and West Duke Buildings was abandoned. In 1910-1912 the two buildings were being completed, as were two new dormitories given by J. B. Duke. The new units helped form a quadrangle. The dormitories were named "Aycock" and "Jarvis," and Few recommended that the ground within the quadrangle be named "The Yard." *Minutes*, Executive Committee, Sept. 9, 1912.

tion was the inability at this time to secure a definite pledge from the Dukes. The dissolution of the tobacco trust had been ordered, and J. B. Duke was absorbed in the complications of that task. Later he went to England for several months. The college asked for and received an extension of time from the G. E. B. Finally, in the spring of 1913 Toms, who had moved to New York, advised Few that now was the time "to hit fast and hard."[17] The result was an announcement at commencement that the Dukes would guarantee $800,000. The college announced complete returns of $1,400,000 (in pledges) to be paid over a period of years. In the time-honored practice of such campaigns, the records reflect more a demonstration of success than fiscal exactitude,[18] and the sums actually received are not clearly evident. It appears that about one-third of the Dukes' gift was counted in the buildings they were financing. Pledges from others totaled some $150,000; yet by 1914 it appears that only $21,000 of this sum had been paid in cash.[19] The drive produced needed funds, but the returns in spirit and unity probably were as useful as the cash.

The fire and the campaign serve to emphasize the fluctuating financial history to 1918. On paper the college seemed to be moving swiftly ahead, but there were handicaps. One was the failure of dividends from the Virginia-Carolina Chemical Company stock, the security which had been purchased in 1898 in deference to a protest against tobacco stock. The protestants would have helped Trinity if they had encouraged the original investment. As early as 1914 the company was deferring dividends, and soon Trinity was suffering a loss of $10,000 per year.[20] The stock did not recover until 1918 and then only briefly.

Other circumstances were, on balance, unfavorable financially. Up to American entry into the World War, the college enjoyed an agreeable increase in enrollment. The new buildings were quickly filled. However, the students were charged the old tuition fee of fifty dollars per year, and many paid no tuition at all. As in Kilgo's day, the waiving of tuition was almost routine. From 1910 to 1916 enrollment increased by 60 per cent; for the same period income from tuition increased only 30 per

17. C. W. Toms to Few, March 24, 1913, Few Papers.
18. *Statement of the Trustees of Trinity College Called Forth by Recent Gifts* Durham, June 3, 1913), Trinity College Papers; Treasurer's Report, 1910 ff.
19. Treasurer's Report, 1914.
20. Few to W. R. Odell, March 27, 1915, Few Papers.

cent.[21] The larger numbers also meant higher maintenance costs and a larger faculty. Small annual surpluses tended to go into buildings and grounds. It was easier to secure single gifts from the Dukes for such purposes than to obtain funds which would have to be recurring, i.e., for salary increases. The new buildings were put up by the Dukes but had to be furnished by the college, and sometimes sums needed were borrowed on short-term notes. For the period the total assets rose from $1,400,000 to $2,500,000, but much of the increase was reflected in the increased value of the plant, not in income-producing investments. In fact, the college listed its dormitories as endowment because they yielded an income, some of which of course had to be applied to their operation.[22]

Like each of his predecessors, Few constantly sought to modify the old habit of giving free tuition, but the college and the clientele were used to it. In 1912 free tuition to seniors was stopped, and students were urged to borrow what they needed or get a part-time job. This last proved more difficult as larger enrollments increased the competition for work. There was an annual scramble in the fall for coveted posts such as flagraiser, bellringer, and (until the campus became fully electrified in 1913) lamplighter. In spite of all this activity, the Trinity student was a greater financial liability than an undergraduate college might reasonably expect to endure. In 1917 Few reported that for every dollar a student paid, he cost the college from six to ten dollars.[23]

Plainly, the financial situation did not provide hope for increased salaries. At the time of the endowment campaign Few had drawn up a dream for the future. He hoped for professors' salaries of $3,000.[24] It was not to be. The range was essentially constant, from a minimum of $1,600 to a maximum of $2,500 for full professors.[25] The significant improvement lay in the fact that more of the faculty began to receive pay near the top of the range. It is clear, however, that several were receiving promotions in lieu of cash. The pressure was apparent when the college entered the market for younger men. Few wrote Kilgo

21. Treasurer's Reports.
22. Few to James E. Dickey (president of Emory College), Feb. 4, 1913, Few Papers.
23. Few to J. H. Reynolds (president of Hendrix College), Feb. 13, 1917, Few Papers.
24. W. P. Few, memorandum, Trustee Records, 1912-1913.
25. *Minutes,* Executive Committee, 1910-1919.

that the time had passed when "a man who knows something about his subject and is somebody" could be hired for $1,200.[26] The first break in salaries came in the fall of 1917, when 10 per cent bonuses were voted for everyone. The bonuses were repeated in 1918 and 1919 and were provided from a small building surplus.[27] After 1919 the increases were funded by gifts from Ben Duke and his brother.

In spite of a tight budget, Few preached optimism to the constituency. Repeatedly he assured his friends that he saw no reason why the college ought not "in our lifetime to become one of the foremost colleges in the country."[28] Although it is doubtful if he had promises from the Dukes, he had constant evidence of their interest in Trinity. Aside from their regular annual payments, Ben and his brother continually gave sums for landscaping or land. In 1915 Ben Duke provided a granite wall that eventually surrounded the campus. Few was particularly grateful for Toms's friendship and aid. As a former educator and a successful businessman, Toms had the ability and opportunity to interpret the work of the college to the Dukes, and to James B. Duke in particular. He was a hardworking trustee, and Few saw to it that he was kept fully informed.

Perhaps on Toms's advice, Few adopted a policy of caution and patience. He did not believe it wise to ask J. B. Duke specifically for gifts, preferring "to let him see the growing needs of the College and then follow his own impulses."[29] He cautioned others against harassing the Dukes for aid. As early as 1915 Duke had asked Few for a statement of what Trinity was achieving. Few said later that during the next year he began to work "definitely" on a plan for a university.[30]

Kilgo, too, was encouraged about the future at this time. He wrote that he had been in New York, "and I had the chance to do some business, and I used my chance." He predicted, "if we will stay on our job and make things go as they should go we will some day come into a large estate of power and good."[31] In 1917 Few used his president's report to outline in detail Trinity's record since the move to Durham and sent a copy to J. B. Duke. He

26. Few to Kilgo, Aug. 29, 1916, Few Papers.
27. *Minutes*, Executive Committee, 1917-1919.
28. Few to W. A. Neilson, April 21, 1913, Few Papers.
29. Few to S. C. Morris, Feb. 15, 1918, *ibid.*
30. Remarks, opening of the fall session, Duke University, Sept. 16, 1931, Few Papers.
31. Kilgo to E. C. Brooks, July 27, 1915, Brooks Papers.

chose to review the recent history of the college, its influence on education in the state, its development since 1892, its commitment to religion, and its "habit, confirmed in the College through these twenty-five years, of standing alone when cherished causes are at stake. . . ." He paid "frank gratitude" to the Dukes, father and sons, for their support. The family influence always had been "on the side of truth seeking and truth speaking. . . ." He observed that, in contrast, sometimes a patron "has hung his own personality" about a college "like a body of death." He considered the inner impulses of men who gain wealth and power, contrasting selfish motives with the yearning to leave a memory of good deeds. He believed that the wealth of the country needed to be humanized. "The men who succeeded in America are victims in turn of overpraise and bitter denunciation. Colleges and educated men ought to hold a steadier light and become a more constant inspiration to the proper employment of wealth. . . ." He offered as goals for Trinity the perfecting of a model college and the serving of the public welfare.[32]

As early as 1913 Ben's son, Angier B. Duke, was elected to the Board of Trustees. By 1918 J. B. Duke had agreed to become the third member of the family to accept membership. Thus the family ties grew stronger, and the future, though vague, looked promising. Moreover, Few was never in doubt as to the role Ben Duke continued to play. During much of the years 1917-1918 Duke was ill and confined to a hospital. For months he received from Few a remarkable series of weekly letters, full of homely details about the campus and Durham. Few sent snapshots of landscaping projects in progress, wrote of the weather, crops and local marriages, and burdened Ben with no worries. Duke was inclined to be despondent at this time, and Few's letters brought a continuing refrain of reassurance. "Your life has not been in vain," he wrote. "It has set in motion forces that will continue to do good hundreds of years." Again, "I feel sure that Trinity College will keep your name alive a thousand years, and before you and I are through with it, we must do our level best to put it in the way to run its course without hindrance and beyond any chances of uncertainty."[33]

While the college awaited its future, it found it necessary to

32. *Report of the President,* June, 1917.
33. Few to B. N. Duke, Jan. 30, Nov. 30, 1918, Few Papers. Lengthy excerpts from the series appear in Woody, *Few.*

adjust the academic programs to the shifting scene in education. In the Southern Association the colleges were concerned about two problems, the number of conditions granted matriculants and the fields of study required for entrance.[34] In 1911 Trinity admitted students with as many as four conditions. In 1913, in accord with Southern Association action, the number was reduced to two. At the same time the entrance requirement in mathematics was increased to three units by adding a half-year of solid geometry and another half-year of plane geometry. Latin remained the required substitute for Greek. There were no other changes at this time, except an announced intolerance of any abuse of "elective" units.[35] In recent years the public high schools, now coming under the control of state inspectors, were offering a variety of vocational subjects. If a college did not prescribe most of the work to be counted in the fourteen units of admission, it found applicants submitting credits in bookkeeping, machine-tool training, woodworking, or domestic science. In 1911 some colleges were accepting work in twenty-four different subjects. This was possible if the colleges permitted many of the fourteen units to be electives. The number of different subjects one might offer for admission to Trinity was the lowest in the association (ten); only one of the fourteen units could be an elective.[36] Few was sharply critical of the vocational trend and believed the great intellectual need of the schools was a "concentration" of subjects.

By 1916 the faculty had completed a study of admissions and made further changes. There does not appear to have been a single group exerting influence in such work. More commonly, here, as in curriculum changes, individual faculty wishes reached Wannamaker; compromises and agreements were worked out under his influence and guidance.[37] The number of units was increased to fifteen, and there was a retreat from the solid geometry requirement. The new plan also marked a blow to Latin. For admission to the "B" program (where one substituted Latin for Greek), the student might offer the usual four units of Latin or two units each of French and German. Previously both Latin and the modern languages, six units in all, had been required. Finally, the changes made possible more admission electives, but

34. *Proceedings*, Southern Association, 1910-1913.
35. Trinity College catalogue, 1912-1913.
36. *Proceedings*, Southern Association, 1911, pp. 36-47.
37. Interview, W. T. Laprade, Feb. 27, 1961. Wannamaker was dean after 1917, but active in academic administration for many years before that date.

as in the past, electives had to represent advanced work in the required fields or work in the sciences and mechanical drawing.[38] Few was proud of the plan which he thought put the college into closer harmony with the public schools. He likened the faculty action to that taken twenty years before, and, as in 1897, the college printed a brochure of its new requirements for distribution to the schools.[39]

Meanwhile the faculty had been studying the requirements for the bachelor of arts degree. A revision in 1912 represented a swing of the pendulum concerning elective studies, in the direction of further restriction. The new scheme forced candidates into a concentration of subjects by creating a major of twenty-four hours and requiring twenty-four hours in two related minor fields. There were thirty hours of free electives. For the degree one still must have two years of English and a year of history, mathematics, and science. The change marked the beginning of the end of the reign of Greek and Latin. The old requirement in "A" was altered. Instead of two years of each of the classical languages, now one took one year of each. For the second year one was permitted to choose one language, omitting the other altogether. The aim of the major-minor program was to "guard against the evil effects of unrestricted choice," the faculty stated. Controls were kept in faculty hands; no elective could be chosen without the approval of the committee on courses, and the selection of majors and minors required the approval of the men who taught them.[40] The new schedule was in line with trends elsewhere. When the young Association of American Universities published a list of 119 colleges whose bachelor's degrees it regarded as equal to those of its own members, Trinity and eight Southern universities made the A. A. U. list.[41]

One other change represented the further decline of Latin and Greek. By 1915 students in the "B" program found it possible to avoid Latin altogether. One was required simply to take four courses in two foreign languages, choosing from Latin, German, and French—and Greek lost its ancient place of prominence. In

38. *Minutes of the Faculty,* Jan.-March, 1916 (Office of the Secretary, Duke University. Faculty minutes prior to 1911 were destroyed in the fire.); Trinity College catalogue, 1916-1917.

39. Brochure, *Trinity College Admission Requirements,* 1916-1917, Trinity College Papers.

40. *Minutes of the Faculty,* 1911-1912; Trinity College catalogue, 1912-1913; *Report of the President,* June, 1913.

41. *Proceedings,* Association of American Universities, 1913, pp. 56-62.

1912 the Southern Association noted that it had virtually disappeared nationally as a requirement for admission. Trinity's
hold on it for several additional years may have been sentimental.
By 1916 the professor of Greek, Charles W. Peppler, freely acknowledged that so few students came to Trinity with any knowledge of Greek that he was offering a beginners' course.[42] Wannamaker reported that the subject had vanished from the public
high schools and that only 28 of the 440 degree students at Trinity were taking it.[43]

Enrollments for the years to 1916, as noted earlier, rose steadily, from 334 undergraduates to 551. Graduate and law school
enrollments showed little change, both declining slightly for the
period and averaging 13 and 19 students respectively per year.
The college worked at the task of building up the law school but
under a permanent handicap. Students were disinclined to spend
two years in college preparing for law training at Trinity, whereas
a high-school education sufficed at other colleges. There seems
to have been less disposition to enlarge the graduate work. A
few awards were available, and advanced students might be
given duties as assistants, but Trinity was hardly ready for ex-
tensive graduate training. It was not until 1916 that a faculty
committee on graduate training was appointed.[44]

The size of the faculty tended to follow the growth in student
population. Faculty members increased from thirty-two to forty-
one. The additions consisted in the main of younger men who
came as instructors or assistant professors. There was an increasing need for assistants, and increases in the number of full professors came for the most part by promoting older staff members
from lower ranks. The additional staff was distributed throughout all departments, although Kilgo seems to have preferred to
build up three or four departments. He wrote Few at one
point, "We simply haven't the money to do what professors wish
and this is not a problem to be solved but a fact to be obeyed."[45]
Nevertheless, the trickle of new men tended to be directed to the
needs of the college at large.[46] The result was a necessity for

42. Trinity College catalogue, 1915-1916, p. 72.
43. Wannamaker to L. C. Glenn (of Vanderbilt), April 6, 1918, Few Papers.
44. Trinity College catalogues, 1910-1916. Glasson was the perennial chairman. Over the years to 1924 his associates on the committee were likely to be
Wolfe and Cranford. As the committee grew larger, Laprade and Paul M. Gross
were added.
45. Kilgo to Few, Aug. 30, 1916, Few Papers.
46. Trinity College catalogues, 1910-1918.

hard work by all hands, but no retreat from the ideal of the twelve-hour load.

One reason for the insignificant growth of graduate work is apparent in the record of library accessions. For the years 1910 to 1919 the library increased from 42,000 to 55,000 volumes, an average of some 1,400 volumes per year.[47] But the college did not buy that many volumes per year. In 1916 the library received 4,000 volumes from the estate of John M. Webb, the father of Professor Webb. During the next year a stream of books from the Far East began coming to Durham through the beneficence of James A. Thomas, a business associate of the Dukes who worked for many years in the Orient. The Webb library and the Thomas gifts were notable accessions, but they were not supplemented by purchases in sufficient quantity to establish the beginnings of a research library.

Trinity would for some years be preoccupied with undergraduate training, and a continued item of discussion was the co-ordinate woman's college. It will be recalled that in 1910 Kilgo suggested a location near the campus, the old Watts Hospital property. The Executive Committee soon found the site unsuitable. At the same time the new building program required the removal of the one residence for women students, the Mary Duke Building. Few and the Board were discouraged in 1911 and agreed that the admission of women had best be limited, perhaps "positively discouraged," until a co-ordinate college was in sight.[48] Within a year, however, the excitement of the endowment campaign revived the old interest, and the alumnae were active in asking for a co-ordinate college and in offering to try to finance it. Few agreed that at least a modest effort should be made. A local campaign for funds was a quick failure, but the trustees again agreed to endorse the idea and to authorize an approach to a foundation. In the summer of 1914 the college embarked upon an ambitious campaign. A Committee on the Organization of a Co-ordinate College for Women was established. The committee would seek funds for a year; if the money were in sight within that period, the effort would be continued for a second year.[49] Probably both Few and Kilgo were less than opti-

47. *Ibid.*; also Joseph Penn Breedlove, *Duke University Library, 1840-1940* (Durham, 1955), pp. 27-32.
48. Appendix, President's Report, Trustee Records, 1911; *Minutes*, Board of Trustees, June 5, 1911.
49. *Minutes*, Executive Committee, Aug. 21, 1914.

nistic; they had been through it all before. But Few saw nothing to do but go ahead. If it failed, he wrote, "then so far as my lifetime is concerned, I can look forward to no hope along that line."[50]

The college hired an experienced woman educator, Laura Drake Gill, former dean of Barnard, as executive secretary of the organizational committee. Miss Gill provided a brisk, businesslike approach to her task, and she seems to have been given a rather free hand.[51] She began negotiations with the General Education Board and, receiving encouragement there, approached the Dukes. The college approved a plan for four buildings and an endowment, the total cost to range from $380,000 to $645,000 depending upon the size of the buildings and endowment. However, Miss Gill was wont to seek a long range commitment. In a memorandum to Toms she outlined the need for an immediate $500,000 trust fund to be increased to $1,500,000 over a period of years. She offered a new idea of administrative control, by which the woman's college would have a separate endowment administered by a separate committee, only some of whom would be Trinity trustees. She was vigorous in her criticism of the present arrangements for women, which were, she felt, "haphazard" and "unspeakably dangerous to the social outlook of the women."[52]

It is possible that Miss Gill simply scared everyone to death. J. B. Duke was "very much opposed" and quickly told her that she was looking too far ahead.[53] Toms put her off with the excuse that the current business depression made it untimely to search for funds.[54] The plans were scaled down to a goal of $300,000. Few asked the G. E. B. for $100,000. The hope was to provide housing for 50 women and instruction for 125. The enrollment at that time was 92. Lacking any sign of support from the Dukes, the G. E. B. was cautious and postponed action for several months. Finally in January, 1916, Trinity was turned down.[55] The

50. Few to Kilgo, Aug. 14, Aug. 19, 1914, Few Papers. Earlier Few had tried to place the movement for a woman's college in perspective: "I do not consider that the education of women will probably ever be a primary obligation of Trinity College. Our main business is the education of men." *Report of the President*, June, 1912, p. 11.

51. Few-Gill correspondence, June 20, 1914–Sept. 17, 1914, Few Papers.

52. Laura Drake Gill to Toms and memorandum attached, May 15, 1915, Few Papers.

53. Toms to Few (telegram), Jan. 4, 1915; Gill to B. N. and J. B. Duke, Jan. 11, 1915, Few Papers.

54. Toms to Gill, May 21, 1915, Few Papers.

55. Few to Jerome Green and E. C. Sage, May, 1915–Jan., 1916. For the G. E. B. answer, Sage to Few, Jan. 31, 1916, Few Papers.

co-ordinate idea would not be revived until the enrollment of women increased after the war when the need for a dean of women became evident.

Although Few did not have the instincts of a crusader, he was a persistent, nettlesome critic of the evils of intercollegiate athletics. The theme was one he had long since made his own. As early as 1906 he was writing in the *South Atlantic Quarterly* of the "excessive devotion to athletics," linking it to the craze for bigness and attributing excesses in the South to the bad example of the Eastern colleges.[56] Trinity had joined the Southern Intercollegiate Athletic Association in 1902 and accepted its rules against professionalism and its eligibility controls. She was the only college in North Carolina and Virginia to remain in the association,[57] and Few was disposed to remind the universities of the two states of that fact. He believed that objections to joining the association were "nearly always disingenuous." He believed the colleges that would not adopt the rules were responsible for some of the glaring evils: playing men under assumed names, professional recruitment, and inducing athletes to transfer from one college to another. He lumped the "inducing evil" with all improper competition for students, athletes or not, and told an alumnus that Trinity would not "enter into any such scramble."[58]

It is significant to note that Few's efforts to heal Trinity's public relations could not be applied to university-Trinity relations so long as he campaigned as he did for athletic reform. He was not inclined to state his case and go on to other matters. In speeches and articles and in his president's reports he repeatedly expressed his indignation at the "tyranny of public opinion" that he believed brought on athletic excess.[59] He often stated that he always went "to headquarters" with important matters, and he frequently wrote F. P. Venable, the president of the University of North Carolina, or other officers there, protesting athletic policies that he believed to be wrong. When the university established a number of scholarships, said to be fashioned on the

56. *South Atlantic Quarterly*, V (Jan. 1906), 44-49; also VIII (Oct. 1909), 301-310.

57. The University of North Carolina was a member of the association from 1900 to 1902, dropping out because of the expense and distance involved in playing other member schools. Thereafter, the university and the University of Virginia were criticized as being "a law unto themselves." Louis R. Wilson, *The University of North Carolina, 1900-1930* (Chapel Hill, 1957), pp. 148-149. Cited hereinafter as Wilson, *U. N. C.*

58. Few to H. A. Dennis, Aug. 20, 1912, Few Papers.

59. For example, *Report of the President*, 1913, pp. 8 ff.; 1915, p. 6.

Rhodes' model and available to athletes, Few was unconvinced. He wrote a faculty member, "Can't you and others check the movement?"[60] In a speech to Trinity students in the Fall of 1913 he spoke warmly of abuses in the state, especially the sending out of scouts "to buy promising athletes."[61] He did not specify the guilty institutions, but when asked by Julian S. Carr (then president of the U. N. C. Alumni Association) just what he had said, he sent a copy of his manuscript and added:

> I shall no doubt have more to say hereafter. And if I should have occasion to call names and to make charges there will be no possible mistaking of my meaning.
>
> I have strong convictions on the subject; and as a man interested in educational conditions in the State I must, of course, be allowed perfect freedom to express my convictions. I believe that athletic conditions are growing worse rather than better. . . . You could do for the institution [U. N. C.] no truer service than to lighten the over-emphasis put upon athletics there, especially during the last two or three years. . . .
>
> I am not willing to be put in the light of meddling with other people's business. But the welfare of a college depends upon the public opinion that is back of it, and I am now profoundly concerned about improving public opinion at this point. Meantime you can be assured that I have not run amuck, and I am not going to.[62]

It was not surprising, therefore, that when Few asked a friend at the university to help in a movement to secure uniform admissions and athletic standards, he was told plainly that the university was quite willing to work at these problems but was reminded that "mutual confidence" was a prerequisite and that his, and Trinity's, attitude of "sharp hostility" made the idea impossible.[63]

The college continued to play no football, limiting itself to baseball and basketball. Trinity, too, apparently found it expen-

60. Few to A. H. Patterson, April 27, 1912, Few Papers. Patterson, a physicist, was then dean of the School of Applied Science.

61. Charlotte *Observer*, Sept. 22, 1913, p. 1.

62. Few to Julian S. Carr, Oct. 1, 1913, Few Papers.

Like other Methodists with university ties, Carr had long since dropped the earlier intimacy with Trinity. Apart from the Christian education campaign, there was no lack of other reasons: he was a friend and supporter of Daniels and a Democrat with political ambitions. Not least, in the course of time the Bull Durham brand joined the rest of the industry in the trust embrace.

63. Archibald Henderson to Few, Oct. 17, 1913, Few Papers. In 1921 colleges of the state organized the North Carolina College Conference to set uniform standards and to deal with other problems.

sive and troublesome to have to play the distant teams in the Southern Intercollegiate Athletic Association. In 1912 the faculty voted to withdraw from the S. I. A. A. for three years, meanwhile keeping the same regulations, in order to try to develop athletic relations with colleges nearby. The Athletic Council was instructed to make alliances only when they were certain to result in amateur competition. By 1915 a group of colleges in North Carolina had agreed upon rules which did not satisfy Trinity, but which she was willing to accept.[64]

In the meantime the students were perennially in some degree of discontent about the absence of football. There were recurrent protests, and in the fall of 1913 a demonstration on the campus that became a riot. The following spring the current "football club" offered a petition to the trustees, asking again for the reinstatement of football. The petitioners had polled each other and some of the alumni and reported wide sentiment for reinstatement. They felt that the college had suffered from the lack of the game. In any event, as loyal students their wishes should be considered "to some extent."[65] The reply was prompt. On Kilgo's motion, the Board replied that it was "unalterably opposed" and issued a public statement. There was a variety of evils in football: the danger of physical injury, the expense, the immorality in methods used to win victories, the sport's influence over the government of colleges, and the occasional "scandalous conduct" at the games. The peroration sounded very much like Kilgo:

> We have no regard whatever for the argument that [football] is a valuable means of increasing the number of students and as such a means commands consideration. As an argument this is beneath the dignity and the serious aims of an institution of learning. Colleges should be right, and the use of sports to gain the favor of youthful patronage is wholly inconsistent with the standards which the general public demands of a college. We trust that at least this college will never attract to itself a class of students that are even remotely influenced by its standing in athletic contests.[66]

Few believed the statement was bound to have a "tonic effect."[67]

64. *Minutes of the Faculty,* Dec. 5, 1912–Dec. 16, 1915.
65. *Minutes,* Board of Trustees, June 8, 1914.
66. *Ibid.,* June 9, 1914.
67. *Report of the President,* June, 1915, p. 6.

Church and Charter

While the college was resisting pressure for football, it was
trying to manage a serious crisis involving the old question of the
charter and the Church. Few did not echo the Christian education message of Kilgo and in fact tended to resist efforts to revive
it. He was unfitted for the role of campus exhorter that Kilgo
had played, although, like Kilgo, he was sensitive to any suggestion that Trinity was narrow in religion. When his friend, W. A.
Neilson of Harvard, recommended a candidate for the faculty at
Trinity as "open and tactful in religious and sectional matters,"
Few bridled a bit. There was no coercion at Trinity—political,
religious, or sectional. "We are known, I think, of all men for
this."[68]

However, Few was personally committed to religion and did
not want a faculty not "sincerely in sympathy with some one
branch of the Christian church."[69] Nor was there to be any
abrupt change at Trinity. The one-hour Bible course remained,
as did daily chapel. Few sought to emphasize Trinity's role of
service to Methodism, and he wished that role translated into
positive educational work. The department of Biblical instruction received constant support, as did activities related to it, the
Y. M. C. A. and the Ministerial Band (the pre-ministerial group).
Increasingly the aim was to persuade the Church to finance chairs
in Bible. The Conferences accepted the idea, and their annual
gifts were almost exclusively for this purpose during the period
1910-1918.

The college also brought its interest in secondary education
to bear upon the work of the Sunday schools. In 1912 Trinity
offered its campus for a Conference Sunday School Institute, and
by 1915 Edgar W. Knight (Brooks's understudy in education)
was providing courses for Sunday school teachers. Throughout
the period Trinity advertised the quality of its facilities for training young preachers and in 1918 offered summer school work for
preachers and religious workers.[70]

The troubles with the Church during 1913-1915 did not arise

68. Few to W. A. Neilson, Jan. 28, 1913, Few Papers.
69. *Ibid.*
70. Summary from Few Papers, *passim; Reports of the President,* 1910-1918;
Brochure, *Opportunities for the Training of Young Preachers* (Durham, *ca.* 1915),
Trinity College Papers.

from any swing to secularism. The cause lay in the turmoil at Vanderbilt. Over the passage of years Vanderbilt had become in the minds of many Church members a fully "connectionalized" institution, i.e., under the aegis of the entire Southern Church. By 1910, however, the Vanderbilt Board of Trust was resisting claims that the bishops and the General Conference had the right to veto its actions and determine its membership.[71] These were legal questions, and the Church was alarmed. She began to take a second look at the ties that bound other institutions to her. The General Conference of 1910 passed a rule that three-fourths of the trustees of all Church institutions must be Methodist and must be "confirmed, nominated or elected" by an official Church body. Schools and colleges not in conformity were urged to make the necessary changes in their charters and were advised to insert a "trust clause" by which the property of the institution was said to be held by the trustees for the Church. The changes were to become effective in July, 1912.[72]

At Trinity the action could be interpreted as a warning. One-third of her trustees were elected by the alumni, not the Church, and there had been nothing like a trust clause in the charter since Crowell's refinement of 1891. Accordingly, when in June, 1913, the Board issued a "manifesto" to celebrate the completion of the endowment campaign, additional comments were included. Trinity, the Board stated, was not sectarian or narrow, but the college should always avow its "unyielding faith in the Christian religion, its reverence for the Christian church in all its branches, and its belief in the Holy Scriptures as the volume of divine revelation."[73] The statement pleased L. S. Massey, editor of the Raleigh *Christian Advocate,* as well as Bishop Candler, and Few sent a copy to the Church editor at the central Methodist offices in Nashville, Tennessee.

By the fall of that year, Stonewall Anderson, the secretary of the General Board of Education of the Church, had found time to examine the Trinity charter. He noted its nonconformity with the Church "law" and asked Few about it.[74] Few, doubtless with Kilgo's aid, tried his hand at three drafts in making reply. In the final version he answered that the Trinity charter was the crea-

71. Mims, *Vanderbilt,* pp. 291-318.
72. *Journal of the Sixteenth General Conference of the Methodist Episcopal Church, South* (Nashville, 1910), pp. 326-328.
73. *Statement of the Trustees of Trinity College Called Forth by Recent Gifts.*
74. Stonewall Anderson to Few, Oct. 21, Oct. 30, 1913, Few Papers.

ure of both North Carolina Conferences. It had existed, to the
satisfaction of all, for many years. Any effort to change it would
be "an expression of bad faith." He stated that Trinity's Board
was wholly Methodist, as were the great majority of alumni, and
hat the college's loyalty to the Church was absolute. He reminded Anderson that Trinity now possessed a great deal of property, given in the belief that its government was stable, and very
little of it given by the Church. Yet the college had always been
eager to co-operate with Methodism. In an early draft he added,
and later deleted: "Is it too much now to request of you in return
hat you do us as little harm as possible?"[75]

Anderson did not pursue the correspondence, but the issue
came alive again the following spring. The Church had taken its
argument with Vanderbilt to law, and the Supreme Court of
Tennessee had ruled in favor of Vanderbilt. The Board of Trust
was deemed fully self-perpetuating and judged to hold final authority over the institution. One of the bishops wrote Few that
he decision "outraged the moral sense of the Church." At Trin-
ty it was recalled that Washington Duke's early endowment
gifts had carried with them a proviso that should Trinity cease
o exist "as a college of the Methodist Episcopal Church, South,"
he income would go to the Conferences in North Carolina. Few
notified Stonewall Anderson of this fact,[76] and on the same day
Kilgo wrote Ben Duke, suggesting that he and his brother issue
a public statement placing themselves on record in agreement
with the view of their father. He sent along a suggested version.
f this were done, Kilgo wrote, then "for all time there may be
no question" of the family approval of Trinity's tie to the Church.
The Dukes quickly agreed and accepted Kilgo's draft.[77] The
statement was given wide publicity throughout the Church. It
aid:

> Following the example of our father we wish to state that all
> of our gifts have been made to Trinity College with a distinct
> knowledge that it is the property and under the control of the
> Conferences of the Methodist Episcopal Church, South, within
> the bounds of the state of North Carolina, and it is to promote

75. Presumably the letter actually sent was the final draft, dated Nov. 12,
913. Other drafts are dated Nov. 4, Nov. 10, 1913. Few Papers.
76. Few to Anderson, April 15, 1914, Few Papers.
77. Kilgo to B. N. Duke, April 15, 1914; B. N. Duke to Kilgo, April 22, 1914.
Trinity College Papers.

the interest of the college under this ownership and government that we have made all of our gifts to it.[78]

A few weeks later the General Conference of 1914 assembled in Oklahoma City. The reaction to the loss of Vanderbilt was "the all-absorbing question." Now Methodists were asking how they could be sure they "owned" other institutions heretofore thought to be Methodist. The General Board of Education reported that almost all of the charters had been altered to conform to the law of 1910 and was directed to continue its work.[7] At this time the General Conference paved the way for the establishment of two connectional universities, Emory and Southern Methodist, and made sure their charters left nothing in doubt.

On occasion Trinity had been mentioned as a potential connectional university, but Kilgo and Few had resisted the idea. Nevertheless, what the college always feared came to pass in the summer of 1914—public analysis of the Trinity charter. It began with a letter to the *North Carolina Christian Advocate,* organ of the Western Conference, in which the author observed that Trinity's charter appeared to give its trustees all property rights. He asked for information. "This question is being privately discussed from one end of the state to the other."[80] Kilgo issued a reply in which he said that the charter was not new; it had merely been "codified" in 1903. He said, no, the Church did not own the college, but the two North Carolina Conferences did. The Conferences could, and on occasion had, refused to elect trustees. There could be no change in the charter without Conference approval. He cited the stipulation in Washington Duke's gifts and the recent statement of his sons. He leveled scorn on Vanderbilt, charging that the question of the Trinity charter had not come up until raised "to palliate the infidelity of Vanderbilt." He spoke of the "shameful fall" of that institution.[81]

The editor of the *Advocate,* H. M. Blair, soon received a number of rebuttals to Kilgo, but he closed the door to discussion in his columns. When Few thanked him, Blair replied, "I am sitting on the lid but I am convinced that something will have to be done."[82] In the meantime Few had been in correspondence with

78. *North Carolina Christian Advocate,* July 30, 1914.
79. *Journal of the Seventeenth General Conference of the Methodist Episcopal Church, South* (Nashville, 1914), pp. 209-213.
80. D. F. Carver in *North Carolina Christian Advocate,* July 23, 1914.
81. *Ibid.,* July 30, 1914.
82. Blair to Few (postcard), Aug. 18, 1914, Few Papers.

another critic of the charter, Robert R. Taylor, an alumnus and a banker in Gatesville. Taylor had studied the charter and was convinced that Trinity's trustees were clearly self-perpetuating. He believed the Church title "very defective."[83] Taylor developed his arguments in a letter to the organ of the East, the Raleigh *Christian Advocate.* He had found "hardly a shade of difference" between the Trinity and Vanderbilt charters. The Conferences merely held a right of confirmation of trustees; there was no real power to elect or to remove members of the Board. Nor was there a trust clause to guarantee ownership. He noted Kilgo's reference to the Dukes' endorsement of the Church connection and asked the uncomfortable question, "If the cloud over the title is not admitted, what harm can come of removing the suspicion?[84] Editor Massey saw no need for alarm but conceded that the legalities ought to be made more secure.

Few continued to correspond with Taylor, finally advising him sharply that he would only do harm by prolonging the argument. And he opened discussion with Massey. Few said he had talked to "a good many thoughtful and sincere people," and all believed that he "had better let the matter stand as it is." Massey was glad when "the little bluster" in the *Advocate* ended, but he tended to agree with Taylor. Few assured him Trinity would do what was right. On the eve of the annual Conferences, Massey was still fretting about the matter, and Few urged caution and deliberation. It was a bad time for any change, he said. Massey yielded. He recognized Few's concern that a change might "frighten off further financial contributions." He would not press it further.[85]

The General Board of Education had asked all Methodist Conferences to appoint commissions to examine and correct institutional charters. In the fall of 1914 the Western Conference did so, giving the group full power to act. Its membership was suitable to Trinity. Two of the three members were Trinity trustees; the third was a man friendly to Few and unsympathetic to the bishops' desire to run Vanderbilt.[86] The following year, the commission brought in various recommendations, none of them affect-

83. Taylor to Few, July 29, 1914, *ibid.*
84. August 6, 1914.
85. Few-Massey correspondence, Aug. 15–Nov. 12, 1914, Few Papers.
86. *Journal,* Western Conference, 1914. The commission members were W. R. Odell, F. M. Weaver, trustees; and H. H. Jordan, a minister whose son, B. Everett Jordan, was then attending Trinity. For his father's attitude, interview with another son, Charles E. Jordan, Feb. 1, 1961.

ing Trinity, and reported that "the rights of the Conference are fully safeguarded."[87] The Eastern Conference declined to take any action on the question of charters.[88]

Now the matter lay with the General Board of Education, of which Kilgo and Flowers were members. When Anderson reported the actions of the two North Carolina Conferences, noting that the Trinity matter was unresolved, the question was referred to a committee, of which Flowers was chairman. The committee reported that it believed no action was necessary "as it is assured that all rights of the Church will be fully protected."[89] Trinity had long since learned that the church relationship required her officers to be strong churchmen.

The "Buffalo" Trouble

In the charter question as in many other matters after 1910, Kilgo and Few worked together successfully. Kilgo's long experience at Trinity, his ties with the Dukes and the Church continued to be of benefit to the college and to Few. As a trustee he played an active role in the annual meetings. In the Executive Committee he provided a strong second voice of authority from the college. By early 1914 Kilgo's residence in Durham was proving taxing to him. His episcopal duties required constant travel, mostly to the West, and Durham was out of the way. He decided to move to Charlotte,[90] and in June, 1915, on Few's recommendation, the Board elected him president emeritus, a salaried position with the duties of advising and assisting the Executive Committee and the president.[91] He continued to hold membership on the Board and on the Executive Committee.

Before he moved from the campus Kilgo precipitated his last controversy at Trinity College. It was one of those petty incidents blown large by emotion, and it centered on student discipline. It led to Kilgo's final, sad break with the college.

It is probable that the two presidents did not agree precisely on methods of disciplining students. Kilgo instinctively used a

87. *Journal*, Western Conference, 1915, p. 40.
88. Few to W. R. Odell, Dec. 5, 1914, Few Papers.
89. *Bulletin*, Board of Education of the Methodist Episcopal Church, South, V (July, 1915), 62-64, 92.
90. Kilgo to Few, Feb. 14, 1914, Few Papers.
91. Trustee Records, June, 1915; *Minutes*, Executive Committee, June 10, 1915.

strong hand. As president he had warned students that he was "chief priest and coroner," and the students had put it this way: "Few catches 'em, and Kilgo shoots 'em."[92] After 1910 there was a hint that the retired president would not have dealt with the football riot of 1913 as patiently as had Few: "Such acute ailments call for quick treatment. The rest cure will not work."

Indeed, at least by the time he became a bishop, Kilgo had changed in a variety of ways. His old tolerance of liberal Biblical studies, "the higher criticism," had disappeared. When he sought to reconvert his old students, he met with difficulties: "There was a looseness about that liberty that we liked." Soon he was lukewarm to the unification of the Northern and Southern branches of the Church and later opposed it as vigorously as he had once supported it. To some of his old friends and former students, it was a tragic instance of lost leadership.[93] However, if there were undercurrents of serious disagreement at Trinity, on discipline or any other matter, they are unrecorded. It was not until 1914 and the "Buffalo" incident that a breach developed between Kilgo and the college.

On the evening of Thanksgiving Day two students hoisted a sophomore class pennant, bearing the numerals "17," to the top of the campus flagpole. The Bishop was in town and, as he often did, delivered a chapel talk next morning. Kilgo had long made much of Trinity's flagpole and the ceremonies attached to it; he had regarded it as another example of the college's national spirit, in contrast to Southern provincialism. He was angry at the "treasonable" act and challenged the sophomore class to find the guilty parties. He asked, "Are they sons of buffaloes?" (an old colloquialism for turncoats). "Are they the descendants of Benedict Arnold?" If the Trinity community did not find and drive out the culprits, he said he would "wash my hands of it forever."[94] The story quickly reached the newspapers, and the account emphasized his strictures against the sophomore class. His reference to buffaloes was made more pointed and more accusatory than it actually had been.[95] The sophomores held a meeting and replied

92. Interview, H. E. Spence, Nov. 13, 1959.
93. Interview, Gilbert T. Rowe, Sept. 14, 1959; also Garber, *Kilgo*, pp. 311-314, 318. Kilgo said that as bishop he held an "official influence" and did not have the right to express personal opinion. Kilgo to R. S. Hyer, July 26, 1910, Kilgo Papers.
94. Later the text of Kilgo's remarks was published. Charlotte *Observer*, July 1, 1917.
95. Greensboro *Daily News*, Dec. 1, 1914.

with a public statement. "No man of unbiased judgment could possibly interpret" the act as an insult to the flag, they said. It was not their duty to find the guilty parties. Besides, there was "no proof" that a sophomore had done it. Finally, they expressed resentment of Kilgo's words as "unwarranted interference by an outsider who occupies no executive position in the college management."[96]

Few soon prepared a statement, defending Kilgo and giving his exact words. He denied that in over four years the Bishop had ever been guilty of interference.[97] The statement was not printed, perhaps at Kilgo's request. Few replied to a number of parents and friends who inquired about the incident that it was "just another example of fervid oratory and sensational journalism."[98] There for a time the matter rested. Few and Kilgo continued to work together, even after the Bishop's move to Charlotte, but perhaps under some strain. Later Kilgo remembered his disappointment that the Board had taken no notice of the students' comments about him. He also advised Few "in perfect kindness and yet with all sincerity" that "the chief complaint among students and others concerns the matter of discipline. . . . Yea and nay are hard tasks to follow but they make the only right way at times. . . ."[99] In later months, if not before, faculty members felt free to approach Kilgo directly in Charlotte on financial and other matters. The existence of "two presidents" held inherent hazards.

More important, Kilgo was unwilling to forgive or forget. Apparently the two guilty students admitted the action but later withdrew their confession. In view of the admission, Kilgo wanted a retraction by the class of 1917 of their statement that there was "no proof." In March, 1917, he suggested as much to Few, who agreed and sought to secure a retraction.[100] The students, now seniors, refused, and Kilgo went into the board meeting of June, 1917, convinced that the members of the class should not receive their degrees. The chairman of the Board, James H. Southgate, had died some months before, and Kilgo was elected chairman at the opening session. Joseph G. Brown, a Raleigh

96. *Ibid.*, Dec. 2, 1914.
97. Statement, dated Dec. 14, 1914, Few Papers.
98. Few to E. C. Ivey, Dec. 4, 1914, Few Papers.
99. Kilgo to Few, Sept. 11, 1915, Few Papers.
100. Kilgo to M. B. Andrews, and accompanying statement, Dec. 14, Dec. 17, 1917, Kilgo Papers.

anker, was named vice-chairman. Few of course knew of Kil-
;o's attitude, but the students had met the academic require-
nents, and the faculty had approved the degrees. He duly
rought in the names for final approval. Kilgo was adamant.
;raduation from Trinity, he said, "should carry with it a moral as
vell as intellectual value." The class knew of the confessions
nd should repudiate their earlier statement. He would not vote
or the degrees. The Board overruled him and directed the vice-
hairman to sign the diplomas.[101]

In the ensuing proceedings, Cranford resigned as dean, and
Vannamaker was elected in his place. A committee recom-
nended that the post of secretary of the college, held by Flowers,
·e made second in rank only to the president. The full Board
ecided against the change, although the trustees gladly gave
'lowers a vote of approval. After the adjournment apparently
nost of the trustees went home. However, on the next day Kilgo
nd four other trustees met and abolished the office of secretary
nd elected Flowers vice-president.[102] During a commencement
athering Kilgo announced the administrative change.

The events at commencement were too exciting to keep, and
vithin four days the story was out in at least two state papers.
'he most elaborate account was by W. T. Bost, the Raleigh
orrespondent for the Greensboro *Daily News*. For several
nonths Bost had been receiving a monthly retainer from Trinity
ɔ publicize the twenty-fifth year in Durham. Presumably this
ist service was gratis. He had learned about the events in the
oard meetings and had of course attended commencement. His
ccount was ironic and largely critical of Kilgo. He observed that
: the class of 1917 had thought Kilgo impotent at Trinity, they
ad learned better. He described the Bishop as "the ruling spirit
f the executive committee which fixes salaries and isn't liable to
nake any mistakes in their apportionment."[103] Bost followed the
tory for a few days, reporting resentment of Kilgo among some
f the parents of the seniors. Later he picked up a rumor that
he Bishop would move back to Durham, become chancellor, and
ake over the college.[104]

As soon as the story appeared, Few prepared a statement of
xplanation. He wrote Kilgo in Charlotte that he had tried to

101. *Minutes*, Board of Trustees, June 4-6, 1917.
102. *Ibid.*, June 7, 1917.
103. Greensboro *Daily News*, June 10, 1917.
104. *Ibid.*, June 11, June 18, 1917.

keep "the floating rumors" out of the papers. Now he hoped
Kilgo would approve the statement and let the college handle
the matter from Durham.[105] Few also sent Toms a copy of the
statement and asked for his reaction. The reply came quickly.
Toms was strongly opposed to any comment. Trinity College was
too big "to pay any attention to the barking or snapping of the
ordinary man."[106] Toms also wrote Kilgo, reassuring him and
urging him to forget the matter. For his part Kilgo was deeply
hurt. The record shows no direct comment from him about the
statement, but he told Few he believed that he had received "a
raw deal from Trinity."[107] Soon it was apparent that he suspected
that someone in the college had released the story to the press,
and he was irritated when no statement of explanation came from
Trinity. But it was not a personal matter, he insisted, and he
would make no "personal requests." Within a few days he sent
the vice-chairman his resignation as trustee and president-emeri-
tus. He told Toms, "I am tired of being nagged at and misrepre-
sented."[108] Few was sorry. He had tried to do right, and he
believed that he had. He wrote Kilgo, "The time will come when
all this will appear to you in better light."[109]

Soon Few was busy calming irate parents. He urged that
they remember the Bishop's long service to Trinity, and he assured them that the degrees had been conferred and were in
perfect order. Shortly Kilgo left for an episcopal assignment in
the Far East, but before his departure he issued a brief statement.
Press comment had been almost wholly against him; Bost had reported that his resignation "did not create a ripple" among Trinity supporters in Raleigh. Kilgo would not specify the reasons
for his resignation, except to say that it was based, not upon the
events of commencement, but on "facts which have taken place
since. . . ." He was making the statement because of misrepre-
sentations that had appeared. "There are others who might have
made it [the statement] and perhaps should have. . . ."[110] Within
a few days he sailed for the Orient and was gone for four months.

105. Few to Kilgo, June 11, 1917, Few and Kilgo Papers. In his statement
Few tried to soften the sharpness of the newspaper stories and emphasized that
he believed Kilgo's position to be conscientious and consistent. He appealed to
the sons of Trinity to appreciate Kilgo's services. The statement, undated, is in
the Few Papers.
106. Toms to Few (telegram), June 4, and letter, June 15, 1917, Few Papers.
107. Kilgo to Few, June 14, 1917, Few Papers.
108. Kilgo to Toms, June 16, 1917, Few Papers.
109. Few to Kilgo, June 25, 1917, Few Papers.
110. Charlotte *Observer*, July 21, 1917.

In Northampton, Bassett heard about it all from Boyd and from his perspective offered a word of comment:

> Of course the Bishop is very impetuous, and he does not know how to curb his will. He got the fixed idea, evidently, that someone had insulted him, and he now feels that his influence is gone if he does not make that person smart for it. . . . On the other hand, he has many good qualities, and you and I have been the beneficiary of them. Let us respect him for the good he has done and cover the nakedness of his weakness.
>
> Does he mean to oppose Trinity in the future? If he drops out quietly, and does not use his influence against the college, it may be for his happiness. If he carries the fight into the future —and I fear he is not the man to drop a fight—he will promote his own dissatisfaction. I hope he will let the matter drop. . . . The whole thing brings Trinity very close back to my eyes. . . .[111]

During the summer there was pressure, especially from the class of 1917, for a meeting of the Board to act upon Kilgo's resignation and to disavow his position with regard to the students. In late August Toms reported that he had had "a very satisfactory talk" with J. B. Duke,[112] and within a few days the Executive Committee agreed to call a Board meeting for November 21. The Committee also observed that the action of the five trustees in June (in creating the vice-presidency) was not in accord with the college by-laws. A two-thirds' vote was required to make such a change, and the matter was referred back to the full Board.[113]

By mid-November Kilgo had returned to Charlotte and found there a letter from Toms advising him that the Board would meet on November 21, "to accept your resignation." Toms hoped that Kilgo would always help Trinity, even if he were not directly connected with the college.[114] The Board duly met and accepted the resignation. Brown was elected chairman. The demands of the class of 1917 were heard and referred to a committee where they quietly died. Resolutions of appreciation of Kilgo's services were passed. He was described as "the real builder of the new Trinity," and his moral leadership was singled out as his most significant contribution.[115] The matter of the vice-presidency was

111. Bassett to Boyd, July 1, 1917, Bassett Papers.
112. Toms to Few, Aug. 20, 1917, Few Papers.
113. *Minutes,* Executive Committee, Sept. 1, 1917.
114. Toms to Kilgo, Nov. 14, 1917, Kilgo Papers.
115. *Minutes,* Board of Trustees, Nov. 21, 1917.

given to the Executive Committee, which later recommended no change in the duties of the college officers.[116] Few drafted a personal letter to Kilgo, but Toms advised him not to send it. "You have acted nobly; you have always done the best you could. . . ." He urged Few to go on and say nothing.[117]

Kilgo chose not to attend the meeting, but he could not conceal his bitterness. He was angered by Toms's letter and its positive prediction of the Board's action. He returned the honorary degree Trinity had given him in 1916, "the only mark of favor I ever received from the College."[118] Brown, who had long been his friend, urged him to reconsider. "Is it not possible for you to be mistaken and for all of these men [the trustees] to have struck it right?"[119]

By now the Bishop was beyond an appeal to moderation. He looked upon the press criticism as "brutal, vicious" attacks by Trinity College. He hinted darkly of an undercover fight that had been going on for years.[120] When an alumnus, one of his Old Boys, asked for information, Kilgo sent him a lengthy summary of the events. Trinity was an "ingrate." For years he had given Few advice and help almost every day, at Few's request. He believed he had "saved" the college on occasion recently (apparently referring to the charter trouble). Yet, to his astonishment, at no time in this matter had Trinity risen to his defense. The entire affair reflected a moral failure of the college. And then Kilgo made a statement that was unworthy. He said that now only one class of men could influence him to help Trinity, "My Old Boys, God bless them, for their sakes I am willing to contend for the fair name of their College if they call on me to do it." He repeated the hint a few days later: "If her truth-loving sons call me to join them in a fight for the character of their College I will join them."[121]

In the months and years that followed, Kilgo received frequent assurances from the Trinity faculty, from Ben Duke and his family, from alumni, and others of his place in the memory of the college.[122] There seems to have been no correspondence be-

116. *Minutes,* Executive Committee, May 29, 1918.
117. Toms to Few, Nov. 30, 1917, Few Papers.
118. Kilgo to Joseph G. Brown, Dec. 17, 1917, Kilgo Papers.
119. Brown to Kilgo, Dec. 19, 1917, Kilgo Papers.
120. Kilgo to "Dear Joe" (Brown), Dec. 22, Dec. 28, 1917, Kilgo Papers.
121. Statement and letters, Kilgo to M. B. Andrews, Dec. 17, Dec. 20, 1917, Kilgo Papers.
122. Kilgo Papers, 1917 ff., *passim.*

tween him and Few. Soon the Bishop was deeply involved in the Church battle on unification, which he and his friend Bishop Candler strongly opposed. Kilgo once threatened to organize a separate church if unification were approved.[123] After 1918 he was frequently ill, and gradually his health failed. By 1920 he was relieved from his episcopal duties. Few felt it necessary to make inquiries indirectly about his condition but was able to help in arranging for a disability compensation from the Church. In 1922, while returning from the General Conference at Hot Springs, Arkansas, Kilgo became seriously ill. Few and others helped settle him in a hospital at Memphis. Kilgo was grateful, and at the end the two were reconciled.[124] After months of lingering, the Bishop returned to Charlotte, where he died on August 11, 1922.

It is not necessary to evaluate Kilgo in detail. His actions were not shrouded in mystery, and the previous pages suggest something of his character and life. Indeed, he was always a little larger than life to those who knew him.[125] One evaluation is precise; his greatest gift was "the ability to inspire other men to do difficult things."[126] His faults were clear, but the personality lingered longest. The enigma and the power lay in the contradictions.

Trinity and the War

When the World War erupted in the summer of 1914, the academic community at Trinity College was divided in sympathies, as were the American people.[127] Professors who had studied abroad or knew the German intellectual heritage could not but lean toward the Central Powers. A greater number were pro-British from the beginning. Few did not advertise his feeling, but he sent word abroad that most of the people he knew were wholly with England.[128] As the months of American neutrality passed and as the United States' involvement became more cer-

123. Kilgo to "Brother Augustus," Sept. 11, 1919, Kilgo Papers.
124. Plato Durham, a friend of both men, said that shortly before his death Kilgo spoke gratefully of Few's kindness to him. Woody, *Few*, p. 82.
125. H. E. Spence, "*I Remember*": *Recollections and Reminiscences of Alma Mater* (Durham, 1954), p. 7.
126. Gilbert T. Rowe to Kilgo, March 18, 1910, Trinity College Papers.
127. Interview, W. T. Laprade, Jan. 28, 1961.
128. Few to Sir Gilbert Parker (London), Oct. 19, 1914, Few Papers.

tain, college sentiment hardened into support for the Allies. After this country became a combatant in the spring of 1917, Few was prompt in registering his conviction that the world now had "a sickening sense of the moral failure" of German "efficiency."[129] He wrote his father that "perhaps no war was ever more just or more inevitable."[130]

The college was quick to catch the spirit of service in wartime. Some twenty acres of the campus were planted in crops as a contribution to the food conservation program. Students needed in agricultural work were released early, and those who enlisted, and whose records were satisfactory, received credit for a full term's work. The women students maintained an auxiliary Red Cross chapter, and soon the faculty was making speeches in the interest of Liberty Bonds. During the war Trinity counted a thousand sons in service; twenty-two died.[131] Several faculty members were young enough to enlist, and those with permanent appointments were promised that their places would be held for them.[132] As noted earlier, in the fall of 1917 and for the next two years, the college was able to give a 10 per cent bonus to all of the faculty and staff. When Bassett heard of it he told Boyd it was "the only thing like it in the country. . . . You are lucky."[133]

Even before the American involvement, the students had asked for military training on the campus, and Flowers and W. H. Hall (in engineering), both graduates of the Naval Academy, began giving three hours of drill per day. The faculty granted three hours credit to those who took it. By the fall of 1917 drill became the substitute for physical education and was required of all who were physically fit. Soon classroom work was added, the whole making up a course in military training and tactics. In physics, Edwards designed a course in "war engineering," to provide preparation for the signal corps.[134]

As the students began to trickle away, Few found himself operating a placement agency. He was beseiged for recommendations from recent graduates and older alumni seeking govern-

129. *Report of the President*, June, 1917, p. 26.
130. Few to B. F. Few, April 6, 1917, Few Papers.
131. Few Papers; *Minutes of the Faculty; Trinity Alumni Register*, 1917-1918, *passim*. The war at Trinity is well summarized in the *Report of the President*, June, 1919.
132. Few to W. J. Martin (president, Davidson College), April 25, 1917, Few Papers.
133. Bassett to Boyd, Oct. 12, 1917, Boyd Papers.
134. *Minutes of the Faculty*, 1917-1918; Trinity College catalogue, 1917-1918.

ment and military positions. The major problem, however, was to devise a means of keeping the students in college, in particular to hold them long enough to maintain enrollments and, incidentally, to prepare them for officer candidate's school. Few worked hard in a campaign for "enlistment for college." The situation was serious by the spring of 1918; the enrollment had dropped by over one hundred. Most of the law students were gone, and the faculty relaxed its rules to permit undergraduates to elect as many as two courses in law. Student fees were declining, and prices were rising. The college sought to become the site of one of the new Student Army Training Corps units. By 1918 these units, staffed with military personnel, were scattered on campuses about the country. The S.A.T.C. protected college enrollment. Students who joined were exempt from the draft and were considered potential officer candidates. A college with such a unit might also hold its faculty from a call to service, or bring them back from service. In the Summer of 1918 Trinity was approved for an S.A.T.C. unit, and several professors went off to camp at Plattsburg, New York, to become "indoctrinated" and to study the military approach to education.

With the arrival of the S.A.T.C. the college assumed the manners and methods of an army post. About 80 per cent of the undergraduate men (280) signed up and fell under the complete disciplinary control of the Army. By contract the college provided the instruction, and the government paid tuition and fees. The faculty was responsible solely for teaching duties. Wannamaker temporarily retired as dean to take a commission and to become personnel officer for the S.A.T.C. The college assumed for the first time the responsibility of providing dining facilities, converting for this purpose the basement of the West Duke Building.[135]

Boyd was named director of the academic program of the S.A.T.C. A quarter system was established, and four schedules of courses were set up, preparatory to service in the infantry, or in the engineering, medical, or naval branches. Essentially the programs were much the same. Common to all was an emphasis upon mathematics and the sciences, English, modern languages, drill, and a course on the "Aims of the War," shared by

135. *Report of the President,* June, 1919, pp. 5-7. There had been various dining arrangements in campus buildings from time to time, but they were privately managed, sometimes by students.

the history and economics faculties.[136] The war offered no place for the ancient languages, Bible, or education. Professors in these fields taught the women, the non-S.A.T.C. students, or shifted to another field for a time. Brooks, for example, taught history. The general prejudice against teaching German, Wannamaker's field, won no adherents at Trinity. The college declined to discontinue it. German was offered as in the past and remained, with French, one of the modern languages one chose to satisfy regular degree, as well as S.A.T.C., requirements.

The S.A.T.C. never got going. The nationwide epidemic of influenza hit the campus in September, 1918, and over 40 per cent of the community was infected. (Few was proud that there was not a single death.) By November 11 the armistice had been signed. The military unit was demobilized, and by spring the college was operating again on a prewar basis. The military interest lingered for a bit, and the college retained the S.A.T.C. commandant to serve for a time as head of an R.O.T.C. department. But the reaction against all things military soon swept the R.O.T.C. away. By early 1919, with veterans back at Trinity, Few was commenting on the extreme sentiment against military discipline in any form.[137]

Plainly, at Trinity as across the nation, the war had made a difference. Few conceded that the mingling of the military and the college had provoked some misunderstandings,[138] but there were benefits. One was a new respect for systematic exercise and physical training. In 1919 the faculty voted to require physical training of all students and to give academic credit for it. Again, the required army mess had given the college experience in managing such facilities; high prices and labor shortages had hurt the private boarding houses that had long served the campus. After the war Trinity established institutional dining operations on a permanent basis.

Two larger lessons lay in the new emphasis upon science and upon women's education. The war had unleased new and wider applications for science. It was "the demand of the age," and

136. Brochure, *Program of Courses,* S.A.T.C., *Trinity College, 1918-1919* (Durham, Sept. 25, 1918), Trinity College Papers.
137. Few to W. J. Martin, Feb. 18, 1919, Few Papers.
138. *Report of the President,* June, 1919, p. 5. There was a brief flurry when the military scheduled a dance at Trinity, and the faculty and administration canceled it.

Trinity's long-felt need for a science hall, more equipment, and additional science facilities never was more apparent. Similarly, the broader role women had played in the war and the current suffrage movement emphasized the need for women's education. Few took occasion again to sound the call for a woman's college.[139]

139. *Report of the President,* June, 1919, pp. 6-13.

Chapter VII

The College Becomes a University
1919-1924

From the 1890's and Crowell's brave dream of a university, the hope of larger things for Trinity could not be forgotten.
The college's continued access to the wealth and family interest
of the Dukes made this unavoidable. On the other hand, it is far
from the mark to suggest a determined university-mindedness;
one could enjoy only vague hopes. The significance of Trinity's
last years lies in the maturing of the college academically, in its
growing familiarity with the problems of research, and in the desire of some of its faculty to participate fully in the rewards of
modern scholarship. In 1924 the shock of conversion from college
to university would be cushioned by assets in men and experience
already in the possession of Trinity College.

In 1919 the hopes released by the World War were met immediately by two uncomfortable problems, inflated prices and inflated enrollments. By the fall of that year and for years after-
ward the continuing plaint was, "We are overrun." A renewed
enthusiasm for college training everywhere, the existence of more
Southern high schools, and a quantity of returning servicemen
combined to produce larger freshman classes than ever before.
Annual increases of more than 100 became the rule. In 1924 Trinity had 980 undergraduate students.[1]

The problem was to recruit more faculty and to retain those
on the staff—and at a time of sharply rising prices. Even a short,
violent depression in 1921 did not rescue the salaried man, whose
income had never caught up with the inflation. It has been estimated that for several years the purchasing power of the dollar
was one-third that of 1914.[2] Institutional investments with fixed
rates of interest were reduced in value, yet books, equipment,
and other items cost more.[3] At Trinity the students began wear-

---

1. Trinity College catalogues, 1919-1924; Few Papers, *passim.*
2. Chester W. Wright, *Economic History of the United States*, pp. 882-883,
951-968.
3. W. H. Glasson, "Price Inflation: Its Beneficiaries and Its Victims," *South
Atlantic Quarterly*, XIX (April, 1920), 118-130.

William Preston Few

ing overalls in protest of the high cost of clothing. It seemed to Few as if the situation had changed almost overnight. Salaries were rising everywhere; Trinity found it difficult to meet the competition. In 1920 Few offered a new salary goal, $4,000 for professors.[4] The "normal" salary was then $2,750.[5] To help meet the objective, tuition and fees were increased in 1921 and again in 1923.

The college sought help from the General Education Board, the Church, and the alumni. The G. E. B. had received additional funds, and Few and Toms prepared a request for $300,000 toward a million dollar endowment goal. The request was granted on assurances from James B. Duke that he would back up the college on its promise to get $700,000.[6] In the emergency the foundation gave Trinity the annual income on the grant until the total sums were paid in. Trinity's hopes also rested on a large Methodist campaign, the so-called Centenary Fund, which began after the war. The Southern Church hoped to collect in five years $32,000,000 for its educational institutions.[7] Few counted on at least $500,000 from this source. As always, he was especially anxious to get Church funds "to convince our benefactors that they can go on with their support of the College without causing the Church to rely solely upon them. . . ."[8] It was not to be. Great optimism in the tide of war prosperity washed away in the depression that followed. The Conferences received pledges of no more than one-third of their goal and could not collect all that had been pledged.[9] Ultimately, Trinity's share of the agreement with the G. E. B. was met by the Dukes, in particular in 1922 by James B. Duke's gift of one million dollars, to be paid over a period of years.

The economic troubles emphasized the need for intensive cultivation of the alumni. Immediately after the war a full time alumni secretary, B. W. Barnard, was employed, and soon the

4. *Report of the President,* June, 1920, pp. 4-5.
5. Few to Edgar O. Lovett (president of Rice Institute), April 12, 1920, Few Papers.
6. Few-E. C. Sage correspondence, Nov.-Dec., 1920; Few-Toms correspondence, March, 1920–Dec., 1921; for J. B. Duke's support, see Few to J. G. Brown, July 3, 1922, Few Papers.
7. Harry North on the "Education Movement" in the *Trinity Alumni Register,* VII (April, 1921), 11-13; *Journals,* Western and N. C. Conferences, 1918-1920.
8. Few to Stonewall Anderson, Sept. 2, 1919, Few Papers.
9. *Journals,* Western and N. C. Conferences, 1921-1926. In 1927, at the end of the campaign, less than one-fourth of the total goal had been actually collected. *Christian Education Magazine* [formerly *Bulletin,* Board of Education] XVII (Aug., 1927), 24.

college sought to launch an annual giving program. Alumni were asked to give ten dollars per year to a revolving fund for current expenses.[10] In 1922 most of the trustees joined "the revolvers," but the records show no similar response from alumni in general. It would take years to develop such a fund, and before it could be done, there would be a university whose reputation for wealth would be a handicap.

With the aid of the G. E. B. grant and continued supplements from the Dukes, the college rode out the boom and the bust. Support from Ben Duke tended to be made in the name of his family. His children were grown now and began to make individual gifts of their own. During the Centenary Campaign the family gave for Trinity through that agency, combining their Church interest with that of their favorite philanthropy. Ben's son, Angier B. Duke, died in 1923 and left Trinity $250,000 in his will. All of this assistance kept the college going and made a larger faculty possible, but it did not result in rapid salary increases. Even in 1925, after the establishment of the university, full professors were being brought to Durham at salaries as low as $3,000 and assistant professors as low as $2,500. The upper range was higher, the typical professor's salary being about $4,000-$4,500.[11] The average professorial salary in the colleges of the Southern Association at the time was $4,100.

Since the college lacked extra funds, the unsolved co-ordinate plan remained unsolved. Trinity tried to encourage the admission of women during the war but with slight success. Later, the numbers rose steadily, increasing from 148 in 1922 to 245 in 1924. A series of women deans had been employed, although none was given complete faculty status; their duties lay largely in the area of discipline. However, by 1922 Few had made contact with a trained scholar, Alice M. Baldwin, who had both academic and administrative experience. She had headed the department of history at the Baldwin School, Bryn Mawr, Pennsylvania, and later took her Ph.D. at the University of Chicago. Miss Baldwin came to Trinity in 1924 and the following year was given the responsibility of implementing the co-ordinate idea.[12]

Few's position on co-ordinate education was not hostile to co-education. Indeed, he agreed that coeducation was "the logic of

10. *Minutes,* Board of Trustees, June 4, 1922.
11. *Minutes,* Executive Committee, 1923-1933.
12. Few Papers, *passim*; interview, Alice M. Baldwin, Sept. 5, 1959.

the future." He believed, however, that "we have to reckon with the prejudice of most men and many women through all the Eastern states." It would be easier for Trinity, he said, for a generation at any rate, to provide separate but equal classwork.[13] The first permanent facility for housing the larger numbers of women came with the construction of the Southgate Building, established as a memorial to the late chairman of the Board of Trustees. Southgate's friends in Durham, headed by Julian S. Carr, raised over $100,000 for the structure. An additional $100,000 from Ben Duke made the venture possible, and the building was occupied in the fall of 1921.

The war influence on academic programs was substantial. As early as 1919 the faculty began a series of studies and revisions, seeking to design a curriculum to meet the "modern world." In admissions there was a concession to the high schools. By 1921 the four admission electives might be filled with high school credits in agriculture, woodwork, or household economics. Credit was given for commercial subjects as well, but electives from such areas were limited, from one to three units, depending upon the subject. Again the language requirements were made more liberal. Candidates for admission need offer but four units of language, all in Latin, or two years of two languages, choosing from French, German, or after 1919, Spanish.[14] By 1922 entrance examinations were abandoned altogether. A high school certificate was sufficient. Probably the change was in accord with practices at most other colleges,[15] but it was out of step with the burgeoning testing movement led by the College Entrance Examination Board, a movement still centered in a few Eastern colleges.

The growing enrollments, however, helped Trinity to become acquainted with the new idea of selective admissions. Facilities were continually strained, and Few began to resist the pressures for ever-increasing numbers. His hands were strengthened by the past: Trinity's devotion to smallness had long since become an article of pedagogical faith. Moreover, Few was always anxious that the Dukes should not feel that the college was intoxicated with size. They too understood that if there was expansion, in all

13. Few to J. H. Reynolds (president, Hendrix College), Aug. 18, 1921, Few Papers.

14. Trinity College catalogues, 1919-1923; *Minutes of the Faculty*, 1919-1922.
15. Few to Raymond Binford, April 10, 1922, Few Papers.

likelihood they would pay for it. As early as 1920 Few wrote Toms that soon Trinity might have to set enrollment limits.[16] Neither the times nor the college were equipped with tested techniques or general respect for selection procedures, but the selective idea was to find its way into the indenture that created Duke University in 1924.

In the program for the bachelor of arts the faculty made rather sweeping changes. Again, leadership and influence came from Wannamaker's office. He and Few were the perennial members of the Committee on Courses of Instruction, with Boyd and James J. Wolfe, a biologist, the usual additional members. Soon after the war, physical education became a required course, given for credit. Spanish was added, and beginning courses in science were increased to four hours. A new career emphasis was encouraged. In 1920 the old "A," "B," and "C" groups disappeared, to be replaced by Group I (for the general student) and by Group II, in which were offered specialized courses, tailored for careers in business administration, religion, engineering, premedical and general science, and teaching. Group II was designed, the faculty said, "for the mature and well-prepared students who have already made up their minds as to their life work." At the same time the old one-hour course in Bible disappeared; in its place came a comprehensive three-hour course, one of Boyd's crusades, also required of all students. In the fall of 1923 a uniform requirement of 126 hours for the degree was established. Courses were organized on a semester-hour basis, and a prelegal group was added. All work, in whatever group, was classified as required, special (the major field), and elective. The electives might vary from eleven hours in engineering to twenty-eight hours in business administration.[17]

Many of the changes came from the work of a faculty commission that also considered other academic problems, especially the size of sections and staff load. In 1923 enrollments had increased to the point that the commission believed fourteen new men were required. The science faculties were overloaded. Enrollments were largest in English and history, but these departments had larger staffs or were free of laboratory teaching.[18]

16. Few to Toms, March 24, 1920, Few Papers.
17. Trinity College catalogues, 1919-1923; Minutes of the Faculty, 1919-1923
18. Report on the commission, Wannamaker, Boyd, and Gross to Few, March 26, 1923, Few Papers. Commission reports and recommendations are also found in the faculty minutes, 1921-1923. The commission was created Dec. 1, 1921.

The war also influenced the separate disciplines. A reorganization in history placed new emphasis upon modern Europe at the expense of the ancient period. As compared with 1914, Boyd said, "the whole curriculum is centered on the modern world and its development." In physics Edwards believed his field was in a decline. There had been little money for equipment for many years. On the other hand, Paul M. Gross, a young chemist who came to Trinity in 1919, reported that chemistry was on the ascendancy. Gross had taken his doctorate at Columbia and came to succeed Professor W. H. Pegram, who retired after forty-six years of service. Gross observed that the war emphasis was being felt in industrial development, in food and medical research. He soon launched the beginnings of a "research foundation" through a co-operative effort in tobacco research between the college and the Liggett and Myers Tobacco Company. It was one of the early efforts to bridge the distance between the academic scientist and the industrial laboratory.

The developments in the department of education were most influential on the college at large. Brooks became superintendent of public instruction in North Carolina in 1919, to be succeeded by Millard L. Lowery for two years and then by Holland Holton, a Trinity graduate and former Durham County school superintendent. As the public schools grew and as the demand for teachers rose, Holton's department received an inordinate share of the enrollment pressure. He had seventy-six students in 1920 and 191 in 1921. By 1924 more than half of the graduate work was given in education.[19]

Simultaneously, a movement developed for a more demanding graduate degree. Even during the war and before, Boyd and Laprade had urged a required thesis for the master of arts and greater concentration in a major field. By 1923 the faculty had approved new requirements. A thesis and examination were required, the major and minor were delineated, and residence and foreign language requirements established. For the first time a clear-cut distinction was made between undergraduate and graduate work.[20] In January, 1924, the pressure for advanced training in education suggested the need for a professional degree, and the faculty approved the master of education "for superior pro-

19. Summaries of departmental developments, written by members of the faculty, appear in the *Trinity Alumni Register*, X (Jan.-May, 1924).
20. *Minutes of the Faculty*, Jan. 31, 1924; W. H. Glasson in the *Alumni Register of Duke University*, XIV (May, 1928), 157-161.

fessional preparation for teaching." On the eve of Trinity's conversion to university status, the college had forty-one graduate students. Twenty-six master's degrees were conferred in 1925.

Holton's work in education reflected his experience in public education and more particularly his success in building a summer school. Before the war the college had considered the idea. Occasionally summer training was available for students who sought to work off admission conditions. After the war inflation and poor salaries squeezed many teachers out of the profession. When the schools expanded, a large number of vacant teaching positions existed. As economic conditions improved, more teachers sought to fill them, but many were ill-prepared, especially those in the rural areas.[21] In 1919 Trinity, remembering again its historic interest in education, opened an experimental summer school. The aim was to provide courses for the returning veteran, for the high school student—and the teacher. After 1920 Holton's energy and the existing demand soon made the school primarily a teacher-training enterprise. By the third summer there were 257 students, three-fourths of them teachers. The college insisted that the work be equal to regular collegiate instruction. By 1924 the enrollment was over 800, and a branch, a "Seashore Summer School," had been established at Oriental on the North Carolina coast. There were plans for another branch in the mountains, at the Methodist retreat at Lake Junaluska.[22]

Directly related to the growth in public education was the decline of the Trinity Park School. After 1920 enrollments at Trinity Park dropped sharply, from 235 to 145 in one year. The end of the school had been foreseen. Public high schools were in operation everywhere, and the college badly needed the plant for undergraduates. In the summer of 1922 the Board of Trustees discontinued Trinity Park.[23] It would be remembered as an advance unit in the battle for adequate college preparation. It had held the line for Trinity until the public schools could arrive.

The emphasis on physical education revived the old issue embodied in the query of generations of students, "Why Can't Trinity Have Football?" The subject was alive after the war. The

21. *Proceedings,* Southern Association, 1920, p. 77; *Report of the President,* June, 1922, pp. 10-11.
22. *Trinity Alumni Register,* V (April, 1919), 63-64; Holland Holton to Few, Aug. 7, 1923, Few Papers; *Minutes,* Executive Committee, Sept. 20, 1923, Feb. 27, 1924.
23. *Minutes,* Board of Trustees, Aug. 4, 1922; *Report of the President,* June, 1923, pp. 3-5.

military had made much of football as a camp sport, and Trinity was almost alone among colleges in rejecting it. In 1918 the Board agreed that a trustee-faculty-alumni commission should study the matter. The next year the commission recommended a policy of "athletics for all" and resolved to encourage intramural sports. Sports for public amusement and high-priced coaches were condemned, but it was agreed that Trinity again might have football. "The game can be kept clean and manly. It must be shorn of the exaggerated and fantastic importance that clings to it . . . and it must be kept in its proper place."[24] The faculty approved the change, and in the Fall of 1920 Trinity played Guilford College (Trinity won, 20-6) and finished the season undefeated. Soon athletic relations with the University of North Carolina, suspended since the stormy days of 1898, were resumed.

The new athletic interest revived a campaign Kilgo had begun in 1916 to build a new gymnasium. The war had intervened, but in 1919 the Board endorsed a "whirlwind campaign" to be conducted among the alumni. The gymnasium would be a memorial to Trinity's war dead. M. E. Newsom, the mayor of Durham and a new member of the Executive Committee, headed the drive. Again, the postwar economic slump intervened, and the whirlwind barely stirred the air. Gifts from Angier Duke, his sister Mary, and from the Duke brothers made it possible to begin construction by 1922, and the college borrowed the rest. The gymnasium was still unfinished although in use by the fall of 1923.[25]

In its last years as a college, Trinity had no new crises with the Church. The emphasis was upon positive service. Few was determined to expand the religious work through academic, extension, or special programs, to "reach directly to every nook and corner of the State."[26] In 1922 he asked the Conferences to underwrite two more chairs in the department of religion, which they shortly did, and soon he outlined his hopes for a School of Religion. He looked to a gradual expansion that would include work in church history, public speaking, and missionary training —in short, a seminary. The school would be named for Kilgo, and the hope was that funds from the Centenary Campaign would

24. *Minutes*, Board of Trustees, June, 1919.
25. *Report of the President*, June, 1923, pp. 7-18; Trinity College catalogue, 1923.
26. *Report of the President*, June, 1922, pp. 6-9.

underwrite the enterprise,[27] but the plan lay dormant, unfinanced until 1924.

Trinity's services to the Church were not always free of complications, however. Increasingly, the college's approach to religion was more scholarly than spiritual, and on occasion Few found it necessary to fend off a minority who found it difficult to appreciate the distinction. There were occasional letters about faculty members whose dedication to the "higher criticism" offended someone, or others who were "not positive in their Christian life and teachings."[28] Usually the criticism was vague. Few sought to reply gently but without giving ground. "I think you overestimate the dangers of intellectual misconceptions about the Bible," he wrote once. "I think it is largely a matter of moral attitudes; and if these are right, the dangers from misinformation and misconception are perhaps not as great as you seem to think."[29] He once cautioned a critic to remember that teachers, like preachers, depended heavily upon their good names and deserved "aggressive cooperation." Few's own efforts for unification of the Methodist Church may have occasionally alienated some churchmen. By 1920 L. S. Massey was uncertain that Trinity could be depended upon to "hold true to the faith. . . ."[30]

Clearly, the community's permanent population was becoming larger and more complex. The number of teaching faculty increased by 90 per cent from 1919 to 1924 (enrollments rose by 65 per cent). However, in 1924 over one-third of the 103 faculty members were listed as assistants. There was a faculty club by 1919, and a fixed sabbatical leave policy by 1923. When the Carnegie pension scheme became the Teachers' Insurance and Annuity Association, Trinity studied the retirement plan with the aim of joining.[31] The details were worked out and agreed upon by 1924, but final arrangements delayed until 1926. When the American Association of University Professors was organized in 1915, a new power for professorial interests was available. "The truth is that we are a single profession, . . ." the founders stated. Perhaps the truth is, and was, that the American professoriate is better understood as a complex of discrete professional disciplines.

27. *Ibid.*
28. Leon M. Hall to Few, Jan. 19, 1921, Few Papers.
29. Few to Alan Browning, Oct. 30, 1916, Few Papers.
30. Massey to W. A. Candler, June 29, 1920, Lucius S. Massey Papers (Duke University Library).
31. *Minutes,* Executive Committee, May 14, 1924–June 7, 1926; Few to Henry S. Pritchett, March 23, 1925, Few Papers.

However, the bond of common employment was sufficient, and the association quickly began to study problems of tenure, pensions, salaries, and college government.[32] Membership in the A.A.U.P. at Trinity was minimal until 1924. No more than three professors joined until that year, when the Trinity delegation rose to fifteen. A local chapter was established at Duke University in 1926.

In 1920 an A.A.U.P. survey of the role of faculties in college government concluded that generally the legal structure was autocratic everywhere, but "in the best institutions, more or less democratic in practice." Trinity was fairly typical of most of the reputable institutions studied, although its faculty had less power than the few "best institutions." Educational policies "to a very large extent" still were in faculty hands, and there were occasional faculty-trustee conferences. Few said he had never used his presidential veto. However, unlike a few institutions, Trinity did not give the faculty much voice in the selection of administrative officers, and none at all in the selection of presidents. As with the great majority of other institutions, there was no provision for a faculty voice in the budget.[33] On the question of honorary degrees there long had been more constant faculty control, and for many years the policy had been one of determined conservatism. In the twenty years before 1924 the college gave but fifteen honorary degrees; in thirteen of these years none was conferred.[34] As early as 1912 the faculty refused to confer degrees upon anyone whose work they had not observed at first hand. There were frequent pressures on behalf of individuals, but for the most part they seem to have been resisted. The problem was always a vexatious one. In 1922 as an experiment, a joint faculty-trustee committee was named and was still being tried in 1924.[35]

During these years the most significant academic development lay in a new interest in research. Long ago Bassett had counseled Boyd to "make your stand for scholarship; it is what Trinity needs most and what the South needs most. They need it more than influence or numbers, or even religion."[36] To the historians at Trinity, this meant first building up the library and collecting

32. *Bulletin,* American Association of University Professors (March, 1916), 10-12.
33. *Ibid.,* X (May, 1924), 23-104.
34. Trinity College catalogue, 1904-1924.
35. *Minutes of the Faculty,* 1911-1924; *Report of the President,* June, 1924, p. 18.
36. Bassett to Boyd, Sept. 22, 1907, Boyd Papers.

220

manuscripts in "the joy of rescuing the perishing." When Boyd became editor of the *South Atlantic Quarterly*, it meant a revived attention to Southern social problems. But others were not passive. In 1919 a faculty Committee on Research was appointed with Wolfe as chairman.[37] The impetus had been an inquiry from the National Research Council, asking what was being done to foster original investigation. The committee discovered that Trinity "was unable to answer a single question in such manner as to reflect credit upon the College."[38] Following a series of studies, the committee recommended, and the college provided, a number of new policies and research aids. A small research fund was established to pay travel expenses to professional meetings and to award research grants to faculty members (1920). The college agreed to underwrite a series of research monographs; the first was a volume bearing the imprint "Trinity College Press" (1922).[39] The sabbatical year was instituted, providing a year's leave at half-salary, a half-year at full salary (1923).

There were other committee recommendations less easily granted, in particular, a plea for reduced loads for professors active in research. Always from the historians there came pressure for more library support. The college had not kept up in this area, even in comparison with other Southern colleges. Immediately after the war the inflated German mark made possible a few good bargains abroad, and the pressure was renewed. Sometimes "you had to punch Few" on this sort of thing, and this time he responded. He secured special funds for other purchases as well, and the library was revived.[40] In 1924 there were 87,000 volumes, far from what was desired, but at least a well-selected nucleus.

In 1923 Boyd was telling others of Trinity's answer to the research weakness in most small colleges, faculty public opinion. Looking back to the days of Weeks and Bassett, he advised that the easiest approach was through history. If one organized a

37. *Minutes of the Faculty,* Sept. 25, 1919. The other members were Boyd and Thornton S. Graves, professor of English, a Ph.D. from Chicago.
38. *Ibid.,* Nov. 6, 1919.
39. *Ibid.;* reports of the committee are in the faculty minutes and the Few Papers. The volume was Randolph G. Adams, *Political Ideas of the American Revolution* (Durham, 1922). By 1924 three books had been published, and the faculty committee on publication was pressing hard for the establishment of a college press. There was a well-authenticated rumor that Adams' volume had just missed winning the Pulitzer prize for 1922. The failure was attributed to its mechanical appearance, the result of necessary economies. W. T. Laprade, quoted in *Report of the President,* June, 1924, pp. 7-11.
40. Interview, W. T. Laprade, Jan. 28, 1961; Boyd Papers, 1921-1922, *passim.*

course in local history and solicited books and manuscripts, "the administration is bound to take notice. That has been our salvation here. . . ."[41]

There were tentative movements toward excellence beyond the routine work of the college. On rare occasions a student might accelerate and take a degree in less than four years. Few began to speak of the needs of "the superior student." Trinity had its first Rhodes Scholar (Bryan Bolich) by 1921. Laprade worked for years to make graduation with honors more than a reward for high marks in regular courses. By 1923 the faculty approved modifications that required honors students to complete individual work beyond the graduation requirements. Finally, after years of waiting in line, in 1920 Trinity acquired a Phi Beta Kappa chapter.[42]

Few's Medical School Plan

Like the co-ordinate college idea, the notion of a medical school at Trinity was long-lived and stubborn. Crowell had busied himself briefly with it in the nineties, and Kilgo gave it the status of a dream in 1901. It came up periodically through the years but gained new force after the famous Flexner Report of 1910. Abraham Flexner had prepared for the Carnegie Foundation an analysis of medical education and made the nation conscious of the need to improve its quality.[43]

In North Carolina the need was acute. There were too few doctors, inadequate hospital facilities, and no four-year program in medical education. The University of North Carolina operated the principal two-year medical school but was handicapped in transferring its graduates into already crowded four-year schools. It became apparent that the state soon must have its own four-year school with clinical facilities.[44]

41. Boyd to W. Kirk Woolery (at Bethany College), May 22, 1923, Boyd Papers. At this time Boyd was chairman of a research committee of the American Historical Association.

42. Few Papers; *Minutes of the Faculty,* 1917-1925; documents dealing with the Phi Beta Kappa matter are found in the Few and Glasson Papers. The first application was in 1912.

43. Abraham Flexner, "Medical Education in the United States and Canada," *Bulletin No. 4,* Carnegie Foundation for the Advancement of Teaching (New York, 1910).

44. Wilson, *U. N. C.,* pp. 558-568; Woody, *Few,* pp. 96-103. The story of Few's proposal is well told, from different perspectives but without material difference, in the two volumes cited.

At Trinity Few had long felt the pressure. In 1916 he was being repeatedly urged to establish at least a two-year school.[45] After the war he began to revive the idea. As a part of the pre-medical curriculum, Trinity students already were taking laboratory work at Watts Hospital. A useful relationship between the hospital and the college had been suggested before. By 1920 Few was discussing with George W. Watts, the Dukes' business associate and founder of the hospital, the possibility of making Durham "a hospital, medical and public health centre. . . ."[46] Now, apparently, he was thinking of a four-year medical school, and he was getting advice from Flexner and keeping the officers of the General Education Board informed of his hopes. The Rockefeller Foundation was then moving strongly into the support of medical schools.

George Watts died in March, 1921, but there was hope that his widow might take up the project. The record is not clear, but it appears that she was willing to guarantee land for the site. In the spring of 1921 Few told the trustees of his general plans[47] and soon began collecting data on population distribution, numbers of physicians, and other material. He sought the support of Durham citizens, in particular that of John Sprunt Hill, Watts's son-in-law. By fall he was able to report to Flexner that "the time is ripe for launching our medical school."[48]

In December, 1921, the University of North Carolina began an intensive study of medical needs, and six months later, a committee recommended the establishment of a four-year medical school and teaching hospital as a part of the university. The question of location was left unsettled.[49] Few thus faced the possibility of a confusing competitive situation. He was convinced, as were others, that the state needed one but not two medical schools.

Therefore, in December, 1922, he offered a plan to unite the two movements. The idea of co-operative medical schools had been in the air for some time, encouraged by Pritchett and the Carnegie Foundation. Few and others talked with Governor Cameron Morrison and with Harry W. Chase, the president of

45. Few to Simon Flexner, March 18, 1916, Few Papers. Simon Flexner was Abraham's brother, a physician and a Rockefeller Foundation trustee.
46. Few to E. C. Sage, Feb. 15, 1921, Few Papers.
47. Appendix, Report of the President, Trustee Records, June, 1921.
48. Few to Abraham Flexner, Oct. 17, 1921, Few Papers.
49. Wilson, U. N. C., pp. 560-561.

the university, and proposed that U. N. C. and Trinity share one medical school and divide equally the expense of establishing it—which he estimated at eight million dollars. He did not reveal his source of funds publicly but spoke with some assurance of his belief that Trinity could provide its share. He proposed that Wake Forest and Davidson Colleges, both of which had experience in operating two-year schools, might wish to join the movement. The school would be located in Durham, where the facilities of Watts Hospital could be used, and would be operated by a joint board representing the university and Trinity—and the other colleges if they joined.[50] Later Few suggested that the president of the University of North Carolina be elected the head of the medical school.[51]

The record does not show a specific commitment from James B. Duke, although in 1921 the G. E. B. promised three million dollars if it could be matched. Few had talked to Duke and found him willing to confer with the Rockefeller officers. He said Duke "has it pretty definitely in mind to give sooner or later considerable sums of money to public causes such as hospitals and Trinity College. . . ."[52] It seems certain that the remaining million dollars, and perhaps more, were to be provided by Duke, although he was insistent that his name not be used.[53]

Few was encouraged when the governor and President Chase both approved of his plan. It seemed an ideal solution. The governor was planning to run for the Senate and welcomed the establishment of a medical school as a part of his record.[54] Chase had numerous other budget items to take up with the legislature that would convene in 1923. The chance to share the cost of starting a medical school was attractive. There were also realistic considerations at Trinity. The college could not ignore the opportunity for a school and if there were to be one, wished to have a part in it. But Few had learned of the costliness of medical education. He was now confident that Duke soon would do something large for Trinity. Here, then, was a chance to asso-

50. W. P. Few, "As To a Medical School in North Carolina," memorandum sent by Few to newspapers and others following the confusion of December, 1922, Few Papers.
51. E. C. Brooks to Few, Jan. 11, 1923; Brooks was Few's emissary to the governor, interview, W. T. Laprade, Dec. 8, 1960.
52. Few to Wallace Buttrick, Sept. 29, 1922, Few Papers.
53. Interview, W. T. Laprade, Dec. 8, 1960.
54. The best sources for Few's private judgments of the varying attitudes in the state are his letters to Flexner and to B. N. Duke, Dec., 1922, to Feb., 1923, Few Papers.

ciate the college with medical education without the expense of
sole ownership. He candidly stated as much: "We are planning
for large expansion here, but I am anxious to get rid of the necessity of Trinity College tackling a medical school."[55] Nor was
Few disturbed about the hazards of joint control. He had learned
much in his talks with Flexner and said once that, in any event,
"the doctors will manage the medical school."[56]

The reaction to what was called Few's "bombshell" was confused. Newspaper reports carried garbled versions of his offer.
He was variously reported to have said he had the money in
hand and to have been so vague that some questioned his claim
that he could get it. He was perhaps handicapped by Duke's restriction on the use of his name, although it seemed to be understood that his sources were the G. E. B. and James B. Duke.

In Raleigh Josephus Daniels, then a trustee of the university,
did not encourage the idea. He favored a University of North
Carolina medical school controlled by the university. He thought
Few's offer had sounded like an "ultimatum," and his newspaper
reported "an almost unanimous sentiment" among the Baptists
(the Wake Forest constituency) against any mingling of church
and state.[57] There was similar institutional loyalty among some
Trinity alumni, who believed that Trinity alone should control
the school.[58] The discussion was further complicated by the vigorous campaigns of several cities that wanted a medical school,
Few's or the university's, located within their precincts. In Durham, even college pride was buried in civic unity when Trinity
and U. N. C. alumni resolved to endorse the co-operative plan.

Few tried to set the record straight as to what he had implied
and what he had actually said, but it probably did not make
much difference. In January he told Ben Duke, "I do not care
very much now what they do about it."[59] Chase was having difficulties and above all was unwilling to endanger appropriations
for other matters soon to come before an economy-minded legislature. By mid-January he too was discouraged about the plan
and believed the matter should be postponed. The next month
the university trustees rejected Few's proposal. Chase explained

55. Few to R. M. Johnston, Jan. 15, 1923, *ibid.*
56. Interview, W. T. Laprade, Dec. 8, 1960.
57. *News and Observer*, Dec. 20, 1922, to Feb. 10, 1923.
58. Few Papers, *passim.*
59. Few to B. N. Duke, Jan. 11, 1923, *ibid.*

that there were too many difficulties of joint control, but he appreciated Few's "high-minded" offer.[60]

Few was disappointed, of course, but not unhappy. He wrote the president of the state medical society, "You can safely assume that Trinity will build a medical school without too much delay."[61] Later he observed that "the state was not then ready for cooperation," but he thought that the plan had served two purposes: "It kept the road open for a first-rate School of Medicine later on, and it put Mr. James B. Duke on his mettle."[62]

The Duke Endowment

When Trinity College became Duke University in 1924, the philanthropy that made the change possible represented the culmination of a habit of giving by one family. There was nothing inevitable about James B. Duke's decision to make Trinity a university, but the past was on Trinity's side.

By 1924 the Duke interests were helping the Carolinas revolutionize their industrial capacity, and the medium was capital, in quantity sufficient to support an electric power industry. As early as 1899 the Dukes had become interested in water power as a means of generating electricity with which to turn machinery in the mills they and others had built. From Durham Ben Duke was in frequent contact with men throughout the Carolinas, and he, his brother, and George Watts began buying sites along the swift rivers that drained the mountains in western North and South Carolina. In the nineties James B. Duke had developed a personal interest in the mechanics of water power when he built an electric plant on the Raritan River to serve his farm in Somerville, New Jersey.[63]

Perhaps in anticipation of the dissolution of the tobacco combine (which came in 1911), the Dukes expanded their holdings and their plans. A small American Development Company, capi-

60. H. W. Chase to Few, Feb. 13, 1923, *ibid.*
61. Few to Dr. J. W. Long, March 23, 1923, *ibid.*
62. "The Medical School," a chapter in Few's unpublished and unfinished history, "The Beginnings of an American University," *ca.* 1939-1940, *ibid.* Cited hereinafter as Few, "History."
63. B. N. Duke Papers, especially 1900-1905; John Wilbur Jenkins, *James B. Duke, Master Builder* (New York, 1927), pp. 172 ff. (cited hereinafter as Jenkins, *Duke*). For a less sober treatment of Duke, see John K. Winkler, *Tobacco Tycoon: The Story of James Buchanan Duke* (New York, 1942).

talized at $170,000 in 1903, led to a consolidation of power proper-
ties and a definite move to enter the power business in 1905. In
that year the Southern Power Company (later the Duke Power
Company) was formed; by 1908 the enterprise was furnishing
power to textile mills. During the next five years James B. Duke
directed the investment of some $25,000,000 in water power and
related interests in the Carolinas; in a few years the sum had
trebled. He said that his decision was both sentimental and
practical. He hoped to see his old homeland prosper but once
warned that his willingness to keep providing the capital "must
necessarily be limited by the appreciation shown and the co-
operation afforded the investments already made."[64]

Unhappily, James B. Duke remains a personality incomplete-
ly understood. There is no rounded biography of him, and the
few personal papers he left were destroyed. He has been well
served neither by his admirers, whose estimates have been on
the whole eulogistic, nor his critics, who have drawn stereotypes
of the ruthless capitalist. Duke never made speeches, rarely
issued public statements. Yet he does not appear to have been
uncandid by nature. He was the subject of sharp criticism during
most of his life but was said to be as indifferent to it as he was to
the desirability of improving, in the modern manner, his "image."
His wealth and the aura of important affairs that surrounded him
contributed to the stereotype, as did his appearance: he was
large, commanding in appearance, often photographed with a
cigar in hand. The general effect would have been intimidating,
even to newspaper reporters.

Shortly before his death Duke gave a lengthy interview; some
of the comments attributed to him are of value in the attempt
to understand him:

"Americans don't work enough. They are too careless. They
can't make this car. No man ought to be allowed to live if he
will not work. No matter if he has millions or if he has nothing."
He called off numbers of idling millionaires, devastating them
with a gesture. Work. That is the passion of Duke's life.
"If you like the thing you are doing, it is enough. You will
succeed at it, and you don't need to do anything else." Fish?
Well, maybe for some who have not learned to work. These mill
people here can swim and frolic in Mountain Island lake when it
is done.

64. J. B. Duke to John A. Law, Oct. 23, 1912, Robert Lee Flowers Papers
(Duke University Library).

Millions have come to him because he worked for them, and because he had the judgment to buy the right sort of men to work for him. He believes that very firmly. "Cheap men don't pay. Build up your organization with costly men. Let them make profits. Give them part of yours and you will get it back." Time and time over he reiterated that philosophy of business. "They pay me good profits," he would say of some of his best men.[65]

When one sifts the fragments of plausible evidence, the impression that lingers is of a tough-minded, ambitious man of property, indifferent to theory and abstraction, dedicated, rather, to putting to use his gift of discerning the means by which material progress can be made to happen. And in the picture there was habitually a disposition to share the rewards on the same large scale.

As he built his utility properties, it is probable that also in Duke's mind was an idea that later became reality, a union of his philanthropy and his business, as he put it, to make the "economic resources of a community administer to its philanthropic needs . . . a dream of mine for many years."[66] His close associates long had been aware of his intention to direct—in some fashion and at some time—a large share of his wealth to charitable purposes.[67] Few also knew of Duke's general intention; Duke had spoken of it "definitely" to him in 1916. Talks between the two men had been "more or less incidental." Duke made it clear that when he converted his wealth to philanthropic uses he would want to include the electric power interests, and he would not do this until they were strong enough to pay dividends. The nature of the charities was also uncertain. Few and Duke had talked about enlarging Trinity, but not about a university.[68]

Immediately after the World War the discussions were revived, and Few proposed a plan by which Trinity College would be linked with the foundation Duke had in mind. The property of the foundation might, he thought, be administered under the

65. Jenkins, *Duke*, pp. 210-211.

66. J. B. Duke to J. J. Eads, Jan. 10, 1925, Few Papers.

67. For example, G. G. Allen, "James B. Duke: the Man," *Ninth Anniversary, the Duke Endowment*, addresses, Greenville, S. C., (n.p., 1933); and *The Duke Endowment Established by James B. Duke* (n.p., n.d.). The latter volume contains the text of the indenture that created the endowment and a useful explanatory address by William R. Perkins. Cited hereinafter as *The Duke Endowment*. Perkins said that as early as 1914 a document had been prepared that embodied an early version of what eventually became the endowment plan, *The Duke Endowment*, p. 55.

68. "In the Beginning," Few, "History."

Trinity charter; if not, then the members of the college's Executive Committee would be the trustees of the foundation.[69] This was a natural suggestion to make. For years Duke had been giving money to the North Carolina Conferences for retired preachers and for building rural churches. He had channeled these funds through the Trinity Board of Trustees, and Few himself had mailed the checks to individual recipients.

By the fall of 1919 Duke and his legal advisers, in particular William R. Perkins, his personal counsel, were making progress, Toms reported confidentially, "on the formation of the Trust to be administered by the College. . . ." Toms was keeping in close touch with the plans and commented that Furnifold M. Simmons, now a Senator, also was being consulted. He suggested that Flowers see that Simmons was fully informed about the college, and Toms strongly urged that everything be kept quiet: "I think it would weaken the College position materially for any part of it to be known."[70] Few was very hopeful. He wrote Ben Duke, who was privy to all the discussions, that he was sure Trinity was now "on the eve of developments almost beyond our dreams."[71] It was clear that nothing could be consummated until the income from the power properties was increased. Meanwhile, Few arranged for a landscape architect to prepare a general plan for the future development of the campus and grounds.

When the North Carolina legislature met in 1921, Few and others accompanied James B. Duke to Raleigh to work for higher power rates for the Southern Power Company. Apparently in doing so, Few saw no conflict in his official responsibilities. He reported to Ben Duke that his brother had made an admirable impression and that the legislature "stood by the Southern Power Company in great state."[72] Soon after the visit to Raleigh, Few fell ill with pneumonia and in his convalescence had time to reflect. He prepared for the first time a plan for a university and showed it to Ben Duke, who approved of it. Few took the plan to New York and offered it to James B. Duke. The document drafted for Duke's signature, was simple enough:

69. Woody, Few, p. 94.
70. Toms to Few, Sept. 17, 1919, Few Papers.
71. Few to B. N. Duke, Oct. 9, 1919, ibid.
72. Few to B. N. Duke, March 4, March 9, 1921, ibid. Perkins observed later that the increase finally came "after a bitter fight." The Duke Endowment, p. 58.

I wish to see Trinity College, the law school & other schools expanded into a fully developed university organization. It has been suggested to me that this expanded institution be named Duke University as a memorial to my father whose gifts made possible the building of Trinity College in Durham, and I approve this suggestion. I desire this university to include Trinity College, a coordinate College for Women, a Law School, a School of Religious Training, a School of Education, a School of Business Administration, a School of Engineering (emphasizing chemical & electrical engineering), a Graduate School of Arts & Sciences, and, when adequate funds are available, a Medical School. I desire this enlarged institution to be operated under the present charter with only such changes, if any changes at all, as this enlargement may require. To this university that is to be thus organized I will give ———— millions of dollars. I agree to pay in within ———— years ———— millions either in cash or good securities.[73]

At this time Few was convinced that Duke had decided to include a university as one of the beneficiaries of the coming philanthropy. It was not certain that Trinity would become that university, and it became Few's task to induce him to build it around the college.[74]

Next, the Trinity president spoke to his Board of Trustees about his general hopes for expansion and of the possibility of a university at some time in the future.[75] The Board approved the idea of extending the work of the college, and Few kept Toms well supplied with memoranda and suggestions. By the fall of 1922, it will be recalled, he was involved in the medical school discussion and was able to write his friend Buttrick, "I think you can count on getting reasonable assurances [from the Dukes] as to the future of Trinity College."[76] Early the next year James B. Duke asked Few for more details of his hopes for Trinity, and within a few weeks Few was referring to plans "for reorganizing the whole institution."[77] By this time, April, 1923, one surmises

73. Few's account appears in "In the Beginning," Few, "History," and in the *Duke University Alumni Register*, XVIII (Dec., 1932), 341-342. The document, perhaps the original, is in Few's hand. He filed it under "Initial Steps toward Foundation of D. U.," Few Papers.
74. Few to Henry W. Farnam, Jan. 28, 1925, Few Papers.
75. Few's notes for his remarks to the Board of Trustees, June 6, 1921, Trustee Records. Few noted the "possibility of assuming the name of University when *the thing* is achieved."
76. Few to Buttrick, Oct. 17, 1922, Few Papers.
77. Few to J. B. Duke, April 28, 1923, *ibid*.

it had been decided that Trinity would become the university Duke had in mind. In June, George G. Allen, a business associate of Duke's, came on the Trinity Board of Trustees. Allen and Few were in constant contact after this time. Later Few said Allen had been of particular help in pressing Duke to hasten his arrangements. With his hopes so stimulated, Few was conscious of the unpredictability of life: "We are all growing older and what we get done in our lifetime we must do now without undue delay."[78]

In early 1924 the plans were accelerated. Duke made frequent visits to the campus with his architect, Horace Trumbauer of Philadelphia. Few and Toms conferred about necessary administrative changes. The organization, Few said, should be capable of managing "a great institution." At the top level Flowers would continue to be in charge of business operations, and Wannamaker would be the chief educational officer under the president. The three men, "the triumvirate" who had presided at Trinity, together would direct the new university. Few and Frank Brown, professor of English, visited Eastern colleges to study their buildings and landscaping. Brown had long been an adviser about the physical facilities at Trinity. During the spring and summer Trumbauer drew up general plans for buildings. It was determined that they would be of stone and of Gothic architecture. The college sought to acquire, quietly, options on land near the Trinity campus. By September the Executive Committee had established a building committee composed of James B. Duke, Joseph G. Brown, G. G. Allen, and Few.[79]

In the fall Duke was ready to move. During October and November he and his business associates studied the Trinity College organization and its financial structure. At this time Flowers was in Philadelphia visiting his brother, who was seriously ill, and he had an opportunity to go to New York. He and Toms were on hand to explain in detail the operation of the college. Toms was disturbed at some of the questions. Once, during an analysis of the budget, the question was asked, "Is it necessary to spend $14,000 for library purposes? Do you have more than one book of a kind in the library?" The situation produced a mingling

78. Few to B. N. Duke, July 16, 1923, *ibid.*
79. Few Papers, *passim,* especially Few's correspondence with Toms, B. N. and J. B. Duke.

of the worlds of education and large business enterprises, and there was need for interpretation.[80]

Flowers reported to Few that James B. Duke was concerned about the Trinity charter but soon said that he had been able to explain it satisfactorily. The major item of discussion of course was the administration of the foundation. Conferences were held with Rockefeller officials and doubtless with others. The final decision was to give control of the foundation to fifteen self-perpetuating trustees. Flowers hoped that this would not leave the college Board and the foundation board "too widely separated."[81] It was not what Few had originally planned, but he saw no objection to a separate board, "provided this is carefully arranged for." Later it was clear why the decision had been made. The document creating the foundation directed the trustees to so invest the funds that control of the Duke Power Company would rest in the hands of the foundation. In effect, then, the trustees were to operate a public utility, a task requiring considerable business talent and experience.[82] It is also possible that there were legal difficulties. To hand such an assignment to the trustees of an educational institution, whatever their business acumen, might have given them conflicting responsibilities and in fact would have placed Duke University directly in the power business.

The work in New York was done with great attention to secrecy. There were many meetings; when it was necessary to correspond, comment was guarded. From Trinity's point of view, this probably was essential. Until the plans were complete and could be explained, it would have been hazardous to confuse and possibly offend alumni or the Church. When the Trinity Board met in November, Few spoke generally about his hopes for expansion. The chairman believed that he handled it well: "You told them enough to let them anticipate what was coming and did not tell them anything that could react on the plans for the future."[83] Presumably this last comment meant that there had

---

80. Flowers reported to Few in a series of undated letters whose envelopes are postmarked Oct. 29–Nov. 1, 1924, Flowers Papers.
81. Flowers to Few, "Wed. Night" (Oct. 29, 1924), Flowers Papers. Few said that Duke's "first wish" was to let the Trinity College trustees administer the foundation. Few to R. J. Bateman, Dec. 17, 1924, Few Papers.
82. The indenture recommended Duke Power Company securities as "the prime investment" and discouraged the liquidation of such holdings. *The Duke Endowment*, pp. 8-9, 60. See also W. P. Few, *The Duke Endowment and Duke University* (n.p., ca. 1929).
83. Joseph G. Brown to Few, Nov. 5, 1924, Few Papers.

yet been no reference to the fact that Trinity's name might be changed to Duke University.

By December, 1924, the document was ready. The news was too good to keep, and reports of the forthcoming philanthropy leaked out in the newspapers on December 9. On December 11 the document was signed. It was an indenture of trust creating a perpetual foundation, The Duke Endowment.[84]

The beneficiaries fell into three general groups, educational institutions, hospitals, and the Methodist Church. Securities worth approximately $40,000,000 were turned over to the Endowment trustees, and the income was to be distributed as specifically stated in the indenture. Twenty per cent would be set aside and added to the principal until an additional $40,000,000 had accumulated. The remaining 80 per cent, "the net income" was to be distributed as follows:

Forty-six per cent would go to educational institutions. Trinity College, when and if it became Duke University, would receive 32 per cent; Davidson College and Furman University, 5 per cent each; and Johnson C. Smith University, an institution for Negroes in Charlotte, 4 per cent.

An additional 32 per cent of the net income was set aside for every hospital, of both races, in the two Carolinas. Provision was made for free care and for applying any surplus to the erecting of new hospitals.

Twelve per cent was earmarked for Church purposes, 10 per cent for building and maintaining rural Methodist churches in North Carolina and 2 per cent for payments to superannuated Methodist preachers in North Carolina. Ten per cent was directed to the benefit of orphans, white and Negro, in the Carolinas. The trustees also would receive payment for their services, in accord with a fixed percentage of the annual income of the foundation.

As noted, Trinity College would become a beneficiary when its name had been changed to Duke University and when its charter was altered. Other than the change of name, only the addition of the words that the institution "shall have perpetual existence" would be required. Once this was done, the trustees of the Endowment were instructed to provide the sum of $6,000,000 for erecting and equipping the new university. Duke added a gift of an additional $2,000,000 for this purpose.

84. Summary following from *The Duke Endowment, passim.*

The recommended component parts of the university were very much as Few had outlined in 1921. Trinity would become the undergraduate college for men. To the college and the law school would be added a co-ordinate woman's college, schools for religious training and for training teachers, a school of business administration, a school of chemistry, and a graduate school. As funds became available, medical and engineering schools would be included.

The new university would receive the stipulated income so long as its name remained the same and so long as it was not operated for private gain. In memory perhaps of the old mortgage of 1893, it was specified that the institution must not incur debt beyond its resources. The income might be withheld under one additional condition, if in the judgment of the trustees the university was "not operated in a manner calculated to achieve the results intended hereby."[85]

The results intended were stated in Duke's expression of his hopes for the university, which Few believed constituted a "chart" for the institution.

> I have selected Duke University as one of the principal objects of this trust because I recognize that education, when conducted along sane and practical, as opposed to dogmatic and theoretical, lines, is, next to religion, the greatest civilizing influence. I request that this institution secure for its officers, trustees and faculty men of such outstanding character, ability and vision as will insure its attaining and maintaining a place of real leadership in the educational world, and that great care and discrimination be exercised in admitting as students only those whose previous record shows a character, determination and application evincing a wholesome and real ambition for life. And I advise that the courses at this institution be arranged, first, with special reference to the training of preachers, teachers, lawyers and physicians, because these are most in the public eye, and by precept and example can do most to uplift mankind, and, second, to instruction in chemistry, economics and history, especially the lives of the great of the earth, because I believe that such subjects will most help to develop our resources, increase our wisdom and promote human happiness.[86]

85. *Ibid.*, p. 15; for Perkins' reference to the matter, p. 73.
86. *Ibid.*, p. 24. Few always interpreted the "chart" in broad terms, including the words "sane and practical, as opposed to dogmatic and theoretical." For a narrower interpretation, see Perkins' comments in *The Duke Endowment*, pp. 79-80.

What motivated the great gift? Duke was not inclined to expand on the subject, but the mixture suggested in his own words is probably as reliable as any:

> I was born in North Carolina and I am sixty-six years old. . . . It is time I was beginning to think about a monument. I want to leave something in the State that five hundred years from now people can look upon and say Duke did that. Every man owes something to the State he was born in, and this is what I want to leave North Carolina.[87]

Duke did not long survive his handiwork. He died on October 10, 1925. By his will the Endowment, the university, and the hospital program gained more. He left $10,000,000 for the building of a medical school and hospital at Duke University. The remainder, the "residuary estate," was added to the Endowment and probably amounted to as much as the original $40,000,000.[88] The income from two-thirds of the residuary estate was designated as follows: 90 per cent for hospitals and 10 per cent for Duke University. The Endowment trustees were instructed first to provide $11,000,000 more for building the university and to charge this against the university's 10 per cent.

Few and Flowers attended some of the last-minute meetings in Charlotte during the early days of December, 1924, and Few, of course, was ecstatic. He saw "not one particle of difficulty in arranging all our affairs" and wrote Ben Duke, "after all, my dream and your dream is to be realized in full. Isn't it glorious?"[89] The Executive Committee met and adopted the necessary resolutions for changing Trinity's name. All legal procedures were carefully checked, and a call was issued for a meeting of the full Board.[90] Few drafted a statement that the Board would be asked to approve, and on December 29, 1924, the Trinity trustees (twenty-nine present and five present by proxy) met, approved all the necessary changes, and issued a public statement of their acceptance of Duke's offer.

The statement observed, "We have found that the University is to be developed according to plans that are perfectly in line with our hopes for the expansion of this historic College. . . ." The

87. Jenkins, *Duke*, p. 212.
88. *Ibid.*, p. 59.
89. Few to B. N. Duke, Dec. 13, 1924, Few Papers. Appropriately, within a few days he was to send his first letter on the new Duke University stationary to Ben Duke.
90. *Minutes*, Executive Committee, Dec. 16, 1924.

trustees expressed their gratitude and reported that the charter changes had been made. They noted, "The control of Duke University and all its relations to its constituency will remain identical with the control and relations to constituency that Trinity College has had." Trinity, they explained, would become the college of arts and science within the new University. "It [Trinity] remains as it has always been—both the name and the thing—except that henceforth it will be a college around which is built up a complete university organization."[91]

All of the schools and colleges were accepted as parts of the university organization, and the institution's aims were outlined:

> This University in all its departments will be concerned about excellence rather than size; it will aim at quality rather than numbers—quality of those who teach and quality of those who learn. It will be developed with a view to serving conditions as they actually exist. It will be for the use of all the people of the State and Section without regard to creed, class or party, and for those elsewhere who may seek to avail themselves of the opportunities it has to offer.[92]

With the formalities taken care of, the trustees appointed a committee to study the organization now to be created, and Few busied himself to give the widest possible dissemination to the facts as to what had been done. There had been a brief flurry among a minority of alumni who regretted the change of name. More important, Few was anxious to explain that the university government was not different and that Duke had not sought to create a memorial to himself. Few long remembered the criticism that followed the announcement of December, 1924—and that was to follow the university later. In the course of time the dispassionate, the shrill, and the envious were all heard from. There were frequent reminders that it took time to build a real university. Few recalled a visit from Buttrick in the early years: "As he told me good-by he said, 'The universities of the country will tell you they are for you but,' he added slyly, 'they won't be.' "[93]

The major item for analysis was the structure of government. Sober observers could and did ask, did not the Endowment's power to withhold funds open up dangers of dual control? Was

91. *Minutes*, Board of Trustees, Dec. 29, 1924.
92. *Ibid.*
93. Few's efforts to reach the varying groups within the Trinity constituency are evident in the *Report of the President*, June, 1925. See also "In the Beginning," Few, "History."

there a possibility of friction between the university and the Endowment trustees? Where did the ultimate control lie?

Few faced these questions and others when he discussed the university with educators and foundation officers. Soon he reported to the trustees that he had discovered three areas of doubt.[94] First, as to the government structure, he found opposing views. "Ninety per cent of the leading educators" did not approve of the Church's power to confirm trustees. On the other hand, he heard objections that the Endowment trustees were businessmen and therefore untried in educational affairs. In reply, Few cited the record of the Trinity Board in its long relation with the Church, and he noted the diligence and interest of the Endowment board in things educational. He was certain the two boards would find a safe working procedure. Second, there was wide sentiment that the university did not have the funds to do what had been charted for it. He agreed, but noted that the policy was to move slowly and limit undertakings to resources in hand. Third, there was "uncertainty, based on lack of knowledge," as to the fitness not only of the members of both boards but of the administrators of the university. Few could only say that the answer must come from the efforts of all concerned in the immediate period ahead.

For several years Few worked at the major item, the alignment of power between the two boards, and was willing to analyze it publicly.[95] He urged the university trustees to study the matter as well. He said that he did not believe there was a real hazard and in fact found a positive advantage for the university. There existed a kind of check and balance system between the boards that would make, not for conflict, but for stability. At the same time he sought to insure stability by bringing the Endowment trustees more intimately into the operation of the institution. By 1935 the university had changed its by-laws to provide that three of the Executive Committee would be chosen from among the trustees of the Endowment. As in the past the seventh member was the president.[96]

Of special importance in 1925 was the land the college would need. Earlier Few had hoped that it might be possible to con-

94. Memorandum: "for frank criticism—corrections and additions—concerning questions that I am obliged to meet and concerning which I need to know the wisest answers." Ca. 1926 or 1927, Few Papers.
95. W. P. Few, The Duke Endowment and Duke University.
96. Minutes, Board of Trustees, March 27, 1935.

demn real estate for the expanding college; Durham was building
up around the existing campus. It could not be done, and in
1924, at Duke's instructions, the college was taking up options
for land near its campus. As rumors of an expansion spread, the
prices soared, and it was clear that Duke University would pay
dearly for building space. Few "rediscovered" a handsome wood-
land tract to the west of the campus, and the site appealed to
James B. Duke. Great care was taken to keep the decision to
buy it a close secret. While the college continued to negotiate
for land near the campus, Flowers quietly secured the large acre-
age to the west at reasonable prices.[97] The operation took several
years and in the end provided the new university with a rare
luxury, more than five thousand acres of land into which to expand.

In the heady period of reaction to the establishment of the
university, Few and his associates found themselves in the spot-
light. There were bushels of applications for jobs, and there was
a quantity of free advice. For months Few had to fend off sup-
pliants who were sure that his connection with Duke would un-
lock funds for their projects. There were frequent complaints
that the institution could not succeed in its Durham location, or
even in the South. Vexed beyond patience by one alumnus, Few
finally said that once he had suggested Asheville as a location,
but Duke had not approved. Few added, "When you go out to
get $40,000,000 from a man you will find that he has some ideas
of his own."[98]

The opportunities seemed so new and so challenging that it
was natural for the casual observer to forget some realities, especially that there had been a past. Bassett of course did not
forget. There was talk of bringing him and Mims back to Durham
and into the university organization. Both were now past fifty,
and they briefly toyed with the idea. It would come to nothing,
but it provoked nostalgia in Bassett:

> You and I once had a dream of doing something for our peo-
> ple through the development of the Trinity of the early nineties.
> I think we did some of the things we set out to do, but we always
> felt that there was much that we could not do. Wouldn't it be

97. "Building," Few, "History"; Few Papers, Flowers Papers, *passim;* interview, Charles E. Jordan, Jan. 28, 1961. Jordan was then assistant secretary. On
occasion his signature was necessary to validate documents, and he was brought
into the negotiations in 1925 and later.
98. Few to J. L. Jackson, Nov. 16, 1925, Few Papers.

interesting to be there again in the sunny September and October of life trying to do what we first set out to do? And if old Walter H. Page could be alive to see it, wouldn't he smile?[99]

Nor did Crowell forget. Still dreaming at age sixty-seven, he offered a vision to the alumni. The new Duke University should reach for a world view and toward world interest. "Let no petty narrowness from any quarter ever lay its cold, freezing hand upon those who aspire to make a great and noble institution."[100]

The voices from the past would find echoes within the new institution. Few, Flowers, and Wannamaker, all were over fifty; Few was fifty-seven. There was a nucleus of mature scholars. Together with a corps of new arrivals they would seek to build a university. Their personal resources would be what they had known and what they could learn. Few reminded all that "to walk in the ways of progress" was a heritage of the years that had gone before. In the new enterprise much of the past would accompany the adventurers.

99. Bassett to Mims, April 13, 1925, copies in Boyd and Bassett Papers.
100. *Alumni Register of Duke University,* XI (April, 1925), 171-174.

Appendix

Trinity College and Academic Liberty[1]

The editor has been requested to publish the subjoined statement, memorial, and editorial. He is glad to comply with the request, both because of its respectable source and because he desires to make THE SOUTH ATLANTIC QUARTERLY an open forum for the presentation of all questions which concern the life of the common country. It is proper to add that the article written by the editor and published in the QUARTERLY for October, 1903, under the title "Stirring Up the Fires of Race Antipathy" was followed by such criticism that he offered to resign his professorship of history in Trinity College. The Board of Trustees of the college on December 1, 1903, considered the offer and by a vote of 18 to 7 adopted the following statement.

THE STATEMENT OF THE TRUSTEES.

We, the Board of Trustees of Trinity College, duly conscious of the charge committed to us, and moved by a single desire to promote those high and beneficent purposes which the college is set to cherish, have at all times exercised our best care in the tasks belonging to our office. We have had before us the offer of Dr. John S. Bassett to resign his professorship of history, and it is made clear to us that it was not presented out of a voluntary decision to sever his connection with the college, but that it was tendered under coercive influences from the outside, and because of a feeling that his further connection with the college might bring injury to it. Candor impels us to admit our regret that Professor Bassett has expressed certain opinions which give offense to many, and we are glad to find that these opinions were expressed solely on his own authority, through a medium which is in no sense an organ of the college, and not at all in his capacity as a college official, so that neither this Board nor the college can be held in any way to have approved or countenanced them, or to be in any degree responsible for them.

On the contrary, it clearly appears that the faculty and the students disagree with certain of Professor Bassett's opinions—so far as we can ascertain, unanimously. Neither do we agree with them. Nevertheless, both faculty and students, with equal unanimity, have manifested their desire that this Board decline to accept Professor Bassett's offer

1. From the *South Atlantic Quarterly*, III (Jan., 1904), 62-72.

of his resignation, and for the following reasons, which seem to us high and vital, we do decline to accept it:

1. Any form of coercion of thought and private judgment is contrary to one of the constitutional aims of Trinity College, which is "to cherish a sincere spirit of tolerance." We prefer to exemplify this virtue rather than hastily to set it aside and thus do violence to a principle greatly esteemed by all men of noble feeling.

2. We are particularly unwilling to lend ourselves to any tendency to destroy or limit academic liberty, a tendency which has, within recent years, manifested itself in some conspicuous instances, and which has created a feeling of uneasiness for the welfare of American colleges. Whatever encourages such a tendency endangers the growth of higher education by intimidating intellectual activity and causing high-minded men to look with suspicion upon this noble profession. We cannot lend countenance to the degrading notion that professors in American colleges have not an equal liberty of thought and speech with all other Americans.

3. We believe that society in the end will find a surer benefit by exercising patience than it can secure by yielding to its resentments. The search for truth should be unhampered and in an atmosphere that is free. Liberty may sometimes lead to folly; yet it is better that some should be tolerated than that all should think and speak under the deadening influence of repression. A reasonable freedom of opinion is to a college the very breath of life; and any official throttling of the private judgment of its teachers would destroy their influence, and place upon the college an enduring stigma. For it is not the business of college professors to provide their students with opinions. American college students would generally resent such dictation if it were attempted. It is the business of colleges rather to provide for young men the material, the knowledge, and the training which will enable them to form and defend their own opinions. Neither, on the other hand, is it the business of governing boards like ours to prescribe opinions for professors. The same broad principle holds both in the college and the state. While it is idle to deny that the free expression of wrong opinions sometimes works harm, our country and our race stand for the view that the evils of intolerance and suppression are infinitely worse than those of folly.

4. The matter which has engaged our attention is of more than local interest and will be far-reaching in its results. It is hard to commend even the slightest measure of coercion or suppression of opinion to the people of this country. But we are particularly regardful of the reputation of the commonwealth from which Trinity College received its academic privileges. We are jealous of its good name, and mindful of its historical struggles and sacrifices in the cause of free speech and freedom of conscience. To subject any citizen of

North Carolina to any form of coercion or persecution for his opinion's sake would be to misrepresent the State, to foster a suspicion of its tolerant spirit, to set our people in a false light before the world. Rights which were bought with blood and suffering must not now be endangered for want of patience, tolerance, and a noble self-restraint. Nor would we do anything which may seem to imply that the social order of our Southern States in general needs to be defended from criticism with any weapons but reason and the truth.

5. Trinity College is affiliated with a great church whose spirit and doctrines are tolerant and generous, and a due regard for the teachings and traditions of this Christian society requires us to exercise our judgment in harmony with its spirit and doctrines.

Viewing the matter in the light of these wider interests, and finding that there is no complaint against Professor Bassett's moral character, his scholarly fitness, his energy, his competency as a teacher, or his command of the confidence of his classes, we are sure that duty requires us to decline the offer of his resignation. Great as is our hope in this college, high and noble as are the services which under God we believe that it is fit to render, it were better that Trinity should suffer than that it should enter upon a policy of coercion and intolerance.

We state as a fact that Professor Bassett does not believe in, nor does he teach social equality, and we have confidence in him, both as a man and as a teacher.

MEMORIAL FROM THE FACULTY TO THE TRUSTEES.

Presented to the Board of Trustees, December 1, 1903.

The faculty of Trinity College deem that the proposal to terminate Professor Bassett's relations with the college involves considerations of the deepest concern to every teacher in the institution and of the most far-reaching importance to its usefulness in the educational life of the South. We believe that these considerations are entirely apart from the wisdom or folly of certain opinions advanced by Dr. Bassett in his article. We do not endorse those opinions, and hence are very far from undertaking any defense of them. The faculty do, however, desire to place upon record their view of the broader aspects of the question under discussion for the information and use of the president of the college and for transmission to the Board of Trustees in the event that the Board shall desire to receive and consider a statement from the faculty. In that event, we wish to urge upon your honorable Board that the important matter at issue in your decision is neither the interest of an individual nor the particular opinions which that individual happens to hold and to express; it is the question of the maintenance of a great principle—a principle vital to the whole work and mission of our college.

But the matter is of far wider importance. It is a question in which every college is concerned—in which every member of every college faculty in the entire country has a personal interest. Other colleges have been called upon to face the same issue which you are to decide. Such as have failed have been disgraced in the eyes of the academic world. It is the cause of academic freedom, and we, the professors of Trinity College, by reason of the very circumstance that we do not assent to the views of our colleague which are being criticised, feel that we are left exceptionally free to devote ourselves to the great and general principle involved. We should be recreant to the principle and false to our brothers in other colleges if we did not now urge upon your body the gravity of the crisis at hand. If American colleges are to be the homes of seekers after truth, their atmosphere must be favorable to the free expression of opinion. It is the duty of a college professor, as of every other citizen, to consider well all his opinions and the form of their expression. If he err, he is subject to criticism, to rebuke, to refutation, equally with all others. The principle of academic freedom, as we understand it, merely requires that while the public hold him to his duty as it holds other men, it shall not invade his rights, which are not less than other men's. To persecute him for his opinion's sake, to drive him into exile, to deprive him of the means of livelihood,—these are invasions of his rights. Such methods, by making men martyrs, have given to their opinions an importance which they could not otherwise have commanded. It is far better to tolerate opinions which seem to be wrong than to punish the expression of opinions because they are contrary to those generally accepted.

And, if this issue appeals to us directly as professors in an American college, it appeals to us no less strongly as citizens of North Carolina and as members of a Southern community. As North Carolina claims from her Mecklenburg Declaration precedence in our national government for political independence and freedom, so may she find in your decision reason to claim among her sister states an honorable distinction in the struggle for freedom of speech. As a Southerner of national and international reputation has written in a private letter to one of our number, you have the opportunity to make a decision which will be "the most important event in the history of North Carolina in our time; for free speech and free teaching will be won there for all time to come." More than that, there is a question in the mind of the world whether there is genuine freedom of speech throughout the South. This college has now the opportunity to show that her campus is undeniably one spot on Southern soil where men's minds are free, and to maintain that the social order of the South need not be shielded from criticism because it has no reason to fear it, because it is not too weak to bear it.

But the immediate concern of your honorable body is for the welfare of Trinity College. We who are day by day giving our lives to her service can scarcely be wanting in solicitude on that score. We realize with you that we may be in danger of losing students, perhaps of losing friends, but we are willing to risk our future standing for the great principle of free speech and to accept all the consequences of this choice. For we believe that our chance to build up here eventually a great institution among the colleges of the world will be far better if we stand for truth and freedom, than if we silently consent to yield our minds to any sort of intellectual bondage. There is, we conceive, a widespread misconception of the true nature of college teaching which, on this question of academic freedom, has misled many honest minds. It is by many thought to be the business and practice of professors in colleges to inculcate opinions on controverted subjects. Such is neither the right nor the accepted practice. It is the constant effort of every enlightened professor to help and to encourage young men to form their own opinions from a fair examination of all available sources of information. That certainly is the conception of their business and their duty which prevails among this faculty. Trinity College has many claims on our affection. The thought of her ever-increasing usefulness, the vision of her future, is to us all a daily inspiration. But it is because she has been thought to rest upon a broad foundation, because she has stood for the open mind, because she has sought only after the knowledge of what is true, because she has been willing to accept and defend the truth in the face of all narrowing influences—it is precisely for these reasons that she has already come to hold a good place among the higher institutions of learning. This reputation is a priceless possession. To lose it would be a calamity, to throw it away would be unpardonable folly. Money, students, friends are not for one moment to be weighed in the balance with tolerance, with fairness, and with freedom. Surely to preserve for Trinity this character and this reputation we should be strong enough to resist the clamor of the open enemies of the college and to rise above what seems to us the mistaken demands of some of her friends.

The undersigned, therefore, members of the faculty of Trinity College, in all sincerity, and with all the emphasis they can command, urge upon your honorable body to decline to accept the resignation of Professor Bassett. We urge you to say of Trinity College what Thomas Jefferson, the founder of American democracy, said of the institution which he established: "This institution will be based upon the illimitable freedom of the human mind. For here we are not afraid to follow truth wherever it may lead, nor to tolerate error so long as reason is left free to combat it."

Signed, W. H. Pegram, Robt. L. Flowers, W. I. Cranford, Edwin Mims, A. H. Meritt, W. P. Few, C. W. Edwards, William H. Glasson, William F. Gill, Plato T. Durham, John C. Ransmeier, Albert M. Webb.

Signed in the order of official seniority by every member of the faculty except one, who is, and for several days has been, out of town.*

EDITORIAL IN THE *ARCHIVE*†

A great fight has been waged and won at Trinity. Free thought and coercion have been engaged in mortal combat, and free thought has triumphed. We rejoice accordingly. For six weeks Trinity has been under a strain, the like of which she has never experienced in all her history. But instead of weakening under it, she has only been made to put her strength to the test; and having stood the test, she rises stronger today than ever before, because she is now conscious of her strength. The great principle of academic liberty, which is the foundation principle of Trinity, has been severely arraigned, and true to herself and her traditions, Trinity has taken her stand for tolerance, and banished intolerance from her halls forever. It must now be our care to guard ourselves against abusing our privileges, and to be calm lest in our enthusiasm for academic liberty we fall into academic license.

Below we have tried at some length to set forth the attitude and actions of the student body during the discussions resulting from the publication of Dr. Bassett's article, "Stirring Up the Fires of Race Antipathy," in the last issue of THE SOUTH ATLANTIC QUARTERLY. We have done this in order that the friends of the college may know the facts in the case, and to relieve them of any wrong impression they may have formed from reading newspaper accounts based on mere rumors.

Especially do we desire that the friends of the college should know the circumstances attending the so-called "Burning of Editor Daniels in Effigy," and the truth about the "Mob Spirit Among Trinity Students." No one regrets the affair more than the large conservative majority of the students. The occurrence has been much exaggerated and consequently misunderstood; and it is principally with the hope of reaching our friends with the truth about it, that the following account is written.

* Membership in the faculty is limited to teachers with the title of professor or associate professor.

† Issue for December, 1903. The *Archive* is published at Trinity College by the senior class and the editorial reprinted above was written by Mr. W. P. Budd, editor-in-chief.

The attitude of the student body of Trinity during these trying times has been a revelation to the friends of the college. Many who have kept posted on the trend of affairs expected and feared that there would be an outbreak of indignation among us against those who have taken advantage of this opportunity to attack the officials and the policy of the college. And indeed many of us have had a desperate struggle with our feelings in our efforts to be calm and dispassionate. But at each new attack we managed to hold in check our rising anger and indignation, and have stood the awful suspense as best we could. And now we congratulate ourselves on our maintenance of a conservative position.

And through it all, the attitude of the student body has been conservative. We realized in the beginning that it was a man's fight, a struggle between the official representatives of the college and men of opposing opinions; and that it was not a matter requiring or even allowing the interference of the students of the institution. At first, when the question at issue concerned only the truth or the untruth of the article causing the discussion, and the right of its author to express his opinions, we took the view that the article was an honest expression of an opinion by an honest editor; that it was published by him in the capacity of a citizen of the state, and had no connection whatever with his professorship in the college; that as a citizen and editor, he has an inalienable right to have and express his opinions, even though they be, as in this case they were, contrary to our own; but also that his critics have a right to have and express their opinions in the matter; and that in the publication of an opinion so liable to misinterpretation and so radical from a Southern point of view, he had made a grave but not unpardonable blunder. Knowing Dr. Bassett to be a man of irreproachable character and a Christian gentleman, appreciating his worth as a scholar and author, feeling his inspiration as a teacher, and loving and respecting him as a man, we forgave him his mistake and continued to respect him as much as ever.

And then the affair took on a more serious nature; people began to demand that our beloved teacher be dismissed from the faculty of the college and even exiled from the state, because he held and expressed opinions contrary to the current thought, beliefs and convictions of our people. Then we realized that a great principle was involved,—the principle of academic liberty; and individually we protested against the intended outrage on this right, which we have guarded most jealously. We asked ourselves when had it come to pass at Trinity that her professors were changed into mere machines, phonographs, which could do nothing but tell us that this and that is truth, and nothing else is truth; that this is the opinion of the majority, and consequently this is our opinion, and therefore this must be your opinion?

What, we wondered, was to become of the greatest principles of advanced teaching: To throw light on facts, and then leave the conclusion for each student to draw for himself; to throw light on truth, and allow each student to form his own conception of it? If a professor of Trinity was to be deprived of his salaried position and exiled from the state because he entertained as a private citizen ideas contrary to those of the majority, would it not logically follow that a student who formed opinions contrary to those accepted as truth in the college, should be expelled for the expression of them? Were we no more than parrots to be taught to say and think,—if we thought at all,—that this is truth, and that is falsehood? Were we not to be taught how and where to search for truth, and then be free to form our own conception of it? Truly it was hard to go on classes and do routine work with these questions throbbing in our brains and demanding a decision.

At this juncture Dr. Bassett's explanation of his article appeared; and to a man of so sensitive a nature such an explanation is the extremity of humiliation. It was published in the vain hope that it would remove all blame from the college. To those who took it in good faith, it was satisfactory. But to others it only furnished an opportunity for fresh attacks.

Then came the news that Dr. Bassett, fearing that his continued connection with the college would shake the confidence of our people in the institution and thus prevent it from fulfilling its great mission of teaching boys how to become real, true men,—was preparing to present to the trustees his unconditioned resignation. Believing that such a step would be a great mistake, realizing that a greater principle than the mere removal or retention of one man was involved, and holding Dr. Bassett high in our esteem and respect as a scholar, teacher, and man, we met in a mass-meeting of all the students and adopted resolutions expressing our feelings for him as a teacher and a man, and entreating him not to resign. Whether or not these resolutions had any weight in his decision not to resign, we have no positive assurance, but only a verbal expression of his appreciation.

Contemporary with our mass-meeting, the call for a meeting of the Board of Trustees was sent out; and from outside sources it was published that their meeting was for the purpose of expelling Dr. Bassett from the faculty. Then in truth did we have a struggle to hold in check our indignation. We realized more fully than before that it was no longer a question of one man's fitness to teach; but the point at issue was whether tolerance should continue to hold sway at Trinity, or be choked out by intolerance and coercion.

But the crowning indignity of it all came when the attack became general, including the president, faculty, and students, and even the cherished principles of our ALMA MATER. Of this we have nothing to say; we will simply leave it to the calm consideration and just decision of a fair-minded people. It was only by a supreme effort that we controlled our feelings, and let the attack continue unresisted. During the last few days just preceding the meeting of the trustees, the tension among us increased almost to the breaking point. When at last the time for the meeting came, many of us gathered near the door of the faculty room, and waited as patiently as we could for the decision on which hinged the future of Trinity. And a weary wait it was! Gradually, the majority of us, tired out by the suspense, drifted off to our rooms, leaving a few of the faithful on duty. Between two and three o'clock in the morning, our sleep was "cried to wake" by the college bell ringing out the glad news "TRINITY LIBERAL!" In a few minutes we were congregated on the campus, and the pent-up feeling of six weeks of self-restraint broke out into the heartiest cheers that have been heard on the Park in years. Somebody proposed a bon-fire. Immediately we set about making one; and soon a big blaze lit up the whole campus. But its light revealed that some of our number had made a great mistake: hanging from the large persimmon tree back of the Main Building, and from an electric light wire near the Memorial Hall, were two effigies of Mr. Josephus Daniels, editor of the Raleigh, N. C., *News and Observer*, who had led the fights against everything connected with Trinity. We have regretted very much that he has recorded an "Everlasting No" as his answer to the question, "Can anything good come out of Trinity?" We are sorry that he thinks that we are eternally lost. We do not understand why he considers it his duty to his fellowmen to do all in his power to ruin our institution. But we have realized that in all he has said, no matter what may have been or may be his motive, he has only been exercising the right for which we have been contending—freedom of speech; and that to hang a man in effigy because he exercised the right of freedom of speech, would be to give the lie to all our motives.

As soon as we saw the effigies, therefore, the more conservative of us condemned it and tried to take them down,—succeeding, however, in removing only one of them. An impromptu investigation was instituted, and revealed the fact that the effigies had been put up in the early part of the night by a half-dozen students who were bent on a "lark." There were a few feeble efforts at cheering among the more hot-headed of us when the effigies were first discovered; but the conservative element soon prevailed, and the indiscreet action of a few fun-seeking students was and is generally regretted. The next morning the effigies were taken down and destroyed by the janitors under the orders of the first member of the faculty to see them.

And now we have settled down to work again—firm in our conviction that the decision of the trustees was wise, and steadfast in our belief that there is a great future before the Liberal Trinity.

It is with pleasure that we add that not one of our number has left college on account of the "Bassett Affair"; and that so far as we have been able to find out, not one of us doubts the wisdom of the decision of the trustees. On the contrary, we feel nearer to our ALMA MATER in her time of trouble, and she is dearer to us today than ever before. From our hearts we pray, *Long live the Liberal Trinity!*

Bibliographical Note

The fire of 1911 paid off the mortgage but destroyed a quantity of valuable college records. Most of the official documents customarily were kept in a fireproof safe and survived. But the Washington Duke Building, containing faculty and other offices, and its contents were destroyed. Among the known losses were: one volume of the minutes of the Board of Trustees; apparently all of the faculty minutes before 1911; much of Few's early correspondence; and financial, admissions, alumni, and *South Atlantic Quarterly* records.

Thus for the years before 1911 the sources of Trinity College history are not abundant. It is likely that papers from the administrations of Crowell and Kilgo were lost in the fire. Certainly one notes the lack of copies of their outgoing correspondence. As a result, Crowell's personality in particular is less well-defined than it should be. There is one Crowell letterpress book, covering his last months in office; none for Kilgo's time.

As for the manuscript collections, the Trinity College Papers are somewhat uneven in quality, although indispensable for the early years. Later, when the college collection becomes weaker, it is amply supplemented by the comparative richness of Few's presidential papers. Among the stronger personal collections are those of Few, B. N. Duke, and Bassett. The Few papers contain a quantity of letters, memoranda, reports, and other materials. One of the most interesting collections is that of B. N. Duke, which also contains some correspondence of his father and brother. There are no James B. Duke papers of any special value for the period. The B. N. Duke papers have an occasional item of concern to Trinity College, but often the item is useful if only for its rarity. Of more general interest is the fact that the collection contains an abundant record of the impact of the family upon the industry and commerce of North Carolina, in particular for the period 1890-1910.

It should be noted that correspondence with the Dukes always was heavily in one direction. They received a great number of appeals for help and, of course, business correspondence. They did not find time or did not care to reply to more than a fraction of the writers. The pattern applies to their correspondence with the presidents of Trinity. In this case, many of the letters from the college simply sought to inform the Dukes of the status of buildings in process or of general college matters and did not require a reply. Moreover, Ben

Duke was frequently in and out of Durham and inclined to defer college business until he was in town. Again, the family's proximity to the college often made correspondence unnecessary.

Because of the usefulness of the Bassett papers (at Milton, Massachusetts, as distinguished from a small collection at Duke) one regrets that there are not more faculty papers. Apparently, both Bassett and Boyd saved everything of consequence, and both left a valuable record of their activities and personalities. Because Bassett, in his own person, linked Crowell's first graduating class (1888) with the creation of Duke University in 1924, the preservation of his records is fortunate for this study. Nevertheless, the role of the faculty at Trinity would be much more clearly understood with the aid of additional faculty collections.

In common with most minutes perhaps, those of the trustees and the faculty are more useful for dating official action than for the discussion and debate that preceded decisions. As with the financial records, and indeed president's reports and other publications of the college, one must try to find insights between the lines. A word of caution also is to be registered in the use of Few's correspondence with Toms and with the Dukes during the late years before the establishment of the Duke Endowment. At an early point there was acceptance of the need for great secrecy. For many years the plans were indefinite anyway. Therefore, oblique references and guarded statements in the correspondence require care in interpretation as to the exact nature of the business under discussion.

Secondary sources, specialized studies of North Carolina history in particular, tend to be irregular in quality. In general, the reliable materials are those of more recent origin. Even so, it is still something of a test of scholarship to go back into the political turbulence of North Carolina at the turn of the century and maintain detachment—doubly so if one yields to a disposition to separate the heroes and the villains and fit them into classifications that are themselves value judgments. For this reason biographies and personal studies occasionally are defensive or absorb the partisan flavor of the period. A conspicuous exception to this judgment is Orr's thoughtful biography of Aycock, which is exemplary for its forthright scholarship. Another valuable analysis of the emotional torment of the period is that of Cash in his *Mind of the South*, although Cash too had trouble with his classifications (he reasoned that someone else must have initiated the attack against Bassett and that the "liberal" Josephus Daniels must have been swept along in the general current).

I register here my gratitude for the work of many who have made my task easier, Nora M. Chaffin, Paul N. Garber, Robert H. Woody, and others. It has been possible because of their careful labor to gain direct assistance as well as perspective. I believe the text indicates my debt. Naturally there are occasional differences in interpretation.

Bibliography

Manuscripts

(The collections are located in the Duke
University Library unless noted otherwise.)

Herbert Baxter Adams Letters (photostats, Duke University Library; originals, Johns Hopkins University Library)
John Spencer Bassett Papers (in the custody of his son, Richard Bassett, Milton, Massachusetts)
William Kenneth Boyd Papers
Eugene Clyde Brooks Papers
Henry Groves Connor Papers (University of North Carolina Library)
John Franklin Crowell Administrative Papers
Jonathan Daniels Papers (University of North Carolina Library)
Benjamin Newton Duke Papers
William Preston Few Papers
Robert Lee Flowers Papers
William Henry Glasson Papers
John Carlisle Kilgo Papers
Lucius S. Massey Papers
Walter Hines Page Papers, Letters, American Period (Houghton Library, Harvard University)
Thomas J. Shinn Papers
Trinity College Papers
Booker T. Washington Papers (Library of Congress)

College Records and Publications

MINUTES AND RECORDS

Minutes of the Board of Trustees of Trinity College, 1880-1933
> One volume, for the period 1901-1910, was destroyed in the fire of 1911. However, there are scattered notes of the minutes for that period in the Trustee Records.

Minutes of the Executive Committee of the Board of Trustees of Trinity College, 1892-1933 (complete)
Trustee Records, 1901-1922
> This classification refers to a quantity of memoranda, reports, treasurer's records, drafts, and working papers deposited in envelopes, by year, and variously labeled "Board of Trustees: 'Records,' 'Exhibits,' " etc.

(All of the materials listed above are preserved in the Treasurer's Office, Duke University—except for Board and Executive Committee minutes, 1923-1933, which are in the President's Office, Duke University.)

Record of Grades, Trinity Law School. Dean's Office, Duke University School of Law

Minutes of the Faculty, Trinity College, 1911-1928. Office of the Secretary, Duke University

PRINTED MATTER

Annual Report of the President. 1901-1924.
  Reports in manuscript are in the Trustee Records and minutes of the trustees.
Bulletin of Important Facts. 1909.
CROWELL, J. F. *Annual Report of the President of Trinity College to the North Carolina Conferences of the Methodist Episcopal Church, South.* Autumn, 1893.
FEW, W. P. *The Duke Endowment and Duke University* [ca. 1929].
Formal Opening of the Trinity College Library. February 23, 1903.
In Memory of Mr. Washington Duke [ca. 1905].
The Inauguration of President William Preston Few, Trinity College, November 9, 1910.
KILGO, JOHN C. *Christian Education: Its Aims and Superiority.* 1896.
—— *The Lines of the Future Development of Trinity College.* 1902.
Memorial volume, *Samuel Fox Mordecai* [ca. 1932].
Opportunities for the Training of Young Preachers [ca. 1915].
Program of Courses, S. A. T. C., Trinity College, 1918-1919. Sept. 25, 1918.
Report of the Proceedings of the Investigation of the Charges Brought by Justice Walter Clark against Dr. John C. Kilgo. 1898.
Requirements for Admission and Suggestions to Teachers of Secondary Schools. 1898.
The School of Education, Trinity College. 1910.
Statement of the Trustees of Trinity College Called Forth by Recent Gifts. June 3, 1913.
Trinity College Admission Requirements. 1916-1917.

PERIODICALS

Alumni Register of Duke University and *Duke University Alumni Register* (title varies)
Catalogue, Trinity College
Catalogue, Trinity Park School
Christian Educator
South Atlantic Quarterly
Trinity Alumni Register
Trinity Archive
Trinity Chronicle

Interviews

Baldwin, Alice M. Sept. 5, 1959.
Bassett, Richard (Milton, Mass.). Sept. 17-27, 1960.
Jordan, Charles E. Jan. 28, Feb. 1, 1961.
Laprade, W. T. Dec. 8-9, 1960; Jan. 28, Feb. 27, 1961; and numerous conversations, August, 1960, to February, 1961.
Rowe, Gilbert T. Sept. 14, 1959.
Spence, H. E. Nov. 13, 1959.
Webb, Albert M. Sept. 21, 1959.
Womble, B. S. March 15, 1961.

Books

BATTLE, KEMP B. *History of the University of North Carolina.* Vol. II, 1868-1912. Raleigh: Edwards and Broughton, 1912.
BOYD, WILLIAM K. *The Story of Durham: City of the New South.* Durham: Duke University Press, 1925.
BREEDLOVE, JOSEPH PENN. *Duke University Library, 1840-1940.* Durham: Friends of Duke University Library, 1955.
BROOKS, AUBREY LEE. *Walter Clark: Fighting Judge.* Chapel Hill: University of North Carolina Press, 1944.
——— AND HUGH T. LEFLER (eds.). The Papers of Walter Clark. Vols. I and II. Chapel Hill: University of North Carolina Press, 1949.
BROOME, EDWIN C. *A Historical and Critical Discussion of College Admission Requirements.* New York: The Macmillan Company, 1903.
CASH, W. J. *The Mind of the South.* New York: A. A. Knopf, 1941.
CHAFFIN, NORA C. *Trinity College, 1839-1892: The Beginnings of Duke University.* Durham: Duke University Press, 1950.
CORNELIUS, ROBERTA D. *History of Randolph-Macon Woman's College.* Chapel Hill: University of North Carolina Press, 1951.
CROWELL, JOHN F. *Personal Recollections of Trinity College, North Carolina, 1887-1894.* Durham: Duke University Press, 1939.
CURTI, MERLE (ed.). *American Scholarship in the Twentieth Century.* Cambridge, Mass.: Harvard University Press, 1953.
DANIELS, JOSEPHUS. *Editor in Politics.* Chapel Hill: University of North Carolina Press, 1941.
DILLIARD, IRVING (ed.). *The Spirit of Liberty: Papers and Addresses of Learned Hand.* New York: A. A. Knopf, 1960.
DURHAM, ROBERT LEE. *Since I Was Born.* Richmond: Whittet and Shepperson, 1953.
EDMONDS, HELEN G. *The Negro and Fusion Politics in North Carolina, 1894-1901.* Chapel Hill: University of North Carolina Press, 1951.

FOSDICK, RAYMOND B., WITH HENRY F. PRINGLE AND KATHARINE DOUG-
LAS PRINGLE. *Adventure in Giving: The Story of the General
Education Board.* New York: Harper and Row, 1962.
FUESS, CLAUDE M. *The College Board: Its First Fifty Years.* New
York: Columbia University Press, 1950.
GARBER, PAUL NEFF. *John Carlisle Kilgo.* Durham: Duke University
Press, 1937.
GATEWOOD, WILLARD B., JR. *Eugene Clyde Brooks: Educator and
Public Servant.* Durham: Duke University Press, 1960.
*The General Education Board: An Account of Its Activities, 1902-
1914.* New York: General Education Board, 1915.
GOBBEL, LUTHER L. *Church-State Relationships in Education in North
Carolina since 1776.* Durham: Duke University Press, 1938.
GOLDMAN, ERIC F. *Rendezvous With Destiny.* New York: Alfred A.
Knopf, 1958.
HAMILTON, WILLIAM B. (ed.). *Fifty Years of The South Atlantic
Quarterly.* Durham: Duke University Press, 1952.
HENDERSON, JOSEPH LINDSEY. *Admission to College by Certificate.*
New York: Teachers College, Columbia University, 1912.
HENDRICK, BURTON J. *The Training of an American: The Earlier Life
and Letters of Walter H. Page, 1855-1913.* Boston and New York:
Houghton Mifflin Company, 1928.
HOFSTADTER, RICHARD, AND C. DEWITT HARDY. *The Development and
Scope of Higher Education in the United States.* New York:
Columbia University Press, 1952.
—— AND WALTER P. METZGER. *The Development of Academic
Freedom in the United States.* New York: Columbia University
Press, 1952.
HOXIE, R. GORDON, *et al.* *A History of the Faculty of Political Science,
Columbia University.* New York: Columbia University Press,
1955.
JENKINS, JOHN WILBUR. *James B. Duke, Master Builder.* New York:
George H. Doran Company, 1927.
KNIGHT, EDGAR W. *Public Education in the South.* Boston: Ginn
and Company, 1922.
LONG, AUGUSTUS W. *Son of Carolina.* Durham: Duke University
Press, 1939.
MIMS, EDWIN. *History of Vanderbilt University.* Nashville: Vander-
bilt University Press, 1946.
MORDECAI, SAMUEL F. *Mordecai's Miscellanies* [n.p., privately
printed]. 1927.
NEWSOM, D. W. (ed.). *Chapel Talks by John Carlisle Kilgo.* Nash-
ville: Publishing House, Methodist Episcopal Church, South, 1922.

ODUM, HOWARD W. *Southern Pioneers in Social Interpretation.* Chapel Hill: University of North Carolina Press, 1925.
ORR, OLIVER H., JR. *Charles Brantley Aycock.* Chapel Hill: University of North Carolina Press, 1961.
PASCHAL, GEORGE WASHINGTON. *History of Wake Forest College.* Vol. II, 1865-1905. Wake Forest: Wake Forest College, 1943.
PIERSON, GEORGE W. *Yale College, an Educational History, 1871-1921.* New Haven: Yale University Press, 1952.
RAPER, CHARLES LEE. *The Church and Private Schools of North Carolina.* Greensboro: J. J. Stone, printer, 1898.
RIPPY, J. FRED (ed.). *F. M. Simmons: Statesman of the New South, Memoirs and Addresses.* Durham: Duke University Press, 1936.
RUDOLPH, FREDERICK. *The American College and University: A History.* New York: A. A. Knopf, 1962.
SAVAGE, HOWARD J. *Fruit of an Impulse: Forty-Five Years of the Carnegie Foundation, 1905-1950.* New York: Harcourt, Brace and Company, 1953.
SELDEN, WILLIAM K. *Accreditation: A Struggle Over Standards in Higher Education.* New York: Harper and Brothers, 1960.
SMITH, CHARLES LEE. *History of Education in North Carolina, Contributions to American Educational History,* edited by Herbert B. Adams. Washington: 1888.
SNOW, LOUIS FRANKLIN. *The College Curriculum in the United States.* New York: Teachers College, Columbia University, 1907.
SPENCE, H. E. *"I Remember": Recollections and Reminiscences of Alma Mater.* Durham: The Seeman Printery, 1954.
STARR, HARRIS E. *William Graham Sumner.* New York: Henry Holt and Company, 1925.
THWING, CHARLES F. *A History of Higher Education in America.* New York: D. Appleton and Company, 1906.
TILLEY, NANNIE MAY. *The Bright-Tobacco Industry, 1860-1929.* Chapel Hill: University of North Carolina Press, 1948.
—— *The Trinity College Historical Society, 1892-1941.* Durham: Duke University Press, 1941.
WILSON, LOUIS R. *The University of North Carolina, 1900-1930.* Chapel Hill: University of North Carolina Press, 1957.
WINKLER, JOHN K. *Tobacco Tycoon: The Story of James Buchanan Duke.* New York: Random House, 1942.
WOODY, ROBERT H. (ed.). *The Papers and Addresses of William Preston Few.* Durham: Duke University Press, 1951.
WOODY, THOMAS. *A History of Women's Education in the United States.* 2 vols. New York: The Science Press, 1929.
WRIGHT, CHESTER W. *Economic History of the United States.* New York: McGraw-Hill Book Company, 1941.

Articles

CARNEGIE, ANDREW. "The Best Fields for Philanthropy," *North American Review*, CXLIX (December, 1889), 682-698.

—— "Wealth," *North American Review*, CXLVIII (June, 1889), 653-664.

CROWELL, JOHN F. "The Future of the Small College," *Proceedings*, National Education Association, 1894, pp. 797-803.

GLASSON, W. H. "Price Inflation: Its Beneficiaries and Its Victims," *South Atlantic Quarterly*, XIX (April, 1920), 118-130.

MIMS, EDWIN. "Early Years of the *South Atlantic Quarterly*," *South Atlantic Quarterly*, LI (January, 1952), 33-63.

—— "The University in the South," *Annals*, American Academy of Political Science, XXII (September, 1903), 261-265.

——. "Walter Hines Page: Friend of the South," *South Atlantic Quarterly*, XVIII (April, 1919), 97-115.

MORRISON, JOSEPH L. "Josephus Daniels and the Bassett Academic Freedom Case," *Journalism Quarterly*, XXXIX (Spring, 1962), 187-195.

PEACOCK, DRED. "Dr. Dred Peacock on the Early Days of Trinity," *Duke University Alumni Register*, XVI (Jan., 1930), 31.

SLEDD, ANDREW. "The Negro: Another View," *Atlantic Monthly*, XC (July, 1902), 65-73.

STEPHENSON, WENDELL H. "John Spencer Bassett as a Historian of the South," *North Carolina Historical Review*, XXV (July, 1948), 289-317.

——. "The Negro in the Thinking and Writing of John Spencer Bassett," *North Carolina Historical Review*, XXV (October, 1948), 427-441.

TIGERT, JOHN J. "Professional Salaries," *School and Society*, XV (Feb. 25, 1922), 205-208.

Other Printed Matter

Annual Report, Carnegie Foundation for the Advancement of Teaching. New York, 1906-1910.

BABCOCK, KENDRIC CHARLES. *A Classification of Universities and Colleges with Reference to Bachelor's Degrees*. Bureau of Education, Washington, 1911.

BOONE, R. B. [supposed compiler]. *Suppressions and Omissions of the So-Called "Minutes" of the So-Called "Investigation" of Dr. J. C. Kilgo*. [n.p.] 1898.

Bulletin, American Association of University Professors.

Bulletin, Board of Education of the Methodist Episcopal Church,

South. Nashville, 1911-1924. Later entitled *Christian Education Magazine.*

Davidson College *Catalogue.*

The Duke Endowment Established by James B. Duke. [n.p., n.d.].

FLEXNER, ABRAHAM. "Medical Education in the United States and Canada." *Bulletin No. 4,* Carnegie Foundation for the Advancement of Teaching. New York, 1910.

"The Financial Status of the Professor in America and in Germany." *Bulletin No. 2,* Carnegie Foundation for the Advancement of Teaching. New York, 1908.

HAMILTON, WILLIAM B. "Duke University and the Schools: The First Century." *Duke University Centennial Conference on Teacher Training.* Historical Papers of the Trinity College Historical Society. Series XXX. Durham, 1951.

JOHN, WALTER C. *Graduate Study in Universities and Colleges in the United States.* Washington, D. C., 1935.

Journal of the Fifteenth General Conference of the Methodist Episcopal Church, South. Nashville and Dallas, 1906.

Journal of the Sixteenth General Conference of the Methodist Episcopal Church, South. Nashville, 1910.

Journal of the Seventeenth General Conference of the Methodist Episcopal Church, South. Nashville, 1914.

Journal of the North Carolina Annual Conference of the Methodist Episcopal Church, South. [Place varies] 1890-1924.

Journal of the Western North Carolina Annual Conference of the Methodist Episcopal Church, South. [Place varies] 1890-1924.

Journals of the Senate and House of the General Assembly of the State of North Carolina. Raleigh, 1893.

KILGO, JOHN C. *Our Dilemma; Into or Out of Christian Education.* Nashville, 1897.

Laws of North Carolina, Private and Public, 1891. Raleigh, 1891.

Ninth Anniversary, The Duke Endowment. 1933.

Private Laws of the State of North Carolina. Raleigh, 1893-1925.

Proceedings, Association of American Law Schools. 1900-1924.

Proceedings, Association of American Universities. [Place varies] 1908-1913.

Proceedings, Association of Colleges and Preparatory Schools [later, Secondary Schools] of the Southern States. [Place varies] 1895-1924.

REDLICH, JOSEF. "The Common Law and the Case Method in American University Law Schools." *Bulletin No. 8,* Carnegie Foundation for the Advancement of Teaching. New York, 1914.

REED, ALFRED Z. "Training for the Public Profession of the Law." *Bulletin No. 15,* Carnegie Foundation for the Advancement of Teaching. New York, 1921.

Report of the Commissioner of Education, 1884-1885. Washington, 1886.
Statistical Abstract of the United States, 1888. Washington, 1889.
United States Census, 1890.
University of North Carolina *Catalogue.*
University Record, University of North Carolina. Jan. 27, 1897.

Periodicals and Newspapers

Boston *Transcript*
Charlotte *Daily Observer* and Charlotte *Observer* (title varies)
Durham *Daily Sun*
Durham *Daily Globe*
Durham *Morning Herald*
Durham *Recorder*
Greensboro *Daily News*
North Carolina Christian Advocate
Progressive Farmer
Raleigh *Christian Advocate*
Raleigh *Morning Post*
Raleigh *News and Observer*
Webster's Weekly

Index

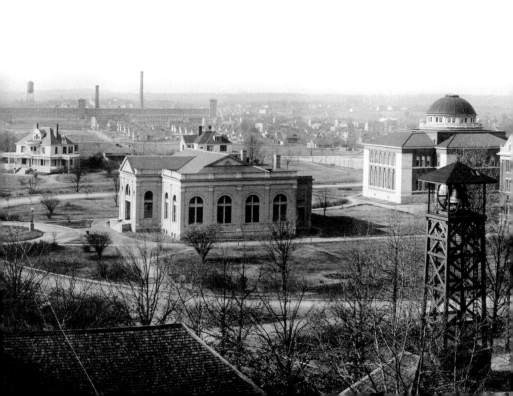